AMERICAN
POTTERY
AND
PORCELAIN

IDENTIFICATION AND PRICE GUIDE

AMERICAN
POTTERY
AND
PORCELAIN

IDENTIFICATION AND PRICE GUIDE

FIRST EDITION

WILLIAM C. KETCHUM, JR.

The CONFIDENT COLLECTOR™

AVON BOOKS ◆ NEW YORK

Important Notice: All of the information, including valuations, in this book has been compiled from the most reliable sources, and every effort has been made to eliminate errors and questionable data. Nevertheless, the possibility of error always exists in a work of such scope. The publisher and the author will not be held responsible for losses which may occur in the purchase, sale, or other transaction of property because of information contained herein. Readers who feel they have discovered errors are invited to *write* the author in care of Avon Books so that the errors may be corrected in subsequent editions.

THE CONFIDENT COLLECTOR: AMERICAN POTTERY AND PORCELAIN IDENTIFICATION AND PRICE GUIDE (1st edition) is an original publication of Avon Books. This edition has never before appeared in book form.

AVON BOOKS
A division of
The Hearst Corporation
1350 Avenue of the Americas
New York, New York 10019

Copyright © 1994 by William Ketchum, Jr.
Interior text design by Suzanne H. Holt
The Confident Collector and its logo are trademarked properties of Avon Books.
Published by arrangement with the author
Library of Congress Catalog Card Number: 93-50203
ISBN: 0-380-77138-1

Library of Congress Cataloging in Publication Data:
Ketchum, William C., 1931–
    The confident collector : American pottery and porcelain
  identification and price guide / William C. Ketchum, Jr.
        p.   cm.
    Includes bibliographical references.
    1. Pottery, American—Catalogs.   2. Porcelain, American—Catalogs.
  I. Title.
  NK4005.K45 1994   93-50203
  738′.0973′075—dc20   CIP

First Avon Books Trade Printing: July 1994

AVON TRADEMARK REG. U.S. PAT. OFF. AND IN OTHER COUNTRIES, MARCA REGISTRADA, HECHO EN U.S.A.

Printed in the U.S.A.

ARC 10 9 8 7 6 5 4 3 2 1

CONTENTS

AMERICAN
POTTERY
AND
PORCELAIN

IDENTIFICATION AND PRICE GUIDE

INTRODUCTION

The world of American ceramics is a wonderfully
exciting one, large enough to offer something for every
collector in almost any taste and every price range. For
those who love sophisticated painting and gilding, there
are the products of American porcelain manufactories
that at times rivaled the output of their more famous
European counterparts like Meissen and Staffordshire.
On the other hand, those who appreciate the simple
and the homespun may be drawn to folksy slipware
plates or blue decorated stoneware or even the humble,
banded yellowware mixing bowl. All are available, at a
price.

1

Ceramics price guides must, of necessity, cover an extremely broad range of items. The field is a huge one, and several of the categories included here—stoneware, redware, and yellow-ware—are individually large enough to justify separate price guides. Consequently, I have selected particular items in each category, such as jugs, plates, or vases, to provide pricing guidelines for many similar items. In most areas this approach presents few problems, since American pottery has been collected for many years and pricing sources are well established. However, it should be noted that two of the categories covered here, sewer tile ware and scroddled ware, are collected by a relatively small number of people and offer only a limited number of forms. In these areas I have tried to be as inclusive as possible.

As I believe that any price guide is of little use unless one has some basic knowledge of the field, for example, how, when, and of what the items were made, each chapter has an introduction covering the history and background of the particular ceramic type. Moreover, within each category, descriptions of the items priced are as detailed as possible, since identification is essential to valuation.

Prices quoted are retail and are given as a range based on the most current auction and dealer prices available for items in good, average condition. Readers should always bear in mind that exceptional quality or, conversely, serious damage may require sharp adjustments. A damaged piece of pottery, for example, may bring no more than 20 to 70 percent of what you might expect to pay for one in good condition.

Damage is a particularly sensitive issue in the ceramics field since some collectors insist on pieces in mint or near-mint condition. Given that many examples are well over a century old and were often subject to hard use in the kitchen and dining room, such high standards are not easily met. They have, however, led to a most lucrative cottage industry—ceramics restoration. Highly sophisticated porcelain restorers have been in the field since the early twentieth century, and within the past two decades numerous individuals have turned their hands to repairing attractive but damaged pieces of redware and, particularly, salt-glazed stoneware.

There is nothing wrong with restoration per se; the problems arise when pieces that have been skillfully reconstructed are offered as undamaged. Since, as a general rule, the more expensive the piece, the more likely it is to have been restored (modestly priced examples do not justify the expense of repair), collectors should always seek a written warranty from the seller confirming that the piece is undamaged and unrestored. One should also own and know how to use a "black light" and should examine any potential acquisition under this light, although bear in mind that some new epoxies and resins used in repair work will not react to the ultraviolet rays. For such pieces one must rely upon appearances, feel, and knowledge of what old surfaces should look like.

Reproductions and fakes are mentioned throughout, as appropriate, focusing on current major problems in the fields of redware and stoneware. Again, insistence on a written guarantee of authenticity is as much a must as is common sense. Any piece offered to you at a price well below the going rate must be viewed with suspicion. Some sellers don't know prices, but most do; few are in business to offer bargains.

The availability of American ceramics varies greatly by category and by location within the country. Early porcelain is hard to come by. If you are knowledgeable and very lucky, you might find a rare piece at a flea market or in a house sale. If not, you will probably have to pay top dollar at an auction, show, or antiques shop. Much the same may be said for scroddled ware and for better examples of Rockingham, spongeware, and majolica.

Redware, yellowware, and stoneware are widely available in the eastern, midwestern, and southern United States. Look for examples at flea markets, tag sales, and local auctions, and through dealers. In most cases you will have to pay the market rate, but some awfully good pieces are still coming out of old houses and barns. Common white earthenware (bowls, plates, platters, etc.) is even easier to find nationwide, as it was mass-produced, and prices here are low. Most sewer tile, on the other hand, was made in Ohio, Pennsylvania, and western New York. Much of it has stayed in those areas, and many collectors elsewhere never see it.

Finally, since the field is so broad, you may find it best to focus your attention on a single category of American ceramics, such as blue-and-white spongeware, or on a particular form, such as a collection of pitchers. A collection of this sort will be manageable while at the same time offering enough variety to be challenging.

How to Use This Book

This book is divided into sections by pottery type. Each section contains photographs and provides pottery prices of different forms and sizes with various amounts of decoration.

An example: If you have a blue decorated stoneware pitcher, turn to the stoneware section and locate pitchers in its alphabetically listed photo section. Examine the items listed therein, and select the one that most closely matches your piece. By this method, you'll be able to have a reasonable approximation of your piece's current value.

STONEWARE

Although blue decorated Northeastern stoneware is among the most popular of all American ceramics, collectors actually have a much wider range of items from which to choose. Southern potteries turned out large numbers of alkaline-glazed pieces in greens, yellows, and browns; and later, kilns in Texas, Oklahoma, and even California produced stoneware with white Bristol slip or brown Albany slip finishes. While jugs, crocks, jars, and churns are most common, many other shapes will be found, including inkwells, statues, mugs, pitchers, bottles, flasks, water kegs, miniatures, and even toys. Prices are given for all items

5

Photograph of potter William Keller, worked, New Albany, Indiana, c. 1844–1875, 3.75 × 6 inches; $80–120.

that change hands frequently enough for a value to be established. There is one exception. No prices are given for stoneware grave markers, though these are often found in the South. These pieces are often initially acquired illegally through theft, and the selling or collecting of them should be discouraged.

As a general rule, the more decoration, the higher the price a piece of stoneware will command. A plain salt-glazed jug might sell for $30, while one with a simple flower could bring $90; another with a large floral design, $200; a well-done bird decoration would be priced in the $350 range, a rarer dog or horse could easily surpass the $1,000 mark, and a spectacular example with large animals or a complete village scene might bring $10,000 or more.

All of the above would fall within the c. 1850–1890 decorative period, the most popular with many collectors. However, there are strong collector subgroups whose members will pay prices in the thousands for such things as pre-1830 ovoid pots with incised decoration, rare Southern alkaline-glazed wares, and even the machine-molded, late-nineteenth-century pieces produced by such firms as White's of Utica, New York, and The Robinson Clay Products Company of Akron, Ohio.

Other factors that may affect pricing are makers' marks and condition. Much stoneware was stamped with the name of the company that made it, and the value of an otherwise unimportant example may be doubled or tripled if it bears the mark of a sought-after maker such as Crolius of New York, Remmey of Philadelphia, or Chandler of Edgefield, South Carolina.

Condition is regarded as extremely important by most stoneware collectors, particularly those who seek elaborate blue decoration. Seemingly oblivious to the fact that these pieces are often 100 to 150 years old and were usually subjected to hard use in the kitchen and dairy, they insist on near-mint condition. A whole repair industry has grown up to satisfy this unreasonable demand. Since the best of these restorations are impossible to detect with the naked eye, few collectors today are safe without an ultraviolet black light to detect hidden repairs.

Another problem is reproductions and fakes. Many contemporary potters are making stoneware, and if not marked (or where marks have been removed), such pieces can confuse inexperienced buyers. There are also rumors of nineteenth-century pieces that have been decorated in blue and then refired. This sort of fraud is not thought to be widespread, but it may prove to be a problem as fakers become more skilled.

Stoneware prices vary greatly, allowing everyone from the most modest collector to the very rich to get into the game. As is the case with other categories of antiques, the middle of the stoneware market has been soft for several years. Pieces in the $200–500 range are often selling for less than they did a decade ago. On the other hand, the most-sought-after examples continue to increase in price, with several trophy pieces having recently brought over $30,000 at auction. Still underpriced categories include brown-and-white slipped wares and early, undecorated ovoid jugs and jars whose classic beauty far surpasses the mundane shapes of the late nineteenth century.

An expanding area of interest is colorful molded stoneware kitchen accessories (pitchers, bowls, storage containers), produced c. 1900–1940 by many Midwestern potteries like Minnesota's Red Wing and the Western Stoneware Company of Illinois. Such pieces are glazed in many colors (greens, reds, pale blues) that nineteenth-century potters could not achieve. Moreover, they are both abundant and inexpensive, making them ideal for the beginning or less-well-to-do collector. Consequently, I have devoted substantial space to pricing this area, one that stoneware price guides usually ignore.

STONEWARE PRICES

Advertisement, lithographed cardboard for "Stoneware, The Best Food Container" (picture of boy and dog at table); 9 × 13 inches; c. 1910–1915; $200–300.

Advertisement, trade card, printed cardboard, for the Walnut Hill Stoneware Company, Des Moines, Iowa; c. 1900–1915; $75–100.

Ant trap, double-walled dish form, salt-glazed stoneware; Richter Pottery, Bexar County, Texas; 6 inches in diameter; c. 1890–1910; $40–60.

Ashtray, molded stoneware glazed in orange shading to gray, embossed logo of the I.O.O.F. fraternal order; by Western Stoneware Company, Monmouth, Illinois; 4 inches in diameter; c. 1910–1930; $90–120.

Baking pan or nappy, dark blue glazed stoneware; by Red Wing Union Stoneware Company, Red Wing, Minnesota; 8 inches in diameter; c. 1910–1920; $50–75.

Baking pan or nappy, Bristol-glazed stoneware; Midwestern; 8.5 inches in diameter; c. 1890–1910; $30–45.

Bank, salt-glazed stoneware, in the form of recumbent pig with railway lines incised on back and filled in with blue; by Cornwall and Wallace Kirkpatrick, Anna, Illinois; 6 inches long; c. 1870–1880; $1,800–2,600.

Bank, Albany slip-glazed stoneware, turnip form; Northeastern; 4 inches high; c. 1840–1870; $60–90.

Ink wells, salt-glazed stoneware, Northeastern, c. 1820–1840: left, *with notched decoration, 3.5 inches in diameter; $100–140;* right, *3 inches in diameter; $60–75.*

Bank, beehive form, Albany slip-glazed stoneware; by Blanck & Jegglin, Boonville, Missouri; 4 inches high; c. 1880–1900; $125–175.

Bank, acorn form, Bristol and Albany slip-glazed stoneware; McDade Pottery, Bastrop County, Texas; 3 inches high; c. 1910–1920; $75–115.

Bank, jug form, Bristol and brown Albany slip-glazed stoneware; by Western Stoneware Company, Monmouth, Illinois; 5 inches high; c. 1915–1925; $35–50.

Basket, hand-shaped tan glazed stoneware with rope twist handle, by H.J. Underwood & Son, Calhoun, Missouri; 7.5 inches in diameter; c. 1883–1891; $250–325.

Batter jug, salt-glazed stoneware with abstract blue "bull's-eye" decoration and date 1790; by Abraham Mead, Greenwich, Connecticut; 8 inches high; c. 1790; $7,500–9,000.

Batter jug, salt-glazed stoneware with double "Man in the Moon" decoration in blue; by Cowden & Wilcox, Harrisburg, Pennsylvania; 8.5 inches high; c. 1863–1887; $13,800–15,000.

Batter jug, blue decorated stoneware, William Roberts, Binghamton, New York, c. 1850–1880, 9 inches high; $250–325.

Batter jug, salt-glazed stoneware with simple blue floral decoration; by Sipe, Nichols & Company, Williamsport, Pennsylvania; 8.5 inches high; c. 1874–1877; $550–650.

Batter jug, brown Albany slip-glazed stoneware; Northeastern; 9 inches high; c. 1870–1890; $45–65.

Batter jug, molded Bristol slip-glazed stoneware; Midwestern; 8.5 inches high; c. 1880–1910; $50–75.

Bean pot, brown Albany slip-glazed stoneware with single handle and wire bale; North Star Stoneware Company, Red Wing, Minnesota; 6.5 inches high; c. 1892–1896; $65–105.

Bean pot, brown Albany slip-glazed stoneware, two free-standing handles; by Western Stoneware Company, Monmouth, Illinois; 6 inches high; c. 1906–1920; $35–55.

Bean pot, Bristol and brown Albany slip-glazed stoneware, one handle; Arkansas; 7.5 inches high; c. 1900–1920; $55–85.

Beater jar, Albany slip-glazed stoneware; Red Wing Potteries, Red Wing, Minnesota; 6 inches high; c. 1936–1944; $40–60.

Bean pot, molded blue decorated stoneware, White's Pottery, Utica, New York, c. 1890–1905, 6 inches high; $400–550.

Beater jar, Bristol-glazed stoneware with blue stenciled advertising logo; by Western Stoneware Company, Monmouth, Illinois; 7 inches high; c. 1920–1940; $55–75.

Bedpan, salt-glazed stoneware with blue squiggle design about top; northeastern United States; 10 inches in diameter; c. 1860–1880; $250–300.

Bedpan, molded brown glazed stoneware; Midwestern; 9.5 inches in diameter; c. 1880–1910; $20–30.

Bedpan, molded Bristol-glazed stoneware; Ohio; 10 inches in diameter; c. 1900–1920; $15–25.

Beer bottle, salt-glazed stoneware with blue glazed blob top; Northeastern; 8.5 inches high; c. 1860–1880; $135–165.

Beer bottle, salt-glazed stoneware, twelve-sided, impressed "DR. CRONK'S SARSAPARILLA"; Northeastern; 9.5 inches high; c. 1870–1890; $90–120.

Beer bottle, brown glazed stoneware, three impressed "X"'s; Midwestern; 8 inches high; c. 1870–1900; $35–50.

Bottles, stoneware: left, *salt-glazed, Hartford, Connecticut, c. 1820–1830, 9.5 inches high;* $70–90; right, *Albany slip-glazed, Crolius Pottery, New York, New York, c. 1830–1840, 10 inches high;* $200–300.

Bottles, salt-glazed stoneware: left and center, *Northeastern, c. 1850–1880, 9 inches, 9.5 inches high,* 15–25; right, *molded, Washington Smith, New York, New York, 1849;* $120–160.

Beer bottle, tan salt-glazed stoneware; by E.H. Merrill & Company, Akron, Ohio; 10.8 inches high; c. 1870–1900; $80–120.

Beer bottle, salt-glazed stoneware, brown at mouth; by Darrow & Sons, Baldwinsville, New York; 9.5 inches high; c. 1855–1872; $90–135.

Bill head, printed paper; for the Albany Stoneware Factory, Albany, New York; c. 1853–1866; $125–175.

Bill head, printed paper; for Cowden & Wilcox, Harrisburg, Pennsylvania; c. 1863–1887; $135–185.

Bill head, printed paper; for C.E. Hathaway & Son's Somerset Pottery, Somerset, Massachusetts; 1904; $45–65.

Pottery bill head, printed paper, Exeter Pottery Works, Exeter, New Hampshire, 1911, 5 × 8.5 inches; $75–100.

Pottery bill head, printed paper, E. Swasey & Company, Portland, Maine, 1905, 8 × 6.5 inches; $60–80.

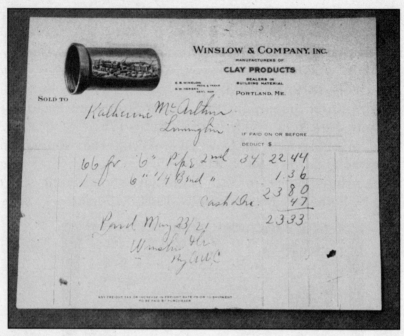

Pottery bill head, printed paper, Winslow & Company, Portland, Maine, c. 1900–1910,
4 × 7 inches; $50–65.

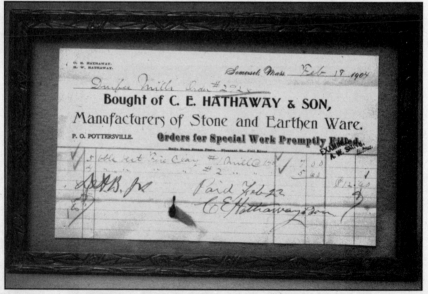

Pottery bill head, printed paper, C.E. Hathaway & Son, Somerset, Massachusetts, 1904;
$45–65.

Bill head, printed paper with view of factory; E. Swasey & Company, Portland Pottery, Portland, Maine; 1905; $60–80.

Bill head, printed paper with picture of stoneware; Exeter Pottery, Exeter, New Hampshire; 1910; $60–90.

Birdhouse, rare beehive form, salt-glazed stoneware with overall blue floral decoration; Pennsylvania or Ohio; 11 inches high; c. 1850–1875; $4,900–5,300.

Birdhouse, conical form, unglazed stoneware; by George W. Suttles, Wilson County, Texas; 9.5 inches high; c. 1870–1900; $235–285.

Birdhouse, conical form, Bristol-glazed stoneware, incised "bricks" edged in blue, other blue highlights; by Ruckel Pottery, White Hall, Illinois; 8 inches high; c. 1890–1910; $600–850.

Birdhouse, molded stoneware with brushed tan glaze and clapboard appearance; by Western Stoneware Company, Monmouth, Illinois; 8 inches high; c. 1930–1940; $90–130.

Bowl, molded Bristol-glazed stoneware with embossed Indian head highlighted in blue; by Western Stoneware Company, Monmouth, Illinois; 6 inches in diameter; c. 1910–1920; $250–325.

Bowl, blue decorated stoneware, Sipe, Nichols and Company, Williamsport, Pennsylvania, c. 1875–1877, 8.5 inches in diameter; $230–280.

Bowl, brown alkaline-glazed stoneware; Seagrove, North Carolina; 7.5 inches in diameter; c. 1840–1870; $350–500.

Bowl (mixing), wide rim, stoneware with rich brown glaze; by Peoria Pottery, Peoria, Illinois; 7 inches in diameter; c. 1863–1875; $40–55.

Bowl (mixing), molded Bristol-glazed stoneware with embossed sawtooth pattern below rim; by Ruckel Pottery Company, White Hall, Illinois; 7.5 inches in diameter; c. 1900–1930; $15–25.

Bowl (mixing), yellow-green Leon slip-glazed stoneware; Meyer Pottery, Bexar County, Texas; 7 inches in diameter; c. 1920–1940; $65–85.

Bowl (mixing), brown glazed stoneware; by Fort Dodge Stoneware Company, Fort Dodge, Iowa; 6 inches in diameter; c. 1892–1906; $55–80.

Bowl (mixing), molded, fluted Bristol-glazed stoneware with pale blue shading down from rim; by Red Wing Union Stoneware Company, Red Wing, Minnesota; 10 inches in diameter; c. 1906–1936; $45–65.

Cake mold, Turk's cap form, salt-glazed stoneware, interior with Albany slip; Midwestern or Southern; 7.5 inches in diameter; c. 1850–1880; $80–120.

Cake mold, brown Leon slip-glazed stoneware; Meyer Pottery, Bexar County, Texas; 9.5 inches in diameter; c. 1890–1920; $125–175.

Cake mold, Turk's cap form, brown Albany slip-glazed stoneware; Whately, Massachusetts; 10 inches in diameter; c. 1840–1860; $90–120.

Canteen, molded Bristol-glazed stoneware, embossed scene of deer and "Bardwell's Root Beer" highlighted in blue; by White's Pottery, Utica, New York; 11.5 inches high; c. 1890–1907; $400–550.

Canteen, molded brown glazed stoneware; by Western Stoneware Company, Monmouth, Illinois; 12 inches high; c. 1907–1914; $130–180.

Casserole, covered molded Bristol-glazed stoneware vessel with fluted sides and printed blue floral design; by Western

Food mold, salt-glazed stoneware, Midwestern, c. 1850–1880, 7.5 inches in diameter; $75–100.

Stoneware, molded with brown Albany slip glaze, Midwestern, c. 1920–1940; left, *casserole, 6 inches high; $30–45;* right, *pitcher, 8.5 inches high; $25–35.*

Stoneware Company, Monmouth, Illinois; 9 inches in diameter; c. 1930–1940; $55–75.

Casserole, molded Bristol-glazed stoneware with encircling blue bands; by Red Wing Union Stoneware Company, Red Wing, Minnesota; 10 inches in diameter; c. 1906–1936; $50–65.

Chamber pot, olive Leon slip glaze; by Meyer Pottery, Bexar County, Texas; 5 inches high; c. 1900–1930; $70–95.

Chamber pot, Bristol-glazed stoneware, blue shading from rim; by Western Stoneware Company, Monmouth, Illinois; 6 inches high; c. 1920–1935; $65–85.

Chamber pot, salt-glazed stoneware; by Charles Baker, Rockville, Indiana; 5.5 inches high; c. 1890–1900; $55–75.

Chamber pot, molded Bristol-glazed stoneware; by Red Wing Union Stoneware Company, Red Wing, Minnesota; 4.5 inches high; c. 1906–1936; $45–65.

Chamber pot, brown Albany slip-glazed stoneware; New York or Pennsylvania; 4 inches high; c. 1860–1890; $30–45.

Chemical dipping basket, brown glazed stoneware perforated basket with handle (often mistaken for cheese-drying baskets); A.J. Weeks Pottery, Akron, Ohio; 8 inches in diameter; c. 1905–1925; $65–85.

Chicken waterer, salt-glazed stoneware with elaborate overall blue decoration; Pennsylvania; 9 inches high; c. 1860–1880; $1,500–2,000.

Chicken waterer, brown glazed stoneware; Midwestern; 8.5 inches high; c. 1880–1900; $30–45.

Chicken waterer, molded Bristol-glazed stoneware with blue band and maker's mark; by Ruckel Pottery, White Hall, Illinois; 9 inches high; c. 1890–1920; $55–75.

Chicken waterer, molded brown glazed stoneware with embossed figures of two doves; Akron, Ohio; 10 inches high; dated 1886; $70–95.

Chicken waterer, yellow-green Leon slip-glazed stoneware; by Meyer Pottery, Bexar County, Texas; 9.5 inches high; c. 1890–1910; $145–195.

Chicken waterer, Bristol-glazed stoneware; by Western Stoneware Company, Monmouth, Illinois; 10 inches high; c. 1925–1945; $25–40.

Chicken waterer, molded horizontal tubular shape, brown glazed stoneware with embossed chicken and 1885 patent date; Ohio; 7.5 inches long; c. 1885–1890; $80–110.

Churn, salt-glazed stoneware with crude incised blue filled leaf; by Francis Nolen, Cloverland, Indiana; 20 inches high; c. 1850–1854; $900–1,200.

Stoneware, brown glazed ware from Missouri, c. 1870–1890. Left to right: *jar, 8 inches high, $65–95; jug, 7 inches high, $75–100; churn, 20 inches high, $300–450; rare scroddled ware jar, 9 inches high, $250–325.*

Churn, brown slip-glazed stoneware; by Daniel Brannon, Oakland, California; 20.5 inches high; c. 1856–1887; $500–750.

Churn, molded Bristol-glazed stoneware with blue band and maker's mark; by Ruckel Pottery, White Hall, Illinois; 19.5 inches high; c. 1900–1920; $75–95.

Churn, Bristol slip-glazed stoneware with blue stamped maker's mark and cast iron gears; by Star Pottery Works, Elmendorf, Texas; 29 inches high; c. 1909–1915; $200–285.

Churn, salt-glazed stoneware with large blue bird on flowering plant; by White's Pottery, Binghamton, New York; 27 inches high; c. 1849–1866; $2,200–2,800.

Churn, salt-glazed stoneware with "Kentucky, 1837" in blue script; by Isaac Thomas, Maysville, Kentucky; 26 inches high; 1837; $2,000–2,500.

Churn, molded salt-glazed stoneware with large parrot in blue; by Minnesota Stoneware Company, Red Wing, Minnesota; 24.5 inches high; c. 1883–1906; $2,300–2,800.

Churn, stoneware with yellow-brown ash glaze, Meaders Pottery, Cleveland, Georgia, c. 1895–1915, 25 inches high; $350–500.

Churn, salt-glazed stoneware, Hirum Wilson, Guadalupe County, Texas, c. 1860–1870, 25.5 inches high; $550–750.

Churn, salt-glazed stoneware with blue slip-trailed representation of large fish; by William Hart, Ogdensburg, New York; 25.5. inches high; c. 1856–1869; $2,300–3,100.

Churn, salt-glazed stoneware with large blue standing lion; by Hubbell & Chesebro, Geddes, New York; 25 inches high; c. 1867–1884; $3,500–4,500.

Churn, salt-glazed stoneware with large standing deer in blue against background of trees and birds; by Ottman Brothers & Company, Fort Edward, New York; 27.5 inches high; c. 1872–1892; $7,500–8,000.

Churn, salt-glazed stoneware, impressed BANGOR; Bangor, Maine Pottery; 27 inches high; c. 1880–1915; $80–110.

Churn, Bristol-glazed stoneware with blue stenciled maker's logo; by Monmouth Pottery Company, Monmouth, Illinois; 16 inches high; c. 1893–1906; $100–150.

Churn, salt-glazed stoneware with blue stenciled maker's mark, by Dawson & Son, Calhoun, Missouri; 17.5 inches high; c. 1872–1874; $200–275.

Stoneware, Missouri, c. 1860–1900. Left to right, *blue decorated jar, 8 inches high,* $225–300; *brown-glazed jar, 5.5 inches high,* $110–140; *blue decorated and stenciled churn, 17 inches high,* $300–450; *brown-glazed creamer, 4 inches high,* $75–100; *jug, 9 inches high,* $135–185.

Churn, salt-glazed stoneware with large cluster of blue slip flowers; by D.P. Shenfelder, Reading, Pennsylvania; 23.5 inches high; c. 1865–1885; $450–550.

Churn, cannon-barrel form, salt-glazed stoneware; by G. Benton & L. Stewart, Hartford, Connecticut; 18 inches high; c. 1808–1818; $300–450.

Churn, salt-glazed stoneware with blue house or fort, American flag, and trees; by Albert O. Whittemore, Havana, New York; 26.5 inches high; c. 1863–1893; $14,000–17,000.

Churn, salt-glazed stoneware decorated with very large and graphic blue rooster; by John Burger, Rochester, New York; 26 inches high; c. 1854–1867; $30,000–33,000.

Coffeepot, molded Bristol-glazed stoneware, blue glazed figure and "Faust Blend," pewter fittings; by White's Pottery, Utica, New York; 10 inches high; c. 1890–1907; $600–750.

Coffeepot, tan alkaline-glazed stoneware; attributed to John Landrum, Edgefield District, South Carolina; 7.5 inches high; c. 1810–1830; $3,000–4,500.

Coffeepot, molded unglazed stoneware with tin fittings and wire bale handle. Midwestern; 9 inches high; c. 1880–1910; $100–150.

Colander, cone-shaped Albany slip-glazed stoneware; Midwestern; 10 inches in diameter; c. 1880–1920; $65–95.

Colander, made by perforating mixing bowl, Bristol-glazed stoneware; Midwestern; 9.5 inches in diameter; c. 1900–1920; $75–100.

Crock, salt-glazed stoneware with matching lid, all covered with blue floral decoration; Pennsylvania; 7 inches high; c. 1860–1890; $800–1,100.

Crock, Bristol-glazed stoneware, blue banded at top and bottom, "BUTTER" stenciled in blue; by Western Stoneware Company, Monmouth, Illinois; 6 inches high; c. 1920–1930; $110–140.

Crock, Bristol-glazed stoneware with blue stenciled maker's mark; by Lowell Pottery Company, Tonica, Illinois; 10 inches high; c. 1895–1915; $30–45.

Crock, blue decorated stoneware, Brown Brothers, Huntington, New York, c. 1865–1885, 11 inches high; $300–400.

Crock, Bristol-glazed stoneware with embossed Indian head highlighted in blue; Western Stoneware Company, Monmouth, Illinois; 7 inches high; c. 1910–1920; $200–285.

Crock, brown glazed stoneware; by George Unser, Jeffersonville, Indiana; 8 inches high; c. 1870–1880; $70–95.

Crock, Bristol-glazed stoneware with blue stenciled maker's logo; by Monmouth Pottery Company, Monmouth, Illinois; 14 inches high; c. 1893–1906; $60–85.

Crock, Bristol and Albany slip-glazed stoneware, blue stenciled maker's logo; by Eben Swasey & Company, Portland, Maine; 8.5 inches high; c. 1886–1891; $55–75.

Crock, Bristol-glazed stoneware with blue stenciled maker's mark; by Fort Dodge Stoneware Company, Fort Dodge, Iowa; 11 inches high; c. 1892–1906; $125–175.

Crock, salt-glazed stoneware with large blue leaf design; by Minnesota Stoneware Company, Red Wing, Minnesota; 13 inches high; c. 1883–1906; $225–300.

Crock, molded blue decorated stoneware, Western Stoneware Company, Monmouth, Illinois, c. 1900–1920, 5.5 inches high; $65–85.

Crock, salt-glazed stoneware with punch work decoration, E.K. Moffett, Moffett's Mills, North Carolina, c. 1850–1870, 10.5 inches high; $500–750.

Crock, salt-glazed stoneware with incised floral decoration filled in blue and brown; by Nathan Clark & Company, Lyons, New York; 14.5 inches high; c. 1825–1835; $14,000–17,000.

Crock, salt-glazed stoneware with large blue rooster, fence, and tree; by Julius Norton, Bennington, Vermont, 10 inches high; c. 1845–1850; $2,400–2,900.

Crock, salt-glazed stoneware with dog carrying basket in blue; by Samuel Hart, Fulton, New York; 10.5 inches high; c. 1840–1876; $2,000–2,700.

Crock, blue decorated stoneware, New Jersey, c. 1870–1890, 8 inches high; $70–95.

Crock, blue decorated stoneware, E & LP Norton, Bennington, Vermont, c. 1861–1881, 10 inches high; $250–325.

Crock or cookie jar, Albany slip-glazed stoneware with applied decoration, John N. Stout, Ripley, Illinois, c. 1865–1875, 8 inches high; $1,000–1,500.

Crock, salt-glazed stoneware with blue floral decoration; by T.S. Balsley, Detroit, Michigan; 9 inches high; c. 1840–1860; $600–900.

Crock, salt-glazed stoneware with abstract blue floral decoration; by N.A. White & Company, Utica, New York; 12 inches high; c. 1865–1867; $175–225.

Crock, salt-glazed stoneware with large blue tulip; by Evan B. Jones, Pittstown, Pennsylvania; 10 inches high; c. 1870–1888; $225–285.

Crock, salt-glazed stoneware with blue bird on stylized branch; by Thomas F. Connolly, New Brunswick, New Jersey; 9.5 inches high; c. 1880–1881 (rare mark); $700–800.

Crock, salt-glazed stoneware with chicken pecking corn, fence in background; by Hover & Fingar's Hudson Pottery Company, Hudson, New York; 11 inches high; c. 1868–1869; $600–850.

Crock, blue decorated stoneware, Brady & Ryan, Ellenville, New York, c. 1878–1897; $350–450.

Crock, blue decorated stoneware, William A. MacQuoid, New York, New York, c. 1863–1879, 10 inches high; $300–400.

Crock, salt-glazed stoneware with blue stenciled maker's mark; by John M. Jegglin, Boonville, Missouri; 12.5 inches high; c. 1867–1880; $175–250.

Crock, salt-glazed stoneware with chicken pecking corn in blue; New York Stoneware Company, Fort Edward, New York; 11.5 inches high; c. 1861–1891; $350–550.

Crock, salt-glazed stoneware with reclining leopard in blue; by Riedinger & Caire, Poughkeepsie, New York; 9 inches high; c. 1857–1878; $2,000–2,700.

Crock, salt-glazed stoneware; by Solomon Purdy, Mogadore, Ohio; 10.5 inches high; c. 1830–1840; $140–190.

Crock, brown glazed stoneware, by Huffman Pottery, Pilot Grove, Missouri; 7 inches high; c. 1880–1890; $75–100.

Crock, salt-glazed stoneware with blue figures of man and woman and words "Willie & Minnie Johnson"; by Fulper Brothers Pottery, Flemington, New Jersey; 12 inches high; c. 1881–1898; $4,800–5,400.

Crock, blue decorated stoneware, Ballard Brothers, Burlington, Vermont, c. 1855–1865, 9.5 inches high; $180–260.

Crock, blue decorated stoneware, Ottman Brothers, Fort Edward, New York, c. 1872–1892, 10.5 inches high; $275–350.

Crock, stoneware decorated with impressed blue-filled cow, Gardiner Stoneware Manufactory, Gardiner, Maine, c. 1880–1890, 12 inches high; $130–180.

Crock, blue decorated stoneware with Centennial design, Lamson & Swasey, Portland, Maine, 1876, 11 inches high; $375–475.

Crock, brown glazed stoneware; by Macomb Pottery Company, Macomb, Illinois; 12 inches high; c. 1880–1906; $40–55.

Crock, salt-glazed molded stoneware with blue filled impressed decoration for "Knickerbocker Catering Co."; by White's Pottery, Utica, New York; 7 inches high; c. 1890–1900; $400–500.

Crock, molded Bristol-glazed stoneware with pale blue shading and embossed classical figure; by Western Stoneware Company, Monmouth, Illinois; 9.5 inches high; c. 1906–1920; $200–300.

Crock, blue decorated stenciled stoneware, Pennsylvania or West Virginia, c. 1870–1890, 9.5 inches high; $400–500.

Crock, molded blue decorated stoneware, White's Pottery, Utica, New York, c. 1890–1905, 5 inches high; $340–390.

Crock, blue decorated stoneware, Haxstun & Company, Fort Edward, New York, c. 1867–1872, 9.5 inches high; $300–375.

Crock, blue decorated stoneware, Riedinger & Caire, Poughkeepsie, New York, c. 1857–1878, 10 inches high; $400–550.

Crock, salt-glazed stoneware with blue eagle carrying banner; by John Darrow & Sons, Baldwinsville, New York; 9.5 inches high; c. 1855–1872; $1,000–1,400.

Crock, salt-glazed stoneware, blue stenciled capacity number in circle; by Torbert & Baker, Brazil, Indiana; 13.5 inches high; c. 1880–1899; $75–125.

Crock, Bristol-glazed stoneware, blue stenciled maker's mark and capacity number; by Ruckel Pottery, White Hall, Illinois; 8.5 inches high; c. 1890–1910; $40–55.

Cruet, Albany and Bristol slip-glazed stoneware, ovoid body, long neck and handle; by Weir Pottery Company, Monmouth, Illinois; 8 inches high; c. 1900–1905; $65–95.

Cuspidor, salt-glazed stoneware with blue floral sprays; Pennsylvania; 8.5 inches in diameter; c. 1860–1890; $135–175.

Cuspidor, brown Albany slip-glazed stoneware; Northeastern; 10 inches in diameter; c. 1870–1900; $40–65.

Cuspidor, olive-brown Leon slip–glazed stoneware; by Meyer Pottery, Bexar County, Texas; 9 inches in diameter; c. 1890–1900; $150–225.

Cuspidor, salt-glazed stoneware decorated with blue banding and incised ribbon work; by Red Wing Union Stoneware Company, Red Wing, Minnesota; 10 inches in diameter; c. 1906–1936; $150–200.

Cuspidor, molded Bristol-glazed stoneware with blue shading and scalloped rim; by Western Stoneware Company, Monmouth, Illinois; 8 inches in diameter; c. 1920–1940; $35–55.

Custard cup, molded brown glazed stoneware; by Minnesota Stoneware Company, Red Wing, Minnesota; 3 inches high; c. 1883–1906; $25–40.

Custard cup, molded Bristol-glazed stoneware with fluted sides and blue stenciled floral pattern about rim; by Western Stoneware Company, Monmouth, Illinois; 3 inches high; c. 1920–1940; $20–30.

Custard cup, salt-glazed stoneware; Midwestern; 2.5 inches high; c. 1870–1910; $15–25.

Doll head and shoulders, salt-glazed stoneware with hair and eyes in blue; Pennsylvania or Ohio; 5.5 inches high; c. 1870–1890; $4,300–4,900.

Doorstop, molded in the form of a sitting poodle, Bristol-glazed stoneware with blue collar; by Lowell Pottery Company, Lowell, Illinois; 7.5 inches high; c. 1895–1915; $225–300.

Doorstop, molded in the form of an owl, Bristol-glazed stoneware with base touched in blue; by Ruckel Pottery Company, White Hall, Illinois; 8 inches high; c. 1890–1920; $165–245.

Doorstop, molded in the form of a sitting spaniel, Bristol-glazed stoneware with spots of blue; McDade Pottery, Bastrop City, Texas; 8.5 inches high; c. 1920–1930; $135–185.

Doorstop, molded in the form of an owl, stoneware covered with dark blue glaze; by August Blanck, Boonville, Missouri; 8.5 inches high; c. 1880–1890; $400–650.

Figurine, recumbent deer, salt-glazed stoneware with blue highlights; Strasburg area of Virginia; 14 inches long; c. 1860–1890; $3,500–5,000.

Figurine, recumbent lamb, molded stoneware with light tan glaze; by Clinton Pottery Company, Clinton, Missouri; 9 inches long; c. 1889–1897; $350–500.

Figurine, cow and calf on oval base, Bristol-glazed stoneware; by Monmouth Pottery Company, Monmouth, Illinois; 6 inches long; c. 1893–1906; $200–275.

Figurine, standing pig, Albany slip-glazed stoneware with embossed maker's mark; by Monmouth Pottery Company, Monmouth, Illinois; 4 inches long; c. 1893–1906; $135–185.

Figural molded stoneware, brown slip-glazes, all from Missouri, c. 1870–1900. Left to right: *lamb, 8 inches long, $350–500; snake jug, 7 inches high, $400–550; owl doorstop, 12 inches high, $275–350; basket, 6 inches high, $250–325; snake jug, 9 inches high, $500–650.*

Figural stoneware, molded brown-glazed door stop, Ohio, c. 1850–1880, 9.5 inches high; $250–325.

Figurine, elephant (part of a bookends set), stoneware with a gray glaze; by Western Stoneware Company, Monmouth, Illinois; 6 inches long; c. 1920–1940; $110–150.

Figurine, boy holding crock on shoulder with dog, Bristol and brown Albany slip-glazed stoneware; by Union Stoneware Company, Red Wing, Minnesota; 7 inches high; c. 1894–1906; $2,000–2,500.

Figurine, man in European dress playing bagpipes, brown glazed stoneware; by Lyons Pottery, Lyons, New York; 10 inches high; c. 1865–1875; $450–600.

Flask, salt-glazed stoneware with incised blue filled flower; New York or New Jersey; 8 inches high; c. 1800–1820; $1,200–1,600.

Flask, round form, salt-glazed stoneware with overall abstract blue decoration and date 1789; by Abraham Mead, Greenwich, Connecticut; 5.5 inches high; 1789; $6,000–7,500.

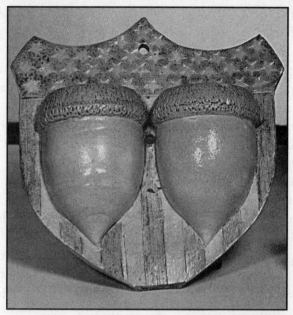

Figural stoneware, molded wall sconce-glazed in red, blue and white Bristol slip, Hyten Pottery, Benton, Arkansas, c. 1880–1885, 8 inches high; $650–950.

Flasks, salt-glazed stoneware, New England, c. 1820–1850: left, *8.5 inches high,* $80–110; right, *6 inches high,* $65–85.

Flask, round form, brown slip stoneware incised "Made by Ira Griffith, Clay City, Ind., Oct. 1888"; by Ira Griffith, Clay City, Indiana; 5 inches high; 1888; $300–400.

Flask, salt-glazed stoneware in the form of recumbent pig with incised blue filled railway lines; Anna Pottery, Anna, Illinois; 5.5 inches long; c. 1860–1890; $2,500–3,200.

Flask, Albany slip-glazed stoneware in form of recumbent pig with incised political slogans; by the Texarkana, Arkansas pottery; 5 inches long; c. 1880; $950–1,350.

Flask, flattened-handle vessel, yellow-green alkaline slip-glazed stoneware with name and date in white slip; by Thomas Chandler, Edgefield District, South Carolina; 8 inches high; 1851; $5,000–7,000.

Flower pot, salt-glazed stoneware with extensive blue floral decoration; by New York Stoneware Company, Fort Edward, New York; 6.5 inches high; c. 1861–1891; $800–950.

Flower pot, unglazed stoneware with brown-slip decoration, Pennsylvania or West Virginia, c. 1860–1880, 8 inches high; $275–350.

Flower pot, Albany slip–glazed stoneware; Northeastern; 5 inches high; c. 1850–1870; $35–50.

Flower pot, molded brown glazed stoneware with embossed encircling swag and tassel design; attributed to Norton Pottery, Bennington, Vermont; 6 inches high; c. 1845–1894; $65–85.

Flower pot, unglazed brown stoneware; by Meyer Pottery, Bexar County, Texas; 9 inches high; c. 1900–1920; $55–70.

Flower pot, brown glazed stoneware with scalloped rim and tooled decoration; by Fort Dodge Stoneware Company, Fort Dodge, Iowa; 5.5 inches high; c. 1892–1906; $90–120.

Flower pot, molded Bristol-glazed stoneware with fluted sides; by Western Stoneware Company, Monmouth, Illinois; 7 inches high; c. 1920–1940; $20–30.

Flower pot in form of tree trunk, unglazed brown-tinted stoneware; by Frank B. Norton & Company, Worcester, Massachusetts; 10.5 inches high; c. 1858–1871; $110–140.

Flower pot, cone form for graveyards, salt-glazed stoneware; by William Saenger, Elmendorf, Texas; 13 inches high; c. 1890–1900; $35–55.

Flower pot, cone form for graveyards, unglazed stoneware; by Western Stoneware Company, Monmouth, Illinois; 12 inches high; c. 1930–1940; $10–20.

Flower pot on stand, two-piece salt-glazed stoneware with scalloped rims and blue floral decoration; attributed to Truman Smith, Clay City, Indiana; 22 inches high; c. 1846–1865; $1,000–1,500.

Foot warmer, brown Albany slip-glazed stoneware, molded tubular shape with embossed leaf design, pewter top, and chain; by Red Wing Union Stoneware Company, Red Wing, Minnesota; 10 inches long; c. 1906–1936; $150–210.

Foot warmer, Bristol-glazed stoneware; by Dorchester Pottery Works, Dorchester, Massachusetts; 9.5 inches long; c. 1900–1920; $25–35.

Foot warmer, Bristol-glazed stoneware with "A Warm Friend" and maker's mark stenciled in blue; Logan Pottery Company, Logan, Ohio; 9.5 inches long; c. 1880–1900; $55–75.

Foot warmer or hot-water bottle, salt-glazed stoneware, Bangor Stoneware Works, Bangor, Maine, c. 1880–1900, 11 inches high; $70–95.

Foot warmer, tubular-shaped Bristol-glazed stoneware with black printed logo; by Western Stoneware Company, Monmouth, Illinois; 10.5 inches long; c. 1920–1940; $20–35.

Fruit jar, Bristol-glazed stoneware, top secured with iron wire bale; by Weir Pottery, Monmouth, Illinois; 7 inches high; c. 1900–1905; $35–55.

Fruit jar, Bristol and brown Albany slip-glazed stoneware, top secured by wire bale; by Peoria Pottery, Peoria, Illinois; 10 inches high; c. 1880–1900; $30–45.

Fruit jar, Bristol and brown Albany slip-glazed stoneware with metal screw top; by Western Stoneware Company, Monmouth, Illinois; 8 inches high; c. 1906–1920; $40–55.

Fruit jar, salt-glazed stoneware with black printed advertising logo; by Red Wing Union Stoneware Company, Red Wing, Minnesota; 8 inches high; c. 1906–1936; $175–235.

Funnel, brown glazed stoneware; Northeastern; 7 inches long; c. 1870–1890; $50–65.

Brown and white Bristol-slip decorated stoneware. Left to right: *bean pot, Ohio,
c. 1900–1920, 7 inches high, $20–30; miniature jug, Ohio, c. 1920–1930, 4 inches
high, $30–45; preserve jar, Weir Pottery Company, Monmouth, Illinois, c. 1899–1905,
$35–50.*

Funnel, salt-glazed stoneware; Denton County, Texas; 8 inches
    long; c. 1890–1910; $70–95.
Funnel, Bristol-glazed stoneware with black stenciled maker's
    mark; by Union Stoneware Company, Red Wing, Minne-
    sota; 6 inches high; c. 1894–1906; $275–350.
Funnel, Bristol-glazed stoneware; by Western Stoneware Com-
    pany, Monmouth, Illinois; 5.5 inches high; c. 1910–1930;
    $50–75.

Gemel or twin bottle, salt-glazed stoneware with incised blue filled
    bird decoration; Absalom Stedman, New Haven, Connecti-
    cut; 8 inches high; c. 1825–1833; $3,000–4,500.
Gemel or double bottle, brown Albany slip-glazed stoneware;
    Northeastern; 9.5 inches high; c. 1860–1890; $80–120.
Grotesque or face jug, alkaline-glazed stoneware with porcelain
    teeth; Brown Pottery, Atlanta, Georgia; 8.5 inches high;
    c. 1880–1920; $750–1,000.

Grotesque or face jug, alkaline-glazed stoneware with porcelain teeth and eyes; by Lanier Meaders, White County, Georgia; 10.5 inches high; 1979; $500–750.

Grotesque or face jug, brown Albany slip-glazed stoneware; Southern; 6.5 inches high; c. 1900–1920; $200–300.

Harvest jug, salt-glazed stoneware with incised blue filled decoration, inscription, and applied face; by Kirkpatrick Pottery, Vermillionville, Illinois; 11 inches high; c. 1836–1871; $3,000–4,000.

Harvest jug, salt-glazed stoneware with blue floral decoration, two spouts, and applied strap handle; New England; 10 inches high; c. 1820–1850; $400–600.

Harvest jug, Bristol and brown Albany slip-glazed stoneware with wire bale handle; by Western Stoneware Company, Monmouth, Illinois; 8.5 inches high; c. 1906–1915; $65–95.

Harvest jug, brown Albany slip glaze with handle and double spout, applied snake decoration; by Erastus Crooks, Claylick, Ohio; 10 inches high; c. 1850–1870; $4,300–4,800.

Harvest jug, wire bale handle, molded Bristol-glazed stoneware; by F.H. Weeks, Akron, Ohio; 8 inches high; c. 1891–1910; $55–75.

Humidor, molded brown Albany slip-glazed stoneware with embossed floral pattern and word "CIGARS"; by Western Stoneware Company, Monmouth, Illinois; 10 inches high; c. 1910–1920; $135–185.

Humidor, molded sixteen-sided brown Albany slip-glazed stoneware; by Edmands & Company Pottery, Charlestown, Massachusetts; 7 inches high; c. 1835–1850; $70–95.

Humidor, molded unglazed stoneware with applied handles in form of mountain-goat heads and horns; by White's Pottery, Utica, New York; 8 inches high; c. 1890–1900; $250–350.

Hunting horn, tan salt-glazed stoneware; by William Grindstaff, Knox County, Tennessee; 16 inches long; dated 1871; $2,600–3,200.

Hunting horn, salt-glazed stoneware highlighted in blue; by Charles Decker, Johnson City, Tennessee; 19 inches long; c. 1872–1900; $3,000–4,000.

Stoneware. Left to right, *brown-glazed ink sander (rare), Northeastern, c. 1800–1830, 3.5 inches high,* $95–135; *blue decorated mug, 4 inches high, Northeastern, c. 1830–1850,* $75–95; *brown-glazed bank, 3.5 inches high, New Jersey, c. 1850–1870,* $55–75.

Ink sander, hourglass shape, salt-glazed stoneware with overall abstract blue decoration; northeastern United States; 4.5 inches high; c. 1820–1840; $2,900–3,400.

Ink sander, baluster form, salt–glazed stoneware with impressed blue filled date and name of owner; by Israel Seymour, Troy, New York; 3 inches high; 1829; $850–1,250.

Ink sander or salt shaker in the form of a duck, salt-glazed stoneware highlighted in blue; Pennsylvania; 4.5 inches long; c. 1830–1850; $1,600–2,300.

Inkstand, salt-glazed stoneware, floral embossing highlighted in blue, oblong stand with two removable wells; Northeastern; 6 inches long; c. 1800–1830; $900–1,100.

Inkstand, oblong salt-glazed stoneware highlighted in blue with applied turtle; by Charles Decker, Johnson City, Tennessee; 5 inches long; c. 1872–1885; $1,750–2,500.

Inkwell, salt–glazed stoneware with incised blue filled flowers, birds, and date 1797; New York or New Jersey; 4 inches in diameter; 1797; $5,500–6,500.

Inkwell, salt-glazed stoneware with blue highlights; by Smith & Day, Norwalk, Connecticut; 4 inches in diameter; c. 1843–1849; $350–450.

Inkwell, salt-glazed stoneware with coggle decoration highlighted in blue; by Ethan S. Fox, Athens, New York; 4 inches in diameter; c. 1838–1843; $350–500.

Inkwell, salt-glazed stoneware; Northeastern; 3.3 inches in diameter; c. 1820–1850; $60–85.

Inkwell, salt-glazed stoneware, decorative notching of rims; Northeastern; 4 inches in diameter; c. 1810–1840; $110–160.

Jar, salt-glazed stoneware, minor blue decoration; by John Bell, Waynesboro, Pennsylvania; 5 inches high; c. 1850–1880; $75–90.

Jar, salt-glazed stoneware with blue stenciled maker's mark and floral pattern; by Richey & Hamilton, Palatine, West Virginia; 10 inches high; c. 1870–1890; $125–165.

Jar, tan salt-glazed stoneware, flaring lip; by Nicholas Fox, Chatham County, North Carolina; 7 inches high; c. 1830–1855; $200–275.

Canning jar, blue decorated stoneware, Pennsylvania or West Virginia, c. 1850–1870, 7.5 inches high; $375–450.

Jar, brown manganese decorated stoneware, Henry Glazier, Huntingdon, Pennsylvania, c. 1831–1854, 8 inches high; $235–315.

Jar, salt-glazed stoneware, Jacob Doris Craven, Randolph County, North Carolina, c. 1855–1885, 9.5 inches high; $90–130.

Jar, salt-glazed stoneware with scene of house and tree in pale blue; New York or Pennsylvania; 9 inches high; c. 1860–1880; $2,500–2,900.

Jar, salt-glazed stoneware with blue deer, fence, and tree; by Edmands & Company, Charlestown, Massachusetts; 10.5 inches high; c. 1852–1868; $1,600–2,200.

Jar, salt-glazed stoneware with blue at handles; by Gordon Purdy, Portage County, Ohio; 11.5 inches high; c. 1855–1865; $80–120.

Jar, salt-glazed stoneware with blue at handles, by Isaac M. Mead, Mogadore, Ohio; 9.5 inches high; c. 1840–1860; $135–185.

Jar, brown glazed stoneware; by Henry Melcher, Louisville, Kentucky; 12.5 inches high; c. 1845–1885; $30–45.

Jar, brown glazed stoneware; by George Husher, Brazil, Indiana; 7 inches high; c. 1870–1875; $80–110.

Jar, salt-glazed stoneware with scene of man and woman in blue, the former holding a gun, 2-gallon size; New Jersey or Pennsylvania; 10.5 inches high; c. 1870–1890; $5,500–6,200.

Jar, brown-glazed stoneware with later hand-painted floral decoration, New England, c. 1890–1910, 4.75 inches high; $70–90.

Jars, salt-glazed stoneware: left, *Benedict C. Milburn, Alexandria, Virginia, c. 1841–1867, 7 inches high, $200–300;* right, *P. Hiser & Sons, Washington, D.C., c. 1870–1885, 9.5 inches high, $100–175.*

Jar, blue decorated stoneware with unusual face, Louis Lehman, New York, New York, c. 1858–1863, 9 inches high; $900–1,200.

Jar, salt-glazed stoneware; by Uriah Kendall, Cincinnati, Ohio; 9.5 inches high; c. 1830–1840; $75–110.

Jar, salt–glazed stoneware with stenciled eagle and freehand decoration, all in blue; by R.T. Williams, New Geneva, Pennsylvania; 23 inches high; c. 1882–1895; $1,300–1,700.

Jar, salt-glazed stoneware, overall blue floral decoration, ovoid form, original lid; New York or Massachusetts; only 5 inches high; c. 1820–1840; $3,400–3,700.

Jar, tan alkaline-glazed stoneware with applied American eagle and classical figure; a presentation piece attributed to John Leopard, Randolph County, Alabama; 17 inches high; c. 1850–1860; $20,000–23,000.

Jar, salt-glazed stoneware; by Truman Smith, Clay City, Indiana; 14 inches high; c. 1846–1865; $135–185.

Jar, salt-glazed stoneware with blue floral decoration; by Samuel H. Sonner, Strasburg, Virginia; 10 inches high; c. 1870–1883; $150–225.

Jar, blue decorated stoneware, Pennsylvania, c. 1860–1880, 15 inches high; $350–500.

Jar, ocher-glazed stoneware, Frederick Carpenter, Charlestown, Massachusetts, c. 1804–1811, 10.5 inches high; $325–425.

Jar, blue decorated stoneware, Morgan Pottery, Cheesequake, New Jersey, c. 1790–1800, 9 inches high; $1,100–1,500.

Jar, tan salt-glazed stoneware, single vertical handle; by James A. Boggs, Randolph County, Alabama; 14 inches high; c. 1890–1910; $135–185.

Jar, dark brown streaky alkaline-glazed stoneware incised "L.M. Dave/April 8, 1858"; by the slave potter Dave, Edgefield, South Carolina; 17.5 inches high; 1858; $8,000–11,000.

Jar, salt-glazed stoneware with floral swag and tassel decoration in blue; by Benedict C. Milburn, Alexandria, Virginia, 13 inches high; c. 1841–1867; $1,300–1,800.

Jar, salt-glazed stoneware with blue floral decoration; by Hugh Smith, Alexandria, Disrict of Columbia; 12 inches high; c. 1825–1841; $2,000–2,800.

Jar, salt-glazed stoneware; by Isaac Thomas, Maysville, Kentucky; 9 inches high; c. 1837–1860; $85–125.

Jar, Bristol slip-glazed stoneware with stenciled maker's mark in blue; by W.H. Bennett, Benton, Arkansas; 12 inches high; c. 1890–1905; $65–95.

Jar, blue decorated stoneware, Thomas Reed, Greene County, Indiana, c. 1865–1880, 9 inches high; $250–350.

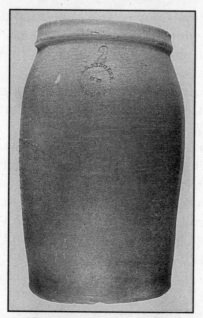

Jar, brown-glazed stoneware, John B. Ziegler, Bellvue, Nebraska, c. 1862–1865 (extremely rare), 13 inches high; $550–750.

Detail of potter John B. Ziegler's mark on jar described above. Marked pieces are almost always more valuable.

Jar, brownish-green alkaline glaze, large tulip decoration in dark-brown-and-white slip; by Colin Rhodes, Edgefield District, South Carolina; 16.5 inches high; c. 1840–1850; $4,000–5,500.

Jar, salt-glazed stoneware with blue parrot on abstract branches; by Frank B. Norton, Worcester, Massachusetts; 11 inches high; c. 1877–1882; $400–550.

Jar, molded salt-glazed stoneware with embossed blue filled horse head; by White's Pottery, Utica, New York; 4.5 inches high; c. 1890–1907; $225–275.

Jar, molded, twelve-sided with rich brown glaze; by Peoria Pottery, Peoria, Illinois; 8.5 inches high; c. 1863–1875; $45–60.

Jar, ovoid tan salt-glazed stoneware; by Daniel Cribbs, Tuscaloosa, Alabama; 12 inches high; c. 1830–1860; $250–325.

Jar, blue decorated stoneware, Centennial piece, A. Haxstun & Company, Fort Edward, New York, 1876, 11 inches high; $350–425.

Jar, blue decorated stoneware, Pennsylvania, c. 1850–1890, 7.5 inches high; $90–110.

Jar, blue decorated stoneware, David & Isaac Wells, Whately, Massachusetts, c. 1857–1861, 10.5 inches high; $185–245.

Jug, salt-glazed stoneware, Goodwin & Webster, Hartford, Connecticut, c. 1810–1840, 12 inches high; $150–200.

Jar, salt-glazed stoneware; by John S. Perry, Putnamville, Indiana; 10.5 inches high; c. 1831–1864; $275–350.

Jar, Albany slip-glazed stoneware; by John M. Jegglin, Boonville, Missouri; 6 inches high; c. 1867–1880; $75–95.

Jar for snuff, brown glazed stoneware, paper label for "Pulaski Snuff"; by Red Wing Union Stoneware Company, Red Wing, Minnesota; 7 inches high; c. 1877–1906; $185–265.

Jar with cover, Bristol-glazed stoneware tinted blue at top and bottom and with blue stenciled "COOKIES"; by Western Stoneware Company, Monmouth, Illinois; 9 inches high; c. 1920–1940; $125–165.

Jug, ovoid salt-glazed stoneware with impressed and incised blue filled floral design; by Peter Cross, Hartford, Connecticut; 14.5 inches high; c. 1805–1815; $900–1,400.

Jug, salt-glazed stoneware with large bird sitting on nest with eggs in blue, 5-gallon size; Pennsylvania; 15 inches high; c. 1870–1880; $5,200–5,800.

Jug, ovoid salt-glazed stoneware with applied clasped hands; by E. Hall, Muskingum County, Ohio; 9 inches high; c. 1856–1860; $1,000–1,500.

Jug, molded Bristol-glazed stoneware with stenciled blue oak leaf logo; by Western Stoneware Company, White Hall, Illinois; 9 inches high; c. 1906–1915; $25–35.

Jug with wire bale handle, Bristol slip-glazed stoneware; by Red Wing Union Stoneware Company, Red Wing, Minnesota; 9 inches high; c. 1877–1906; $60–85.

Jug, ovoid salt-glazed stoneware with impressed blue filled rose; attributed to Fenton & Carpenter, Boston, Massachusetts; 14.5 inches high; c. 1793–1796; $550–750.

Jug, ovoid salt-glazed stoneware with impressed fish and berry-form coggle banding and word "WINE"; Old Bridge, New Jersey; 9.5 inches high; c. 1805–1815; $800–1,200.

Jugs, stoneware. Left to right: *ocher decorated, Frederick Carpenter, Charlestown, Massachusetts, c. 1804–1810, 11.5 inches high, $350–450; dark-brown salt–glaze, Branch Green, Philadelphia, Pennsylvania, c. 1809–1827, 11 inches high, $300–400; blue decorated, Clarkson Crolius, Jr., New York, New York, c. 1835–1849, $265–325.*

Jugs, advertising, white Bristol-slip stoneware; both Ohio, c. 1890–1910: left, *13 inches high, $65–85;* right, *9.5 inches high, $70–100.*

Jug, green and brown alkaline-glazed stoneware, Alabama, c. 1860–1880, 14 inches high; $265–335.

Jug, double-handled, yellow-brown Leon slip-glazed stoneware; by Meyer Pottery, Bexar County, Texas; 17 inches high; c. 1900–1940; $225–300.

Jug, Bristol-glazed stoneware with blue stenciled maker's logo; by Monmouth Pottery Company, Monmouth, Illinois; 13 inches high; c. 1893–1906; $60–90.

Jug, double-handled, yellow-green alkaline-glazed stoneware; by Thomas Chandler, Edgefield District, South Carolina; 13 inches high; c. 1840–1851; $2,800–3,400.

Jug, ovoid salt-glazed stoneware, impressed "Rough & Ready" highlighted in blue; by Samuel Routson, Doylestown, Ohio; 10 inches high; c. 1835–1845; $700–900.

Jug, salt-glazed stoneware; A. Rabine, Calhoun, Missouri; 9 inches high; c. 1871–1875; $100–150.

Jug, salt-glazed with blue floral spray; by Peoria Pottery, Peoria, Illinois; 12.5 inches high; c. 1863–1874; $300–400.

Jug, salt-glazed stoneware with brushed blue feather decoration, ovoid form; by William H. Ingell, Taunton, Massachusetts; 10 inches high; c. 1830–1840; $240–300.

Jug, Bristol-glazed, blue-banded stoneware, Red Wing Union Stoneware Company, Red Wing, Minnesota, c. 1906–1936, 11 inches high; $55–75.

Jug, brown and tan alkaline-glazed stoneware, Georgia, c. 1865–1875, 12.5 inches high; $225–300.

Jug, blue decorated stoneware, Somerset Potters Works, Somerset, Massachusetts, c. 1850–1882, 13 inches high; $275–375.

Jug, salt-glazed stoneware with simple floral design, ovoid form; by Lyman & Clark, Gardiner, Maine; 10.5 inches high; c. 1837–1839; $220–280.

Jug, salt-glazed stoneware with incised blue filled bird on branch, ovoid form; by Calvin Boynton, Troy, New York; 10 inches high; c. 1829–1835; $1,400–1,800.

Jug, salt-glazed stoneware with minor touches of blue; by John B. Ziegler, Clay County, Indiana; 14.5 inches high; c. 1853; $150–225.

Jug, double-handled, salt-glazed stoneware with freehand decoration including maker's mark in blue; by Viall & Ruckel, Middlebury, Ohio; 17 inches high; c. 1860–1880; $1,800–2,200.

Jug, salt-glazed stone with impressed blue filled eagle and swan; Gardiner Stoneware Factory, Gardiner, Maine; 12 inches high; c. 1880–1890; $175–225.

Jug, salt-glazed stoneware with three large trumpet flowers in blue; by John Burger, Rochester, New York; 12.5 inches high; c. 1854–1867; $400–500.

Jug, molded stoneware, Bristol and Albany slip-glaze, Western Pottery Company, Denver, Colorado, c. 1900–1920, 12 inches high; $70–95.

Jug, stenciled brown glazed stoneware, Maryland, c. 1875–1890, 8 inches high; $90–120.

Jug, salt-glazed stoneware; by A.A. Austin & Company, Commerce, Missouri; 12.5 inches high; c. 1840–1850; $250–325.

Jug, brown Albany slip-glazed stoneware in form of man with sculpted face and arms; by William Grindstaff, Knoxville, Tennessee; 14 inches high; c. 1870–1900; $6,000–8,000.

Jug, molded brown Albany slip-glazed stoneware; by Fort Dodge Stoneware Company, Fort Dodge, Iowa; 11 inches high; c. 1892–1906; $75–100.

Jug, ovoid salt-glazed stoneware; by Coffin, Huggins & Company, Etna, Indiana; 9 inches high; c. 1845–1855; $135–185.

Jug, salt-glazed stoneware with blue depiction of "Man in the Moon" figure; by Cowden & Wilcox, Harrisburg, Pennsylvania; 13.5 inches high; c. 1863–1887; $3,900–4,500.

Jug, brown glazed stoneware; by Peoria Pottery, Peoria, Illinois; 8.5 inches high; c. 1863–1875; $50–75.

Jug, olive-green alkaline-glazed stoneware with rare Confederate inscription and date; by Thomas Owensby, Jr., Cherokee County, South Carolina; 13.5 inches high; 1864; $17,000–19,000.

Jug, salt-glazed stoneware with three impressed blue filled stamps in the form of a mortar and pestle; by Jacob Caire, Poughkeepsie, New York; 10.5 inches high; c. 1845–1848; $500–650.

Jug, salt-glazed stoneware with large blue-dot grouse; by Frederick Stetzenmeyer, Rochester, New York; 11.5 inches high; c. 1849–1855; $5,500–6,000.

Lager glass, molded Bristol-glazed stoneware with "Haberle's Lager" in blue; by White's Pottery, Utica, New York; 7 inches high; c. 1890–1907; $200–250.

Lamp base for kerosene lamp, molded Bristol-glazed stoneware with embossed floral pattern and brass fittings; by Western Stoneware Company, Monmouth, Illinois; 9 inches high; c. 1906–1915; $135–185.

Match holder, beehive form, molded salt-glazed stoneware with "American Brewing Company" highlighted in blue; White's Pottery, Utica, New York; 4.5 inches high; c. 1890–1907; $150–225.

Match holder, vase form, unglazed stoneware with coggle decoration; by Meyer Pottery, Bexar County, Texas; 4 inches high; c. 1900–1920; $65–90.

Meat roaster, unglazed stoneware, covered dome-top vessel with wire bale handle; by Minnesota Stoneware Company, Red Wing, Minnesota; 10 inches in diameter; c. 1883–1906; $110–160.

Meat tenderizer, brown glazed stoneware with wooden handle, embossed "Patent, Dec. 25, 1877"; Midwestern; 10 inches long; c. 1877–1880; $90–130.

Milk pan, salt-glazed stoneware with encircling blue leaf decoration and pouring spout; Pennsylvania or New Jersey; 5 inches high; c. 1840–1865; $340–410.

Milk pan, salt-glazed stoneware with blue tulip decoration, semiovoid form; by Sylvester Blair, Cortland, New York; 4.5 inches high; c. 1829–1835; $500–625.

Milk pan with pouring spout, olive-green alkaline glaze with white slip-trailed decoration; Colin Rhodes, Edgefield, South Carolina; 11 inches in diameter; c. 1840–1853; $1,800–2,400.

Match holder, molded blue decorated stoneware, White's Pottery, Utica, New York, c. 1890–1905, 3 inches high; $55–75.

Stoneware, brown-glazed, North Carolina. Left to right: *punch decorated pitcher, c. 1790–1810, 13 inches high, $1,200–1,600; flask incised TH.A. ANDREWS, 1784, 5.5 inches high, $4,000–5,000; milk pan, c. 1830–1860, 15 inches in diameter, $450–600.*

Milk pan with pouring lip, salt-glazed stoneware with blue floral decoration; by Peter Hermann, Baltimore, Maryland; 5.5 inches high; c. 1850–1872; $300–450.

Milk pan, tan alkaline-glazed stoneware; by E.T. Mapp, Bacon Level, Alabama; 5 inches high; c. 1870–1910; $200–300.

Milk pan, stoneware with tan metallic slip; New York or Connecticut; 15 inches in diameter; c. 1830–1850; $185–265.

Milk pan, brown Albany slip-glazed stoneware; by North Star Stoneware Company, Red Wing, Minnesota; 11 inches in diameter; c. 1892–1896; $65–90.

Milk pan, pale blue glazed stoneware; by Western Stoneware Company, Monmouth, Illinois; 9 inches in diameter; c. 1910–1940; $35–55.

Miniature jug, Albany slip-glazed stoneware with incised advertising logo; Indiana; 2.75 inches high; c. 1890–1900; $75–95.

Miniature jug, Albany slip-glazed stoneware; by Blanck & Jegglin, Boonville, Missouri; 2.5 inches high; c. 1880–1900; $65–90.

Miniature jug, brown Albany slip-glazed stoneware with "Little Brown Jug" incised; by Edward Norton Company, Bennington, Vermont; 3 inches high; c. 1882–1900; $65–90.

Miniature jug, stoneware with rich brown glaze; by Peoria Pottery, Peoria, Illinois; 3 inches high; c. 1863–1875; $65–85.

Miniature jug, Albany slip- and Bristol-glazed stoneware with blue stenciled maker's mark; by Weir Pottery Company, Monmouth, Illinois; 3 inches high; c. 1900–1905; $60–85.

Miniature jug, Bristol-glazed stoneware with blue stenciled commemorative logo; by Lowell Pottery Company, Lowell, Illinois; 3.3 inches high; c. 1895–1915; $70–95.

Miniature covered jar, yellow Leon slip-glazed stoneware; by Meyer Pottery, Bexar County, Texas; 4 inches high; c. 1890–1930; $125–165.

Miniature churn, brown Albany slip-glazed stoneware; by Hyten Pottery, Benton, Arkansas; 3.5 inches high; c. 1881–1895; $150–200.

Miniature pitcher, brown Albany slip-glazed stoneware; by Western Stoneware Company, Monmouth, Illinois; 3 inches high; c. 1906–1920; $85–135.

Minature Albany and Bristol slip-glazed stoneware jugs; Bennington, Vermont (except tallest, Midwestern), c. 1880–1900, 1–3.5 inches high; $25–45 each.

Minature Albany slip-glazed stoneware jugs with incised decoration, Bennington, Vermont, Pottery, c. 1876–1893; 2.75 to 3.25 inches high; left to right: *$70–95, $200–275 (very rare), $350–425 (extremely rare), $125–165.*

Brown-glazed stoneware, Missouri, c. 1870–1900. Crocks: 16 inches high, $200–280; advertising jug, 11 inches high, $275–350; preserve jar, 5 inches high, $65–80; bank, 3.5 inches high, $80–120; minature jug, 3 inches high, $70–95.

Miniature crock, Bristol-glazed stoneware with blue stenciled maker's mark; Monmouth Pottery, Monmouth, Illinois; 2.5 inches high; c. 1893–1906; $75–95.

Miniature jug, Bristol and brown Albany slip-glazed, stenciled "Souvenir of Red Wing" in blue; Red Wing Union Stoneware Company, Red Wing, Minnesota; 2.5 inches high; c. 1920–1930; $75–100.

Miniature chamber pot, brown Albany slip-glazed stoneware; by Western Stoneware Company, Monmouth, Illinois; 2 inches high; c. 1910–1930; $45–65.

Miniature bowl, Bristol and brown Albany slip-glazed stoneware; Midwestern; 2.5 inches in diameter; c. 1900–1920; $50–70.

Miniature slop jar, molded Bristol-glazed stoneware with wire bale handle; by Western Stoneware Company, Monmouth, Illinois; 4 inches high; c. 1906–1920; $85–135.

Miniature cuspidor, brown Albany slip-glazed stoneware; Midwestern; 2.5 inches high; c. 1900–1930; $35–50.

Miniature boot, brown Albany slip-glazed stoneware; by Western Stoneware Company, Monmouth, Illinois; 4 inches high; c. 1915–1935; $35–55.

Miniature brown-glazed stoneware, New England, c. 1870–1900. Left to right: *jug, 2.5 inches high, $30–40; food mold, 3 inches long, $45–60; creamer, 3 inches high, $85–115; Bennington, Vermont jug, 3 inches high, $180–220; pot, 3 inches high, $20–25.*

Minature brown-glazed stoneware by Cass Smith, Coalport, Iowa, c. 1875–1885. Left to right: *creamer, 3 inches high, $175–225; saucer, 2.7 inches in diameter, $80–110; crock, 2.2 inches high, $120–160.*

Mugs, blue decorated stoneware; New England, c. 1820–1840: left, *6 inches high, $100–130;* right, *5.5 inches high, $125–175.*

Miniature shoe, green glazed stoneware; by Minnesota Stoneware Company, Red Wing, Minnesota; 3.5 inches long; c. 1883–1906; $100–135.

Mug, salt-glazed molded stoneware with encircling bands of blue and coggle work; White's Pottery, Utica, New York; 5 inches high; c. 1890–1905; $70–85.

Mug, barrel-shaped salt-glazed stoneware with encircling bands of blue; Northeastern; 6 inches high; c. 1820–1850; $110–140.

Mug, stoneware with brown and tan metallic slip; Southern; 6 inches high; c. 1880–1900; $50–75.

Mug, Albany slip-glazed stoneware with so-called "rice graining"; Evans Pottery, Dexter, Missouri; 3.8 inches high; c. 1880–1920; $90–130.

Mug, molded Bristol-glazed stoneware with embossed representation of airplane, car, etc., made for 1933 "Century of Progress" exhibition; by Red Wing Union Stoneware Company, Red Wing, Minnesota; 5.7 inches high; 1933; $40–60.

Mug, baluster-shaped stoneware with tan feldspar glaze; by Beryl Griffith, Clay City, Indiana; 6 inches high; c. 1885–1900; $200–300.

Mug, brown slip-glazed stoneware with applied branch-form handle and rustic barklike inscribing; by William Saenger, Elmendorf, Texas; 6 inches high; c. 1890–1900; $175–265.

Mug, molded blue decorated stoneware, White's Pottery, Utica, New York, c. 1890–1905, 5 inches high; $80–100.

Mug, molded blue decorated stoneware, White's Pottery, Utica, New York, c. 1890–1905, 6 inches high; $200–275.

Stoneware, brown-glazed, Missouri, c. 1875–1885. Left to right, *jug, 10 inches high, $65–95; jar, 7 inches high, $55–75; jug, 12.5 inches high, $75–100; "rice grain" decorated mug, 4 inches high, $125–165; "rice grain" decorated pitcher, 11 inches high, $200–275.*

Paperweight, molded green glazed stoneware with embossed maple leaf logo; by Western Stoneware Company, Monmouth, Illinois; 3.5 inches in diameter; c. 1910–1930; $65–95.

Pie plate, Bristol-glazed stoneware; by Minnesota Stoneware Company, Red Wing, Minnesota; 9 inches in diameter; c. 1883–1906; $70–95.

Pie plate, molded red-orange glazed interior, exterior unglazed stoneware; Eastern or Midwestern; 8 inches in diameter; c. 1880–1920; $30–50.

Pipkin or covered creamer, Bristol and Albany slip-glazed stoneware; by Minnesota Stoneware Company, Red Wing, Minnesota; 4 inches high; c. 1883–1906; $135–185.

Pitcher, molded Bristol-glazed stoneware with embossed representation in blue of Manhattan's Flat Iron Building; The Robinson Clay Products Company, Akron, Ohio; 8 inches high; c. 1900–1915; $200–300.

Pitcher, molded green glazed stoneware with embossed Indian head; by Western Stoneware Company, Monmouth, Illinois; 7 inches high; c. 1920–1940; $45–65.

Pitchers, molded blue decorated stoneware, White's Pottery, Utica, New York, c. 1890–1905; left, 8 inches, right 6.5 inches; each $35–50.

Pitcher, blue decorated stoneware, New York, c. 1840–1870, 11 inches high; $350–450.

Pitcher, molded blue decorated stoneware, Robinson Clay Products Company, Akron, Ohio, c. 1890–1905, 9 inches high; $200–300.

Pitcher, "tanware," unglazed stoneware decorated with dark brown freehand and stenciled designs; New Geneva, Pennsylvania; 8 inches high; c. 1860–1890; $250–325.

Pitcher, black-and-green alkaline-glazed stoneware; by the Meader family pottery, Mossy Creek, Georgia; 11 inches high; c. 1910–1925; $165–245.

Pitcher and bowl set, molded Bristol-glazed stoneware, pale blue shading down from rims, embossed lily pattern; by Red Wing Union Stoneware Company, Red Wing, Minnesota; 14 inches high; c. 1906–1936; $300–400.

Pitcher and bowl set, molded Bristol-glazed stoneware, pale blue shading down from rims, embossed leaf pattern; by Western Stoneware Company, Monmouth, Illinois; 11 inches high; c. 1920–1930; $250–350.

Pitcher, salt-glazed stoneware with elaborate dark blue floral decoration; Pennsylvania; only 5 inches high; c. 1860–1880; $2,700–3,100.

Pitcher, salt-glazed stoneware with stenciled leaf decoration in blue; by Hamilton & Jones, Greensboro, Pennsylvania; 9.5 inches high; c. 1866–1898; $600–750.

Stoneware molded and glazed in shades of green and cream, Midwestern, c. 1910–1930. left to right, *pitcher, 10 inches high, $55–75; pitcher, 9 inches high, $45–65; bowl, 5 inches in diameter, $30–45; pitcher, 9.5 inches high, $60–80.*

Pitcher, blue decorated stoneware, New York or New Jersey, c. 1860–1880, 12 inches high, $250–325; jug, blue decorated stoneware, script "Eats," New England, c. 1870–1890, 10.5 inches high, $180–230.

Stoneware, molded and glazed in shades of pale blue and white, Midwestern, c. 1910–1930: left, crock (missing cover), 5.5 inches high, $35–50; right, pitcher, 10 inches high, $70–95.

Brown-glazed stoneware. Left to right: *jar, Jonathan Stedman, New Haven, Connecticut, c. 1825–1833, 11 inches high, $225–300; jug, New England, c. 1820–1840, 14 inches high, $80–130; pitcher, New England, c. 1810–1830, $95–155.*

Molded blue decorated stoneware, White's Pottery, Utica, New York, c. 1890–1905. Left to right: *pitcher, 10 inches high, $200–280; mug, 4 inches high, $135–185; mustard jar, 4 inches high, $115–165.*

Pitcher, alkaline-glazed stoneware; by Thaddeus Leopard, Winston County, Mississippi; 7.5 inches high; c. 1860–1880; $175–250.

Pitcher, salt-glazed stoneware with overall blue floral decoration; incised "Columbian Regulars #9" and WAP for William A. Parr, Baltimore, Maryland; 10.5 inches high; 1868; $20,000–24,000.

Pitcher, molded brown glazed stoneware with embossed eagle and banner; by Orcutt & Thompson, Poughkeepsie, New York; 9.5 inches high; c. 1830–1831; $1,500–2,000.

Pitcher, salt-glazed stoneware with blue floral freehand and stencil decoration; by A.P. Donaghho, Parkersburg, West Virginia; 13.5 inches high; c. 1874–1890; $350–500.

Pitcher, Albany slip-glazed stoneware with so-called "rice graining"; by Evans Pottery, Dexter, Missouri; 8 inches high; c. 1880–1920; $185–245.

Pitcher, salt-glazed stoneware with blue floral decoration and date 1832; attributed to Johannes Zigler & Andrew Coffman, Timberville, Virginia; 9.5 inches high; c. 1830–1850; $5,000–5,500.

Pitcher, salt-glazed stoneware with overall brown manganese floral decoration; by George N. Fulton, Fincastle, Virginia; 8 inches high; c. 1875–1900; $2,300–2,800.

Stoneware, brown-glazed "combed" ware from Missouri, c. 1860–1900: pitchers, 4 to 12 inches high, $75–225; mugs, 4 to 6 inches high, $90–140; rare miniature bisque jug, 3.5 inches high, $150–200.

Pitchers, molded stoneware with embossed polychrome-glazed decoration, Midwestern, c. 1910–1930, 9 inches high; $85–135 each.

Pitcher, alkaline-glazed stoneware in brown and yellow; by John Leopard, Rusk County, Texas; 10.5 inches high; c. 1865–1880; $235–295.

Pitcher, brown glazed stoneware; by Beryl Griffith, Clay City, Indiana; 9.5 inches high; c. 1885–1900; $75–110.

Pitcher, molded brown glazed stoneware with embossed iris design; by Red Wing Potteries, Red Wing, Minnesota; 9.5 inches high; c. 1936–1945; $60–85.

Pitcher, molded barrel-shaped green glazed stoneware with embossed banding; by Western Stoneware Company, Monmouth, Illinois; 8.5 inches high; c. 1930–1940; $35–45.

Plate, light green Leon slip-glazed stoneware; by Meyer Pottery, Bexar County, Texas; 10 inches in diameter; c. 1910–1930; $225–300.

Plate, brown glazed stoneware; Southern or Midwestern; 8.5 inches in diameter; c. 1840–1880; $60–90.

Pot, salt-glazed stoneware with large blue "star face" design; by Thompson Harrington, Lyons, New York; 13 inches high; c. 1852–1872; $1,700–2,000.

Pot, ovoid salt-glazed, brown-and-tan stoneware with three impressed hearts and "CHARLESTOWN"; Frederick Carpenter, Charlestown, Massachusetts; 10.5 inches high; c. 1812–1827; $600–850.

*Pot, blue decorated stoneware with incised image of running deer, Charles Dillon &
Company, Albany, New York, c. 1834–1835, 8 inches high; $1,600–2,000.*

*Pot, brown manganese-decorated stoneware, John Duntze, New Haven, Connecticut,
c. 1833–1852, 11 inches high; $200–250.*

Pot, ovoid salt-glazed stoneware with blue at handles; by Goodale & Stedman, Hartford, Connecticut; 10 inches high; c. 1822–1825; $150–225.

Pot, ovoid salt-glazed stoneware with blue filled impressed "clam-shell" decoration and words "LIBERTY FOREV/ WARNE & LETTS 1807/S. AMBOY N. JERSY"; by Warne & Letts, South Amboy, New Jersey; 8.5 inches high; c. 1805–1813; $3,000–4,000.

Pot, ovoid salt-glazed stoneware with incised initials "D.S."; by Branch Green, Philadelphia, Pennsylvania; 11.5 inches high; c. 1809–1827; $3,000–3,500.

Pot, ovoid salt-glazed stoneware; by Jacob Bennage, Portage County, Ohio; 9.5 inches high; dated 1836; $200–250.

Pot, ovoid salt-glazed stoneware with blue at handles; by Edwin H. Merrill, Ellet, Ohio; 8 inches high; c. 1833–1845; $125–175.

Pot, blue decorated stoneware, Pennsylvania, c. 1855–1875, 13.5 inches high; $300–400.

Blue decorated stoneware. Left to right: *pot, N. & A. Seymour, Rome, New York, c. 1815–1848, 8 inches high, $150–225; jug, S.S. Perry, Troy, New York, c. 1828–1833, 10 inches high, $90–130; pot, William Warner, West Troy, New York, c. 1835–1860, $75–100.*

Pot, blue decorated stoneware, Calvin Boynton & Company, Troy, New York, c. 1825–1829, 10 inches high; $150–200.

Pot, blue decorated stoneware, A.E. Smith & Sons, Norwalk, Connecticut, c. 1855–1874, 10.5 inches high; $125–175.

Pot, salt-glazed stoneware with simple blue floral decoration; by H. Lowndes, Petersburg, Virginia; 7.5 inches high; 1841; $400–600.

Pot, salt-glazed stoneware with blue floral decoration; Peoria Pottery, Peoria, Illinois; 10 inches high; c. 1863–1875; $250–350.

Pot, salt-glazed stoneware decorated with bands of inscribed lines; by N.H. Nixon, Alamance County, North Carolina; 8.5 inches high; c. 1860–1880; $350–500.

Pot, ovoid salt-glazed stoneware with incised blue filled floral decoration front and back; by John Remmey III, New York, New York; 12.5 inches high; c. 1791–1820; $4,000–5,500.

Pot, ovoid salt-glazed stoneware; by Smith Kelsey, Posey Township, Indiana; 9.5 inches high; c. 1852–1855; $200–275.

Price list, printed paper; Seymour & Bosworth, Hartford, Connecticut, 1874; $175–250.

Price list, printed paper; Hamilton & Jones, Greensboro, Pennsylvania; c. 1866–1898; $150–200.

Price list, printed paper with pottery illustrations; E. & L.P. Norton, Bennington, Vermont; 1866; $300–375.

Price list, printed paper; Eagle Pottery Works, Olean, New York; c. 1860–1869; $200–275.

Price list, printed paper with pottery illustrations; F.A. Plaisted, Gardiner, Maine; c. 1855–1863; $250–325.

Price list, printed paper with pottery illustrations; Fulper Brothers Pottery, Flemington, New Jersey; c. 1880–1890; $275–350.

Pudding pot, salt-glazed stoneware; by A.J. Haws, Johnstown, Pennsylvania; 5 inches high; c. 1860–1880; $100–150.

Pudding pot, brown glazed stoneware; by Levi Brackney, Brazil, Indiana; 5 inches high; c. 1856–1861; $165–245.

Pudding pot, Albany slip-glazed stoneware; attributed to Torbert & Baker, Brazil, Indiana; 4 inches high; c. 1880–1899; $60–85.

Pudding pot, salt-glazed stoneware; Northeastern; 6 inches high; c. 1860–1890; $35–50.

Punch bowl, salt-glazed stoneware with elaborate overall incised blue filled decoration, including flowers and fish and name "Elizabeth Crane"; New York City; 13.5 inches in diameter; c. 1790–1800; $190,000–210,000.

Punch bowl, molded salt-glazed stoneware decorated with nude female figure outlined in blue; White's Pottery, Utica, New York; 7 inches high; c. 1890–1907; $225–300.

Puzzle jug, double handles and spout, brown alkaline glaze; by Sylvanus Hartzog, Lincoln County, North Carolina; 7 inches high; c. 1880–1910; $275–375.

Ring bottle, circular salt-glazed stoneware; North Carolina; 8.5 inches in diameter; c. 1870–1900; $150–225.

Ring bottle with footed base, Bristol-glazed stoneware with name and location in blue; Indiana; 12.5 inches in diameter; c. 1880–1900; $500–750.

Ring bottle, footed, tan salt-glazed stoneware with incised name; by J.B. Rhodes, Harmony, Indiana; 15.5 inches high; c. 1880–1890; $285–365.

Kegs or rundlets: left to right, *brown-glazed stoneware, New York, c. 1820–1840, 4.5 inches high, $130–180; salt-glazed stoneware, Ohio, c. 1830–1850, 8.5 inches high, $150–225; blue decorated stoneware, Clarkson Crolius, New York, New York, c. 1800–1814, 6 inches high (very rare), $1,500–2,000.*

Rolling pin, Bristol-glazed stoneware with stenciled blue floral decoration; Western Stoneware Company, Monmouth, Illinois; 7.5 inches long; c. 1920–1935; $75–95.

Rundlet or keg, brown salt-glazed stoneware decorated with incised bird and fish; Randolph County, North Carolina; 8 inches high; 1846; $3,200–4,000.

Rundlet or keg, light tan glazed stoneware with bands of coggle decoration; attributed to Athens Pottery, Athens, New York; 5 inches high; c. 1820–1840; $200–275.

Rundlet or keg, salt-glazed stoneware banded in blue; by Clarkson Crolius, New York, New York; 7 inches high; c. 1800–1840; $1,500–2,000.

Rundlet or keg, tan salt-glazed stoneware with "ears" for carrying line; Ohio; 8 inches high; c. 1830–1850; $150–225.

Salt box, hanging, molded Bristol-glazed stoneware with blue stenciled "SALT"; by Western Stoneware Company, Mon-
mouth, Illinois; 7 inches high; c. 1920–1930; $65–80.

Shaving mug, stoneware with brownish-yellow feldspar glaze; by
Beryl Griffith, Clay City, Indiana; 3.5 inches high;
c. 1885–1900; $200–300.

Slop jar or "combinette," covered, molded Bristol-glazed stoneware banded in blue and decorated with embossed lilies,
wire bale handle; by Red Wing Union Stoneware Company,
Red Wing, Minnesota; 12 inches high; c. 1906–1936;
$125–175.

Slop jar or "combinette," covered, molded Bristol-glazed stoneware with blue-shaded borders and embossed leaf decoration, wire bale handle; by Western Stoneware Company,
Monmouth, Illinois; 11 inches high; c. 1920–1930;
$100–150.

Smoking pipe, molded salt-glazed stoneware; Ohio; 2 inches long;
c. 1860–1880; $10–15.

Smoking pipe, molded brown glazed stoneware in form of man's
head; Midwestern; 2.5 inches long; c. 1870–1900; $20–25.

Snake jug, salt-glazed stoneware embellished with applied figures
of snakes and humans in blue and brown; Anna Pottery, Anna, Illinois; 10 inches high; c. 1860–1890;
$11,000–15,000.

Snake jug, salt-glazed stoneware with applied figure of black
woman, fly, and words "Shoo Fly," in blue and brown; Anna
Pottery, Anna, Illinois; 6 inches high; c. 1860–1890;
$7,000–9,000.

Snake jug, salt-glazed stoneware highlighted in blue, single snake
curling about top and sides of harvest-jug type vessel; Midwestern; 9 inches high; c. 1870–1890; $800–950.

Snake jug, brown glazed stoneware with curling snake in blue, by
August Blanck, Boonville, Missouri; 9.5 inches high;
c. 1880–1890; $1,200–1,600.

Soap dish, molded octagonal Bristol-glazed stoneware; by Western
Stoneware Company, Monmouth, Illinois; 5 inches long;
c. 1915–1935; $45–60.

Brown glazed stoneware, New York or New England, c. 1840–1870. Left to right: minature creamer, 3 inches high, $85–115; pedestal base soap dish, 5 inches in diameter, $65–90; bank, 3.5 inches high, $75–100.

Stein or pitcher, incised blue decorated stoneware, Wingender Pottery, Haddonfield, New Jersey, c. 1883–1900, 12 inches high; $165–245.

Soap dish, round pedestal form with drain holes, brown glazed stoneware; New York; 5.5 inches in diameter; c. 1830–1850; $70–95.

Stein, molded salt-glazed stoneware with embossed blue filled figure of Teddy Roosevelt; White's Pottery, Utica, New York; 10.5 inches high; c. 1890–1900; $1,900–2,400.

Stein, molded salt-glazed stoneware, embossed Indian head highlighted in blue; by Western Stoneware Company, Monmouth, Illinois; 6.5 inches high; c. 1910–1920; $250–350.

Stein, salt-glazed stoneware with incised blue filled floral and geometric decoration; by Wingender Brothers, Haddonfield, New Jersey; 9 inches high; c. 1880–1920; $165–245.

Stew pan, unglazed stoneware with wire bale handle; by Red Wing Union Stoneware Company, Red Wing, Minnesota; 9 inches in diameter; c. 1900–1905; $90–120.

String holder, jug form, Bristol and Albany slip-glazed stoneware; by McDade Pottery, Bastrop County, Texas; 6.5 inches high; c. 1910–1930; $35–55.

Sugar bowl, matching cover, Bristol-glazed stoneware banded in blue with "Mabelle Dugger/1918"; White Hall (Illinois) Sewer Pipe & Stoneware Company; 5.5 inches high; 1918; $200–275.

Sugar bowl, salt-glazed stoneware, date, inscription, and floral decoration in blue; by Charles Decker, Philadelphia, Pennsylvania; 4.5 inches high; 1856; $1,300–1,800.

Sugar bowl, matching cover, dark green Leon slip glaze; by Meyer Pottery, Bexar County, Texas; 6 inches high; c. 1900–1920; $135–185.

Sundial, salt-glazed stoneware, incised Roman numerals highlighted in blue; Philadelphia, Pennsylvania; 10.5 inches in diameter; c. 1865–1875; $900–1,400.

Teapot, molded salt-glazed stoneware with embossed blue filled figures; White's Pottery, Utica, New York; 7 inches high; c. 1886–1907; $1,500–2,000.

Teapot, Albany slip-glazed stoneware; by Beryl Griffith, Clay City, Indiana; 8 inches high; c. 1885–1900; $90–120.

Tea pot, molded brown-glazed stoneware (with pewter "make do" repair to spout), Ohio or Illinois, c. 1900–1920, 6 inches high; $45–65.

Teapot, Bristol-glazed stoneware; Western Stoneware Company, Monmouth, Illinois; 6 inches high; c. 1930–1940; $40–60.

Teapot, molded brown Albany slip–glazed stoneware with embossed figure of Rebecca at the Well; Northeastern; 7 inches high; c. 1870–1910; $55–75.

Trivet, molded Bristol-glazed stoneware, embossed figure of Indians with tepees and trees, all highlighted in blue; by Western Stoneware Company, Monmouth, Illinois; 6.5 inches in diameter; c. 1915–1936; $300–400.

Toy whistle in form of chicken, green Leon slip-glazed stoneware; by Meyer Pottery, Bexar County, Texas; 3.3 inches high; c. 1890–1920; $300–450.

Toy whistle in form of rooster, salt-glazed stoneware highlighted in blue; Pennsylvania; 3 inches high; c. 1840–1870; $1,000–1,500.

Umbrella stand, molded Bristol-glazed stoneware with embossed alligator in blue; White's Pottery, Utica, New York; 20 inches high; c. 1890–1907; $800–950.

Umbrella stand, unglazed stoneware, Albany slip-glazed interior; Vermillion County, Indiana; 23 inches high; c. 1870–1880; $80–120.

Umbrella stand, molded brown Albany slip-glazed stoneware; by Western Stoneware Company, Monmouth, Illinois; 21 inches high; c. 1910–1930; $100–135.

Vase, unglazed stoneware, painted, applied grape clusters; by Beryl Griffith, Clay City, Indiana; 10 inches high; c. 1885–1900; $60–90.

Vase, handled urn type, salt-glazed stoneware partially dipped in brown slip; by Eli LaFever, Baxter, Tennessee; 11.5 inches high; c. 1900–1925; $110–140.

Brown-glazed stoneware vase or jar, Barnet Ramsey, Halsey, Oregon, c. 1864–1868, 6.5 inches high; $250–350.

Vase, molded blue decorated stoneware, White's Pottery, Utica, New York, c. 1890–1905, 8 inches high; $80–110.

Vase, molded blue decorated stoneware, White's Pottery, Utica, New York, c. 1890–1905, 7.5 inches high; $95–135.

Vase, Bristol-glazed stoneware with embossed cattail·decoration highlighted in bright blue; by Western Stoneware Company, Monmouth, Illinois; 9.5 inches high; c. 1920–1930; $200–285.

Vase, cylindrical Bristol-glazed stoneware vessel with blue printed advertising logo; by Red Wing Union Stoneware Company,

Red Wing, Minnesota; 9.5 inches high; c. 1906–1936; $110–165.

Vase, molded Bristol-glazed stoneware with embossed blue filled Japanese fan decoration; by White's Pottery, Utica, New York; 10 inches high; c. 1890–1907; $100–150.

Vase, blue decorated stoneware, New Jersey or Pennsylvania, c. 1830–1860, 12 inches high; $180–260.

Brown-glazed stoneware grave vase, William Meyer, Atacosa, Texas, c. 1890–1920, 8.5 inches long, $170–230.

Washboard, unglazed stoneware in wooden frame; Midwestern; 12 × 10.5 inches; c. 1850–1880; $70–100.

Water cooler, salt-glazed stoneware with incised blue filled floral decoration, 8-gallon size; marked Cyrus Felton, Ohio; 17 inches high; c. 1830–1850; $5,000–5,500.

Water cooler, brown Albany slip-glazed stoneware with maker's mark stenciled in white slip; by Cannelton Stoneware Company, Cannelton, Indiana; 14.5 inches high; c. 1872–1895; $145–195.

Water cooler, salt-glazed stoneware with encircling blue bands, barrel form; by Clarkson Crolius, Jr., New York, New York; 13 inches high; c. 1835–1849; $700–950.

Water cooler, salt-glazed stoneware, two-piece, bottom with vertical handles, both with extensive blue floral decoration; Pennsylvania; 22 inches high; c. 1850–1870; $900–1,200.

Water cooler, salt-glazed stoneware with large blue deer in front of house and woods; by J. & E. Norton, Bennington, Vermont; 15 inches high; c. 1850–1859; $7,500–9,000.

Water cooler, blue decorated stoneware, New England, c. 1830–1850, 13 inches high; $125–175.

Blue decorated stoneware water cooler, New York or New Jersey, c. 1886–1890, 15.5 inches high; $140–180.

Water cooler, Bristol-glazed, blue decorated stoneware, pewter spigot, Texas, c. 1910–1920, 13.5 inches high; $250–350.

Water cooler, urn form, salt-glazed stoneware with two incised blue filled birds on branches; by Somerset Potters' Works, Somerset, Massachusetts; 15 inches high; c. 1847–1882; $3,500–5,000.

Water cooler, molded stoneware covered with cobalt and pale blue slip, embossed woman at well and house; The Robinson Clay Products Company, Akron, Ohio; 16 inches high; c. 1905–1915; $200–285.

Water cooler, salt-glazed stoneware, front completely covered with incised blue filled leafy tree; by Nichols & Boynton, Burlington, Vermont; 22 inches high; c. 1855; $18,000–21,000.

Water cooler, three sections, greenish Leon slip-glazed stoneware; Meyer Pottery, Bexar County, Texas; 33 inches high; c. 1920–1930; $300–450.

Water cooler, double-handled, greenish alkaline-glazed stoneware decorated with floral banding in white slip; by Thomas Chandler, Edgefield District, South Carolina; 21 inches high; c. 1840–1851; $7,500–9,000.

Water cooler, molded Bristol-glazed stoneware with blue banding and stenciled "WATER COOLER" and maker's logo; Red Wing Union Stoneware Company, Red Wing, Minnesota; 17.5 inches high; c. 1906–1936; $200–260.

Water cooler, Bristol-glazed blue decorated stoneware, Robinson Clay Products Company, Akron, Ohio, c. 1900–1915, 17 inches high; $200–285.

Water cooler, molded blue decorated stoneware, White's Pottery, Utica, New York, c. 1890–1905, 16.5 inches high; $400–550.

Water cooler or "blind pig," blue decorated stoneware (rare), Pennsylvania, c. 1830–1850, 9 inches long; $800–1,200.

Water cooler, ovoid salt-glazed stoneware with matching top and stand, applied, impressed, and blue floral decoration; by Solomon Bell, Strasburg, Virginia; 23 inches high; c. 1840–1870; $15,000–20,000.

Water pump, salt-glazed stoneware with cast iron fixtures; by Weavers & Cordery, Brazil, Indiana; 24 inches high; c. 1873–1910; $250–350.

Water tank float, Bristol slip-glazed stoneware; Rusk County, Texas; 14 inches high; c. 1900–1920; $75–100.

REDWARE

Though more different objects were made in red earthenware than in any other American ceramic body, the medium has never obtained the general popularity among collectors that is enjoyed by stoneware or even yellowware. This may seem odd, since redware was made throughout most of the United States, including many states such as Montana and Utah, where other ceramics were never produced.

This broad range of manufacture is due to the fact that redware is fired from the same common and universally available clay used for bricks and flower pots. Wherever a potter went, he could always find raw material, but he could not always find customers. Because of its relatively fragile body and the poisonous lead glaze with which it was covered, redware was quickly replaced by other ceramics as soon as these became available. In more settled areas this had largely occurred by 1850; consequently, most collectible redware was made in the eastern half of the United States, particularly in New England, Pennsylvania, Virginia, and North Carolina. However, some redware potters in the South and the West worked into the 1880s and 1890s.

The variety of ware manufactured and now available to the collector is remarkable. Many items such as small toy whistles, glasses and mugs, plates, egg cups, washboards, candlesticks, doorstops, buttons, birdhouses, beehives, picture frames, and even coffins were made of redware because nothing else was available at the moment. Once glass, tin, iron, or other, more suitable ceramics could be obtained, the redware potter was confined to the manufacture of jugs, crocks, preserve jars, and especially flower pots. Today, many collectors think of these as "redware"; yet a persistent enthusiast can track down literally dozens of much rarer forms.

These uncommon objects often can be obtained quite reasonably because price in the the field of American redware is determined primarily by decoration rather than by form. As a group, the most highly valued objects are the sgrafitto plates, sugar bowls, and bulb pots produced in Pennsylvania, and rarely in adjoining states. A typical sgrafitto plate will be coated with an opaque white slip through which decorative designs (usually flowers, or human or animal figures) are scratched, producing a contrasting red-white effect. The designs are then glazed in green, yellow, or brown. Names, folksy sayings, and dates are common additions. Most sgrafitto plates were made prior to 1830, and the few that come on the market today usually bring prices in the $10,000–30,000 range.

The second level of desirability includes the slip-decorated redware pie plates, platters, and loaf dishes made primarily in Connecticut and Pennsylvania. These pieces are decorated with flowing calligraphic patterns or with words such as "Mary's Dish" or "Currant Pie" applied in white slip to the red clay body. Occasionally such pieces will also be embellished with birds or flowers in white slip or with glazes of other colors. Prices for this group range from a few hundred dollars up into the low five figures.

A third group consists of a variety of vessels which may be glazed in several colors, rather than in the usual clear lead. Most common are those splashed with black manganese, but other hues—green, yellow, purple, brown, and even blue—may be found. The more color, the higher the price, with most examples bringing from $200 to $2,000.

Yet another pricey category includes the numerous human and animal figurines made primarily in Pennsylvania and Virginia. These pieces may range in size from 2 to 12 inches, and they are usually given a clear lead glaze. Demand from collectors who see them as folk sculpture has boosted prices for such examples into the $1,000–10,000 range, with outstanding pieces bringing even more.

Then there is all the rest: clear lead-glazed pots and jugs; preserve jars in the shiny, overall black manganese glaze which imitated English Jackfield ware; and the numerous pieces which, to save time and money, were glazed only on the interior. Prices here may be extremely low, often no more than $25–100 each. This broad category probably includes 90 percent of all redware available, which largely explains collector attitudes toward the field. If sgrafitto and slipped wares were more easily found, there would no doubt be much greater interest in the ceramic.

Another factor inhibiting collection of redware is the lack of makers' marks. Relatively few pieces bear the name of a potter, so it is usually difficult to determine their origin, which inhibits the collecting by locality so popular among stoneware enthusiasts. Lack of marks may also make it hard to distinguish the occasional pieces of European or South American redware. Abnormally bright glazes, thin walls, and generally poor potting distinguish most Mexican and Central American examples. More difficult to separate out are German examples, which, understandably, look a lot like those from Pennsylvania. English redware may also prove confusing, but as it is quite valuable in its own right, there is little danger of its being intentionally passed for American. Most diffi-cult of all is Scandinavian redware. Undecorated pieces look just like many American forms such as jars and milk pans, and many are marked with names like Carlsen or Johaneson that can make a collector (particularly in Utah, where many late-nineteenth-century Mormon potters were Scandinavian) think he has discovered a rare mark.

Fakes and reproductions must also be watched for in this field. While most collectors do not demand the "mint" condition that has led to so many concealed repairs in stoneware, redware—particularly high-end sgrafitto and slipware—has been widely reproduced. Most contemporary potters mark their wares, which are often sold at craft fairs and through museum shops. However, these marks can be removed; and there have been instances of pieces being chipped or scratched to simulate age, or even being placed in an oven to blacken the bottoms and crackle the glaze. Due to the softer redware body, such false ware is easier to achieve and harder to spot than is the case with stoneware. Collectors should insist on a written warranty of authenticity when buying any expensive piece.

REDWARE PRICES

Apple butter jar, lead-glazed redware, semi-ovoid shape, glazed only on interior; Northeastern; 6 inches high; c. 1820–1880; $25–35.

Apple butter jar, lead-glazed redware, semi-ovoid shape, impressed maker's mark; by John Bell, Waynesboro, Pennsylvania; 6 inches high; c. 1835–1875; $120–160.

Apple butter jar, lead-glazed redware with black manganese splashing, semi-ovoid shape; Connecticut; 4.5 inches high; c. 1830–1870; $80–120.

Apple butter jar, lead-glazed redware, semi-ovoid shape with single handle; Northeastern; 8 inches high; c. 1840–1880; $55–80.

Ashtray, molded unglazed redware with central flower pot form and embossed maker's mark; Western Stoneware Company, Monmouth, Illinois; 4 inches in diameter; c. 1920–1940; $120–160.

Bank, in the form of a bird, lead-glazed redware; Pennsylvania; 4.5 inches high; c. 1830–1860; $1,000–1,500.

Bank, lead-glazed redware in the form of a man's head; Northeastern; 3.5 inches high; c. 1860–1880; $500–650.

Bank, crudely potted standing woman, lead-glazed redware with white slip verse and date; Pennsylvania; 7 inches high; 1831; $3,800–4,500.

Bank, lead-glazed redware, unusual ovoid double jar form with finial in form of a bird; Northeastern or Ohio; 8 inches high; c. 1830–1860; $2,000–2,500.

Bank, redware with yellow slip glaze, New England, c. 1830–1860, 4 inches high, $65–90.

Bank, molded redware in rare form of tree stump, painted brown, New England or New York, c. 1860–1890, 4 inches high, $120–160.

Banks, molded redware in the form of apples, painted in shades of red and yellow, East Brookfield, Massachusetts, c. 1879–1888, 3 to 4 inches in diameter, $75–125 each.

Bank, molded redware in form of Empire chest of drawers, Pennsylvania, c. 1850–1880, 4.5 inches long, $175–250.

Bank, beehive shape, lead-glazed redware with incised name; Northeastern; 3.5 inches high; c. 1850–1880; $75–95.

Bank, barrel shape, unglazed redware, later floral decoration in oils; New York; 3.7 inches high; c. 1870–1910; $20–35.

Bank, lead-glazed redware in the form of an owl head with incised verse and date; Pennsylvania; 3.7 inches high; 1852; $2,800–3,500.

Bank, pear-shaped, lead-glazed redware; Northeastern; 4.2 inches high; c. 1850–1880; $55–85.

Bank, barrel-shaped, lead-glazed redware; Einsiedel Pottery, Egg Harbor, New Jersey; 4 inches high; c. 1880–1920; $70–95.

Barber's bowl or basin, demilune notch out of rim, sgrafitto-decorated redware, floral pattern in green and yellow on white, incised verse; by John Neis, Montgomery County, Pennsylvania; 11 inches in diameter; c. 1800–1810; $15,000–20,000.

Barber's bowl or basin, demilune notch out of rim, lead-glazed redware with concentric bands of brown-and-white slip about rim; North Carolina; 10.5 inches in diameter; c. 1790–1820; $3,000–4,000.

Basket, rope twist handle, redware with green and brown over white glaze; Strasburg, Virginia; 7 inches high; c. 1860–1880; $2,600–3,300.

Bean pot, redware, lead-glazed interior; Northeastern; 5 inches high; c. 1840–1880; $30–40.

Bean pot, redware, lead-glazed interior, impressed maker's mark; by John Safford II, Monmouth, Maine; 5.5 inches high; c. 1830–1850; $300–375.

Bean pot, lead-glazed redware, single handle and matching lid; Northeastern; 6.5 inches high; c. 1840–1880; $50–75.

Unglazed redware, New England or Pennsylvania, c. 1860–1890. Left to right, *bean pot, 6 inches high, $25–35; miniature jug, 2.5 inches high, $10–15; bean pot, 3.75 inches high, $10–15.*

Lead-glazed redware, all attributed to Joseph Oser, St. Charles, Missouri, c. 1855–1885. Left to right, bean pot, *5.5 inches high, $100–150;* preserve jar, *8 inches high, $80–130;* preserve jar, *5 inches high, $60–85.*

Connecticut black manganese–splashed redware. Left to right; child's potty, *6.5 inches in diameter, $55–75;* bed pan, *12 inches in diameter, $40–65;* adult chamber pot, *8 inches in diameter, $50–70.*

Bean pot, lead-glazed redware with green, yellow, and black slip decoration, scalloped rim, and matching lid; Pennsylvania; 7 inches high; c. 1830–1850; $1,500–2,100.

Bedpan, doughnut-shaped, lead-glazed redware splashed with black manganese; Connecticut or Pennsylvania; 10 inches in diameter; c. 1850–1880; $60–85.

Bedpan, doughnut-shaped, lead-glazed redware splashed with green; New Hampshire or Maine; 10.5 inches in diameter; c. 1840–1870; $90–130.

Beehive, domed form like rye straw bee skep, unglazed redware; Pennsylvania; 17 inches high; c. 1850–1880; $250–325.

Birdhouse, beehive shape with wooden perch, unglazed redware; Pennsylvania; 9.5 inches high; c. 1870–1900; $100–150.

Birdhouse, acorn shape with clay perch, unglazed redware; by Henry Schofield, Rock Springs, Pennsylvania; 7 inches high; c. 1938–1943; $80–120.

Bottle, semi-ovoid form with blob top, green glazed redware; Galena, Illinois; 7.5 inches high; c. 1855–1875; $350–500.

Bottle, straight-sided with tapering shoulder, black manganese glazed redware; Northeastern; 5.5 inches high; c. 1850–1890; $45–60.

Chicken waterer, yellow glazed redware, New England, c. 1860–1880, 8 inches high, $130–180.

Left to right: *mustard-glazed redware bottle, Galena, Illinois, c. 1855–1870, 9 inches high, $190–250; brown manganese–splashed keg, Massachusetts, c. 1820–1850, 5 inches high, $200–260; black manganese–splashed flask, Norwalk, Connecticut, c. 1830–1850, 7 inches high, $250–325.*

Bottle, similar in form to glass sack bottle, redware covered with white glaze; New York; 7 inches high; c. 1850–1880; $275–375.

Bottle, similar in form to glass sack bottle, redware with a black manganese glaze; Chesham, New Hampshire; 6 inches high; c. 1845–1865; $200–275.

Bottle, bulbous base and long neck, green glazed redware; Salem, North Carolina; 7 inches high; c. 1800–1830; $375–450.

Bowl, lead-glazed redware with yellow-and-green slip decoration; attributed to Andrew Coffman, Timberville, Virginia; 10 inches in diameter; c. 1830–1850; $6,000–7,000.

Bowl, lead-glazed redware splashed in black; Connecticut or Pennsylvania; 6 inches in diameter; c. 1830–1850; $350–500.

Bowl with matching lid, lead-glazed redware covered with white slip dots; Pennsylvania; 7.5 inches in diameter; c. 1820–1840; $900–1,400.

Bowl with ear handles and matching lid, lead-glazed redware with seaweed type decoration in white-and-green slip; attributed to John Bell, Waynesboro, Pennsylvania; 5.5 inches in diameter; c. 1840–1860; $2,500–3,300.

Bowl, redware with black manganese splotching, Connecticut, c. 1830–1850, 7 inches in diameter, $90–120.

Redware bowls. Left to right: *baking bowl with black manganese splotching, Connecticut, c. 1840–1870, 5 inches in diameter, $70–95; lead glazed milk bowl or pan, 10 inches in diameter, $80–120; eating bowl, New York, c. 1830–1850, 4.5 inches in diameter, $55–85.*

Left, *unglazed redware bowl, Ohio, c. 1840–1870, 6 inches in diameter, $60–90;* right, *lead glazed redware preserve jar, New Jersey, c. 1850–1870, 6.5 inches high, $55–75.*

Connecticut redware with black manganese–splash decoration. Left to right; *crock, c. 1850–1870, 6.5 inches high, $130–180; rare soup bowl, c. 1850–1880, 9.5 inches in diameter, $200–280; pot, 11 inches high, $225–300.*

Bowl, molded, clear glazed redware with two white slip bands; East Liverpool, Ohio; 8 inches in diameter; c. 1910–1930; $35–50.

Bowl, lead-glazed redware with heavy molded rim; Galena, Illinois; 8.5 inches in diameter; c. 1860–1885; $250–350.

Bowl, eight-sided, lead-glazed redware decorated with white slip flowers; Pennsylvania; 8.5 inches across; c. 1840–1860; $1,000–1,500.

Bowl, lead-glazed redware with wavy banding and brushed interior pattern, both in black manganese; North Carolina; 10 inches in diameter; c. 1840–1880; $1,200–1,700.

Bowl, with pouring spout, lead-glazed redware brushed with brown manganese; Osborn Pottery, South Danvers, Massachusetts; 8.5 inches in diameter; c. 1840–1860; $250–350.

Bread basket, round form with flaring sides decorated with pierced work designs, lead-glazed redware; Pennsylvania; 11 inches in diameter; c. 1820–1860; $2,700–3,500.

Bulb vase, perforated ovoid form, redware with unglazed exterior, New Jersey or Pennsylvania; 10 inches high; c. 1800–1840; $200–275.

Bulb vase, perforated ovoid form with pedestal base, lead-glazed redware banded in green-and-white slip; Pennsylvania; 9.5 inches high; c. 1830–1860; $2,400–2,900.

Bulb vase in the form of a rooster, lead-glazed redware splashed with white-and-brown slip; Pennsylvania; 7.5 inches high; c. 1800–1830; $4,000–5,000.

Butter stamp or print, circular disk impressed with geometric forms, lead-glazed redware; Pennsylvania; 4 inches in diameter; c. 1820–1850; $240–310.

Butter tub or keeler, round crocklike form with two upright rope twist handles, redware glazed brown and yellow; Bell Pottery, Strasburg, Virginia; 5.5 inches high; c. 1840–1880; $900–1,400.

Left to right: *mold, black manganese–splashed redware, Pennsylvania, c. 1850–1870, 7.5 inches in diameter, $65–85; jug, black manganese–glazed redware, Pennsylvania, c. 1820–1840, 8 inches high, $110–160; serving bowl, brown manganese–splashed redware, 9 inches in diameter, $200–275.*

Cake mold, Turk's cap form, lead-glazed redware sponged with black manganese; Northeastern; 9.5 inches in diameter; c. 1860–1900; $45–65.

Cake mold, Turk's cap form, fluted sides, lead-glazed redware, impressed maker's mark; by Alvin Wilcox, West Bloomfield, New York; 9 inches in diameter; c. 1845–1860; $500–700.

Cake mold, lead-glazed redware with rare plaster form in which it was cast, Perrine & Company, pottery, Baltimore, Maryland, c. 1850–1870, 7 inches in diameter, $600–800 for both.

Left, mold for cake or food, black manganese–splashed redware, New England or Pennsylvania, c. 1850–1880, 8 inches in diameter, $70–95; right, flower pot, Pennsylvania, c. 1850–1870, 6 inches high, $90–110.

Molds, redware. Left to right: *lead glazed, Pennsylvania, c. 1850–1880, 6 inches in diameter, $80–110; brown splashed, Pennsylvania, c. 1850–1880, 8 inches in diameter, $70–95; lead glazed, Midwestern, c. 1870–1890, 9.5 inches in diameter, $55–75.*

Cake mold, Swirling Turk's cap form, fluted sides, lead-glazed redware splashed with green; Pennsylvania; 8.5 inches in diameter; c. 1830–1860; $90–120.

Cake or food mold in form of fish, lead-glazed redware; Pennsylvania; 12.5 inches long; c. 1840–1880; $300–450.

Cake or food mold in the form of an ear of corn, molded lead-glazed redware; Pennsylvania; 6 inches long; c. 1860–1890; $250–330.

Cake or cookie mold, Springerle type, unglazed redware with embossed representations of birds, people, and flowers; Pennsylvania; 8.5 × 6 inches; c. 1850–1880; $300–450.

Candle holder, tapering cylindrical form with drip pan, lead-glazed redware; Pennsylvania; 6.5 inches high; c. 1830–1850; $275–350.

Candle holder, cuplike form with interior candle socket and ear-shaped handle, lead-glazed redware splashed with brown manganese; Pennsylvania; 2.2 inches high; c. 1840–1870; $300–425.

Candle stick, black manganese glazed redware (rare), Pennsylvania, c. 1825–1845, 5 inches high, $250–350.

Candle holder, cone-shaped form with wide drip pan at top and ear-shaped handle, redware glazed in green spotted with brown; Pennsylvania; 3.5 inches high; c. 1820–1860; $350–500.

Candle holder, tubular form set in dish with loop handle, unglazed redware; North Carolina; 4.7 inches high; c. 1860–1880; $100–140.

Casserole or tureen, semi-ovoid bowl with small handles and matching dome top, lead-glazed redware; Pennsylvania; 8.5 inches in diameter; c. 1850–1880; $450–650.

Chamber pot, lead-glazed redware splashed with black manganese; Norwalk, Connecticut; 5 inches high; c. 1830–1870; $90–120.

Chamber pot, black manganese glazed redware, impressed maker's mark; by Wilmer Cope, Chester County, Pennsylvania; 4.5 inches high; c. 1892–1915; $140–180.

Chamber pot, lead-glazed redware; Northeastern; 4.5 inches high; c. 1840–1880; $55–75.

Churn, yellow-orange lead-glazed redware with swag and tassel coggle wheel banding; Galena, Illinois; 18 inches high; c. 1855–1875; $600–800.

Churn, black manganese glazed redware; New England or Pennsylvania; 15 inches high; c. 1830–1860; $250–325.

Churn, lead-glazed redware, incised banding; New England; 17.5 inches high; c. 1820–1850; $300–450.

Churn, cylindrical with two horizontal lifts, redware brown glazed on interior only; Salem, North Carolina; 20 inches high; c. 1820–1860; $350–500.

Coffeepot, tapering cylindrical form with matching top, redware covered with a cream-colored glaze; Midwestern; 8 inches high; c. 1850–1880; $235–285.

Coffeepot, ovoid form with matching dome-top lid and ear handle, lead-glazed redware streaked with brown manganese; Pennsylvania; 10.5 inches high; c. 1830–1850; $600–750.

Churn, redware with pink and cream glaze, New Hampshire, c. 1840–1870, 16 inches high, $230–280.

Crocks, lead-glazed redware, all by John Eardley, St. George, Utah, c. 1860–1880. Left to right, *14 inches high, $275–350; 7 inches high, $110–160; 11.5 inches high, $200–260.*

Colander, bowl type, lead-glazed redware splashed with green, hand-perforated; Galena, Illinois; 9 inches in diameter; c. 1860–1890; $450–600.

Colander, cup type with handle and three feet, black manganese glazed redware; Pennsylvania; 7.5 inches in diameter; c. 1840–1870; $200–300.

Colander, crock form, redware, lead-glazed on interior; Northeastern or Southern; 6 inches high; c. 1860–1890; $70–95.

Colander, bowl form with heavy rim and small handles, redware glazed in green and brown; Strasburg, Virginia; 11 inches in diameter; c. 1850–1880; $300–450.

Creamer, squat crocklike form with pinched spout and ear handle, black manganese glazed redware; Northeastern; 3.5 inches high; c. 1840–1880; $45–70.

Creamer, squat, bulbous form with ear handle, lead-glazed redware; New York; 3.8 inches high; c. 1830–1860; $65–95.

Crock, unglazed redware, incised "For a Handsome Young Milk Maid"; Virginia; 6 inches high; c. 1860–1880; $400–600.

Crock, heavy rolled rim, lead-glazed redware with splotches of green and yellow; Galena, Illinois; 7.5 inches high; c. 1850–1880; $250–350.

Crock, lead-glazed redware splashed with black manganese, small ear handles; Norwalk, Connecticut; 8.5 inches high; c. 1850–1870; $200–285.

Crock, molded with matching domed cover, embossed decoration, shallow handles, lead-glazed redware; by Carl Mehwaldt, Bergholz, New York; 7 inches high; c. 1851–1885; $400–600.

Crock, lead-glazed redware; by Ephraim Roberts, Vernal, Utah; 6.5 inches high; c. 1860–1890; $200–275.

Cup, lead-glazed redware with incised green filled floral patterns on a white ground; Pennsylvania or North Carolina; 4 inches high; c. 1850–1870; $1,400–1,800.

Cup, lead-glazed redware with stippled bands in black manganese; Pennsylvania; 4 inches high; c. 1860–1880; $275–350.

Cup, lead-glazed redware with marbleized green, white, and brown slip finish; New York; 3.5 inches high; c. 1825–1845; $350–450.

Cup or porringer cup, black manganese glazed redware, Pennsylvania, c. 1820–1850, 3.75 inches in diameter, $90–130.

Cup and saucer, brown glazed redware; by Solomon Bell, Strasburg, Virginia; 3.5 inches high; c. 1850–1870; $250–350.

Cup and saucer, lead-glazed redware mottled in brown manganese; by Carl Mehwaldt, Bergholz, New York; 3.3 inches high; c. 1860–1880; $225–325.

Cup and saucer, lead-glazed redware with small floral decoration in green-and-brown slip; Henry Schaffner, Salem, North Carolina; 3.6 inches high; c. 1850–1875; $350–450.

Cuspidor, green glazed redware with impressed geometric decorative motifs; Pennsylvania; 8 inches in diameter; c. 1850–1870; $550–750.

Cuspidor, heavy molded rim, redware covered with a cream-colored glaze; Galena, Illinois; 8 inches in diameter; c. 1860–1890; $200–275.

Cuspidor, hand-held, lead-glazed redware with coggled rim and ear handle; Northeastern or Midwestern; 4 inches in diameter; c. 1840–1880; $135–185.

Cuspidor, molded, fluted octagonal form, redware covered with a mottled brown glaze; by Solomon Bell, Strasburg, Virginia; 5 inches high; c. 1850–1880; $300–425.

Black manganese–glazed redware, New Jersey or Pennsylvania, c. 1840–1880. Left to right; *preserve jar, 7.5 inches high, $35–45; keg or rundlet, 4.5 inches high, $80–120; preserve jar, 11 inches high, $55–80; cuspidor, 5 inches in diameter, $30–45.*

Left, *cuspidor, black manganese glazed redware, Maine, c. 1870–1900, 7.5 inches in diameter, $35–50;* right, *ovoid jug, black manganese glazed redware, Pennsylvania, c. 1820–1840, 11.5 inches high, $150–225.*

Left, *cuspidor, molded lead glazed redware with shell decoration, Pennsylvania, c. 1860–1890, 7 inches in diameter, $65–95;* right, *preserve jar, lead glazed redware, New Jersey, c. 1840–1870, 6 inches high, $50–75.*

Left to right: *covered jar, manganese-glazed redware, Pennsylvania, c. 1840–1870, 5 inches high, $60–80; custard cup, lead-glazed redware, New England, c. 1860–1890, 3 inches high, $20–30; jug, black manganese–glazed redware, Pennsylvania, c. 1840–1860, 8 inches high, $50–75.*

Custard cup, lead-glazed redware flecked with black; Northeastern; 2.5 inches high; c. 1860–1900; $25–35.

Custard cup, clear glazed redware with two white slip bands; East Liverpool, Ohio; 2.5 inches high; c. 1910–1940; $10–15.

Custard cup, redware glazed only on interior; New Jersey; 3 inches high; c. 1850–1890; $15–25.

Custard cup, lead-glazed redware; Yarmouth, Maine; 2.5 inches high; c. 1850–1880; $40–65.

Deep dish, lead-glazed redware, six wavy lines of white slip radiating from center; Pennsylvania; 10 inches in diameter; c. 1820–1850; $600–750.

Deep dish, lead-glazed redware with radiating bands of brown slip on white interior; Virginia or North Carolina; 10.5 inches in diameter; c. 1825–1855; $1,200–1,700.

Dish or charger, lead-glazed redware with curving spoked wheel design in white slip; Huntington, New York; 13 inches in diameter c. 1830–1850; $700–850.

Dish or charger, redware with sgrafitto decoration of double eagle, green-and-yellow glazing, incised verses, and potter's name; by George Hubener, Montgomery County, Pennsylvania; 12.5 inches in diameter; c. 1780–1790; $25,000–35,000.

Dish or charger, redware with complex sgrafitto design of flowers in pot, green, yellow, and red slip on white ground; attributed to John Monday, Bucks County, Pennsylvania; 12.5 inches in diameter; c. 1825–1830; $15,000–20,000.

Dish, lead-glazed redware covered with dots in white slip; Pennsylvania; 4 inches in diameter; c. 1830–1860; $1,200–1,700.

Dish, lead-glazed redware with central white slip line flanked by four green dots; Pennsylvania; 4 inches in diameter; c. 1830–1860; $900–1,300.

Dish, lead-glazed redware, central star motif in green over yellow; New England or Pennsylvania; 8 inches in diameter; c. 1820–1840; $3,700–4,300.

Dish, lead-glazed redware, manganese brown sponged border, center filled with white slip dots; Pennsylvania; 9 inches in diameter; c. 1830–1860; $900–1,300.

Dish, redware with sgrafitto eagle, potter's name, date, and verse, on white slip; by Samuel Troxel, Montgomery County, Pennsylvania; 9 inches in diameter; 1824; $8,000–12,000.

Dish, redware with stylized sgrafitto leopard and tulip in green and yellow on white ground; attributed to Andrew Headman, Bucks County, Pennsylvania; 10.5 inches in diameter; c. 1810–1820; $9,000–13,000.

Dish, redware with sgrafitto creature (half elk, half fish) and verse on white ground; Friedrich Hildebrand, Montgomery County, Pennsylvania; 10.5 inches in diameter; c. 1810–1830; $18,000–23,000.

Dish, redware with sgrafitto representation of George Washington on horseback, green, yellow, and blue slip on white ground; by John Neis, Montgomery County, Pennsylvania; 11 inches in diameter; c. 1800–1810; $15,000–20,000.

Dish, lead-glazed earthenware, rim decorated with looping bands of brown manganese glaze; by John Loy, Alamance County, North Carolina; 10 inches in diameter; c. 1830–1860; $1,800–2,600.

Dish, redware covered with white slip decorated by flowers in red-and-green slip; Wachovia area, North Carolina; 10.5 inches in diameter; c. 1800–1830; $3,400–4,200.

Doll's head, head and shoulders of lead-glazed redware; Pennsylvania; 4 inches high; c. 1860–1890; $425–550.

Doll's head, head and shoulders of redware covered with white slip, brown manganese slipped hair; Pennsylvania; 3.25 inches high; c. 1840–1870; $500–650.

Door and drawer knobs, redware covered with swirled brown glaze to resemble Rockingham; Norwalk, Connecticut; 1.5 to 2.5 inches in diameter; c. 1825–1840; $10–20 each.

Doorstop, molded Staffordshire type spaniel, black manganese glazed redware; Galena, Illinois; 7.5 inches high; c. 1860–1880; $450–600.

Doorstop, molded recumbent lamb, redware covered with cream glaze splashed in brown and green; Strasburg, Virginia; 11.5 inches long; c. 1860–1890; $1,700–2,500.

Door knobs; molded redware with marbleized Rockingham-type yellow and brown glazes, Norwalk, Connecticut, c. 1835–1855, $10–20 each.

Egg cup, turned, pedestal base, cream glazed redware splashed in green and brown; Strasburg, Virginia; 2.3 inches high; c. 1860–1890; $550–700.

Fat lamp, handled pedestal form with spout, lead-glazed redware, black-spattered; Pennsylvania; 5 inches high; c. 1800–1830; $700–900.

Fat lamp, double spout form, lead-glazed redware, dots and lines in white slip; Pennsylvania; 5 inches long; c. 1800–1850; $550–750.

Fat lamp, jug form with long wick spout and ear-shaped handle, lead-glazed redware; Pennsylvania; 4.5 inches high; c. 1820–1850; $200–300.

Figurine, recumbent lion with lamb, lead-glazed redware incised "And the Lion and Lamb shall lye down together"; Pennsylvania; 12.5 inches long; c. 1830–1850; $6,500–7,000.

Figurine, recumbent whippet dog on oblong base, black glazed redware, stamped "John Bell"; John Bell, Waynesboro, Pennsylvania; 8 inches long; c. 1840–1860; $3,000–4,000.

Figurine, recumbent poodle, lead-glazed redware with tooled hair; Pennsylvania; 10 inches long; c. 1840–1860; $3,500–4,300.

Figurine, poodle standing with basket of fruit in mouth, lead-glazed redware with tooled hair, oblong base; Pennsylvania; 4.5 inches long; c. 1840–1870; $2,500–3,200.

Figurine, sitting poodle, tooled hair, lead-glazed redware; Thorn Pottery, Crosswicks, New Jersey; 4.5 inches high; c. 1820–1840; $2,000–3,000.

Figurine, crudely shaped man's bust, incised initials, lead-glazed redware; Northeastern; 3 inches high; c. 1880–1910; $100–150.

Figurine, sitting man with fiddle, dog at feet, lead-glazed redware; Strasburg, Virginia; 5 inches high; c. 1850–1880; $2,800–3,500.

Figurine, lead-glazed standing lion on oblong base, combed mane, Pennsylvania; 4 inches long; c. 1840–1870; $2,500–3,200.

Figurine, sitting spaniel, redware splashed with brown over a yellow slip; Galena, Illinois; 8.5 inches high; c. 1860–1885; $700–950.

Figural redware, rare molded Whippet dog with salmon-colored glaze, Solomon Bell, Winchester, Virginia, c. 1870–1880, 8 inches long, $3,000–4,000.

Figurine, monkey sitting on elephant and drinking from bottle, lead-glazed redware with incised and impressed details; attributed to Milton Hoopes, Chester County, Pennsylvania; 6 inches high; c. 1842–1864; $4,500–5,500.

Flask, lead-glazed redware, with impressed maker's mark; by John Safford II, Monmouth, Maine; 7 inches high; c. 1825–1850; $450–600.

Flask, yellow glazed redware, slip heart on one side, flower on other; Virginia or Maryland; 6 inches high; c. 1800–1840; $2,900–3,400.

Flask, lead-glazed redware splashed in black; Norwalk, Connecticut; 7 inches high; c. 1830–1860; $200–300.

Flask, molded redware covered with white slip splashed in green, embossed eagle on each side; Virginia or North Carolina; 6.5 inches high; c. 1850–1880; $3,000–4,000.

Flask in the form of a recumbent pig, tooled bristles, spout at rear, lead-glazed redware splashed with brown manganese; Pennsylvania; 6.5 inches long; c. 1830–1860; $1,600–2,300.

Flask in the shape of a standing squirrel, redware covered with white slip splashed with brown and green; Salem, North Carolina; 8 inches high; c. 1790–1830; $3,000–4,000.

Flower pot with attached saucer, lead-glazed redware, impressed maker's mark; by John Bell, Waynesboro, Pennsylvania; 4.5 inches high; c. 1850–1880; $200–300.

Flower pot, semi-ovoid form with attached saucer, redware slipped in green and brown over white; Strasburg, Virginia; 9 inches high; c. 1860–1890; $350–450.

Flower pot with attached saucer, lead-glazed redware with vertical bands of black sponging; Pennsylvania; 7.5 inches high; c. 1840–1870; $250–350.

Flower pot, unglazed redware with pedestal base, wavy incised decoration and heavy molded rim; Galena, Illinois; 11 inches high; c. 1870–1890; $150–225.

Flower pot, black manganese glazed redware with attached saucer; Pennsylvania; 5.5 inches high; c. 1830–1870; $35–60.

Flower pot, molded redware with black splotching, New England, c. 1840–1870, 5 inches high; $110–140.

Flower pot, lead-glazed redware, Galena, Illinois, c. 1850–1870, 6.5 inches high, $175–255.

Flower pots, matching set of black manganese glazed pots, Pennsylvania, c. 1850–1880, each 4.5 inches high, $150–200/pair.

Flower pot, brown manganese–splashed redware with crimped rim and saucer, Pennsylvania, c. 1850–1870, 7 inches high, $130–180.

Flower pot, unglazed redware with separate dish, both having scalloped edges; Pennsylvania; 6.5 inches high; c. 1880–1910; $55–80.

Flower pot with attached saucer, both having double scalloped rims, incised inscription and date, lead-glazed redware; by Enos Smedley, Chester County, Pennsylvania; 7 inches high; 1826; $3,300–4,000.

Flower pot, hanging variety with attached saucer and three holes for cord, lead-glazed redware splashed with brown manganese; Virginia or North Carolina; 5 inches high; c. 1830–1880; $425–550.

Funnel, cone-shaped redware in a white slip flecked with brown; Pennsylvania; 5.5 inches long; c. 1860–1890; $200–275.

Funnel, cone-shaped with small ear-shaped handle, lead-glazed redware splashed with black manganese; Northeastern; 6 inches long; c. 1830–1870; $250–350.

Gemel or double bottle, ovoid black manganese glazed redware; Northeastern; 6 inches high; c. 1830–1860; $300–450.

Gemel or double bottle, molded in the form of two men standing back to back, impressed maker's mark, lead-glazed redware; by Solomon Bell, Strasburg, Virginia; 9 inches high; c. 1840–1870; $6,000–8,000.

Goblet, tapering cylinder, redware sgrafitto decorated with incised tulip in green and yellow on white ground, incised date and verse; Pennsylvania; 5.5 inches high; 1793; $8,000–11,000.

Goblet, pedestal form, lead-glazed redware; Pennsylvania or North Carolina; 4.5 inches high; c. 1830–1850; $400–600.

Grotesque or "face" jug, lead-glazed redware, cigar in mouth; Southern; 9.5 inches high; c. 1920–1950; $200–300.

Grotesque or face jug, salt-glazed redware, porcelain teeth; Georgia; 8 inches high; c. 1900–1930; $450–600.

Harvest jug, strap handle and single spout, lead-glazed redware; Pennsylvania; 9 inches high; c. 1830–1860; $450–650.

Harvest jug, strap handle and two spouts, lead-glazed redware splashed with brown manganese; Bristol County, Massachusetts; 8.5 inches high; c. 1800–1830; $650–800.

Harvest jug, strap handle and two spouts, one much larger than other, impressed maker's mark, black manganese glazed redware; by Samuel L. Daily, Lancaster County, Pennsylvania; 11 inches high; c. 1845–1870; $600–750.

Hot-water bottle, jug form, unglazed redware with tooled decoration and impressed phrase "BABY WARMER"; Northeastern; 7.5 inches long; c. 1860–1880; $220–300.

Hot-water bottle, oval shape with filling hole on upper side, redware with a black manganese glaze; Northeastern; 3.5 × 9.5 inches; c. 1830–1860; $110–160.

Hot-water bottle, shaped like loaf of bread, redware glazed in orange, brown, and green; New Hampshire; 11 inches long; c. 1820–1860; $300–375.

Humidor or tobacco jar with matching dome-top cover, redware with sgrafitto tulips in green and yellow on white, incised name and date; Pennsylvania; 8 inches high; 1822; $10,000–15,000.

Humidor, lead-glazed redware with openwork base, tooled banding and two knob handles, matching top; Pennsylvania; 7.5 inches high; c. 1800–1820; $3,500–4,500.

Ink sander, pedestal-shaped, lead-glazed redware; Northeastern; 3 inches high; c. 1830–1860; $145–185.

Ink sander, cylindrical shape with incised decorative banding, brown manganese glazed redware; North Carolina; 2.8 inches high; c. 1780–1820; $250–325.

Inkstand, molded, oblong with embossed floral decoration and two removable inkwells, lead-glazed redware; by Carl Mehwaldt, Bergholz, New York; 6 inches long; c. 1860–1880; $1,400–1,900.

Inkstand, molded, oblong with two removable inkwells, applied dog, and embossed lion, lead-glazed redware splashed with black manganese; Lancaster County, Pennsylvania; 6.5 inches long; c. 1850–1865; $2,000–2,800.

Inkwell, green glazed redware, impressed maker's mark; by John M. Safford, Monmouth, Maine; 3 inches high; c. 1840–1870; $400–550.

Inkwell, single hole type, lead-glazed redware mottled dark and light brown; New England; 2.5 inches in diameter; c. 1820–1850; $100–150.

Inkwells in redware: left, *black manganese glazed, Pennsylvania, c. 1830–1850, 4 inches in diameter, $80–130;* right, *mottled cream glaze, Middlebury, Vermont, c. 1820–1850, 4.75 inches in diameter, $200–275.*

Inkwell, lead-glazed redware with floral sgrafitto decoration and incised date; Pennsylvania; 3 inches in diameter; 1788; $3,800–4,600.

Inkwell, single hole type, brown glazed redware; Strasburg, Virginia; 1.75 inches high; c. 1850–1870; $90–130.

Invalid feeding cup, cup form with crooked spout at right angle to ear-shaped handle, impressed maker's mark, yellow glazed redware; by John Bell, Waynesboro, Pennsylvania; 5 inches in diameter; c. 1840–1860; $850–1,150.

Invalid feeding cup, boat-shaped with vertical handle, lead-glazed redware; Clark Pottery, Concord, New Hampshire; 7 inches long; c. 1840–1860; $280–330.

Jar, square, molded lead-glazed redware splashed in white, embossed figure of Indian on all four sides, impressed maker's mark; by F.R. Leitzinger, Clearfield, Pennsylvania; 5 inches high; c. 1855–1875; $1,200–1,700.

Jar, lead-glazed redware with black manganese floral decoration, incised maker's mark; by George N. Fulton, Fincastle, Virginia; 8 inches high; c. 1875–1890; $800–1,100.

Jars, black manganese–glazed redware, New Jersey, c. 1830–1860; left, *7 inches high,* right, *9.5 inches high, $45–75 apiece.*

Jars, lead-glazed redware. Left to right: *New Jersey, c. 1850–1880, 8 inches high, $45–65; New England, c. 1850–1870, 4 inches high, $60–75; New England, c. 1830–1850, 9 inches high, $100–130.*

Jar, lead-glazed redware, John Bell, Waynesboro, Pennsylvania, c. 1840–1860, 6 inches high, $160–220.

Jar with handles, lead-glazed redware with red, white, and green slip in bands and sawtooth patterns; attributed to North Carolina; 18 inches high; c. 1820–1840; $2,700–3,500.

Jar with matching cover, lead-glazed redware with green splashing, tooled neck; Maine; 7.5 inches high; c. 1840–1860; $300–450.

Jar, black manganese–splashed redware, New England or Pennsylvania, c. 1830–1870, 8 inches high, $70–100.

Jar, black manganese–glazed redware, Pennsylvania, c. 1850–1880, 5 inches high, $45–75.

Jars, unglazed redware, all Pennsylvania or Ohio. Left to right: 5 inches high, $20–30; 4 inches high, incised "DSB," $30–45; 10 inches high, $35–50.

Jar, brown-glazed redware, H. F. York, Lake Butler, Florida, c. 1880–1890, 17 inches high, $300–450.

Jar, ovoid lead-glazed redware with incised name and date; Northeastern; 7.5 inches high; 1835; $450–600.

Jar, ovoid lead-glazed redware; Northeastern; 8 inches high; c.1820–1850; $55–75.

Jar, lead-glazed redware decorated with tulips in green and yellow; attributed to Morgantown, West Virginia; 9.5 inches high; c. 1790–1820; $2,000–2,800.

Jars, lead-glazed redware. Left to right: *by John W. Bell, Waynesboro, Pennsylvania, c. 1880–1895, 6.5 inches high, $225–300; miniature from Missouri, 3 inches high, $55–85; by Willoughby Smith, Womelsdorf, Pennsylvania, c. 1864–1905, 5.5 inches high, $150–200; New England, c. 1800–1825, 9 inches high, $100–140.*

Jar, cream-glazed redware, New Hampshire, c. 1810–1830, 11 inches high, $180–250.

Jar, redware with a brown-glazed speckled in white, Ohio, c. 1830–1850, 8.5 inches high, $135–195.

Jar, lead-glazed redware, New England, c. 1800–1825, 9 inches high, $100–140.

Jar, ovoid with high shoulder, lead-glazed redware with light sponging in manganese brown; Massachusetts; 6.5 inches high; c. 1830–1850; $175–250.

Jar, lead-glazed redware speckled in green and yellow; Galena, Illinois; 7.5 inches high; c. 1850–1870; $250–325.

Jar, ovoid sgrafitto-decorated redware, incised peacock, trees, and flowers in green and yellow on a white ground; Pennsylvania; 9 inches high; c. 1790–1810; $16,000–22,000.

Jar, straight sides with flaring rim, lead-glazed redware; by James J. Hansen, Hyrum, Utah; 8 inches high; c. 1860–1880; $180–260.

Jelly mold, circular with fluted sides, lead-glazed redware; Northeastern; 4 inches in diameter; c. 1850–1890; $125–175.

Jelly mold, lead-glazed redware, boat-shaped, bottom molded in form of grapes and grape leaves; Pennsylvania; 12.5 inches long; c. 1830–1870; $235–315.

Jelly mold, round, fluted sides, bottom molded in form of swirling star, impressed maker's mark, yellow-glazed redware; by John Bell, Waynesboro, Pennsylvania; 4.2 inches in diameter; c. 1850–1880; $300–450.

Jug, ovoid with freestanding handle, lead-glazed redware splashed with green at neck; New England; 7.5 inches high; c. 1820–1840; $450–600.

Jug, ovoid with freestanding handle, black manganese glazed redware; New England; 11 inches high; c. 1800–1840; $100–150.

Jar, Albany slip–glazed redware, Georgia, c. 1850–1880, 7.5 inches high, $55–85.

Jar, black manganese–splashed redware, Connecticut, c. 1840–1860, 8.5 inches high, $85–115.

Jug, lead-glazed redware, Alvin Wilcox, West Bloomfield, New York, c. 1840–1855, 9 inches high, $350–450.

Jug, cream-glazed redware, Maine, c. 1830–1860, 10 inches high, $175–250.

Jug, white slip–glazed redware, Lorenzo Johnson, Newstead, New York, c. 1850–1880, 11 inches high, $400–500.

Jug, black manganese glazed redware; Pennsylvania; 8 inches high; c. 1840–1870; $60–80.

Jug, ovoid lead-glazed redware flecked with black; Seigeltown, New Jersey; 6 inches high; c. 1840–1870; $200–275.

Jug, lead-glazed redware, yellow slip dripping down over body; Galena, Illinois; 12.5 inches high; c. 1860–1880; $350–500.

Jug, unusual ovoid form with both freestanding and ear handles, redware with a cream-colored glaze; Belmont, Wisconsin; 12.5 inches high; c. 1845–1865; $400–600.

Jug, semi-ovoid form, redware glazed in yellow, green, and brown; Strasburg, Virginia; 6 inches high; c. 1860–1890; $350–500.

Jug, double-handled, redware covered with a gray-green glaze; Porter Pottery, Wiscasset, Maine; 11 inches high; c. 1830–1850; $350–500.

Jug, straight-sided, lead-glazed redware, by James J. Hansen, Hyrum, Utah; 9 inches high; c. 1860–1890; $150–225.

Jug, white slip–glazed redware, Elonzo D. Lewis, Bushnell's Basin, New York, c. 1848–1854, 10.5 inches high, $600–850.

Jug, black manganese–splashed redware, Norwalk, Connecticut, c. 1850–1880, 10.5 inches high, $180–260.

Keg or rundlet, brown-splashed redware, Massachusetts, c. 1820–1850, 5 inches high,
$200–260.

Kegs or rundlets, redware. Left to right: *black manganese–glazed, Pennsylvania,*
c. 1830–1850, 5.5 inches high, $95–135; lead glazed, Ohio, c. 1840–1860, 9 inches
high, $150–200; mustard glazed, New England, c. 1830–1850, 5 inches high,
$250–320.

Keg or rundlet, barrel-shaped, lead-glazed redware decorated with
   white slip flowers; Pennsylvania; 5.5 inches high;
   c. 1820–1850; $500–650.

Keg or rundlet, barrel-shaped, mounted horizontally on three feet,
   lead-glazed redware banded in brown manganese; Pennsylvania; 9 inches long; c. 1840–1870; $400–550.

Keg or rundlet, barrel-shaped, black manganese glazed redware,
   Northeastern; 5.7 inches high; c. 1860–1880; $100–150.

Keg or rundlet, barrel-shaped with decorative tooling, green
   glazed redware; Salem, North Carolina; 6.5 inches high;
   c. 1840–1860; $375–500.

Lampstand or "tidy," for fat or whale oil lamp, lathe-turned lead-glazed redware; Pennsylvania; 7 inches high; c. 1800–1840; $550–750.

Lantern or gigging light for night fishing, cylindrical body with handle and three spouts for fat lamp wicks, lead-glazed redware, Pennsylvania; 13 inches high; c. 1830–1850; $800–1,200.

Lawn vase, molded, heavily embossed vase with flaring rim mounted on pedestal-like stand, unglazed redware; Peoria Pottery, Peoria, Illinois; 40 inches high; c. 1870–1890; $350–500.

Marbles, unglazed redware; Northeastern and Midwestern; .3 to 1 inch in diameter; c. 1850–1900; $2–8.

Master salt, lead-glazed redware splashed with brown manganese; attributed to Solomon Miller, Adams County, Pennsylvania; 2.2 inches high; c. 1865–1885; $250–325.

Master salt, pedestal base form, lead-glazed redware; Pennsylvania; 2.2 inches high; c. 1820–1840; $180–230.

Milk pan, redware, lead-glazed on interior only; New York or New England; 11 inches in diameter; c. 1820–1850; $150–200.

Milk pan, lead-glazed redware, by Frederick F. Hansen, Brigham City, Utah, c. 1855–1875, 12.5 inches in diameter, $300–400.

Milk pan, lead-glazed redware (exterior unglazed), New England, c. 1820–1850, 13 inches in diameter, $110–160.

Milk pan, lead-glazed redware, shaped handles; Eardley Brothers Pottery, St. George, Utah; 12 inches in diameter; c. 1860–1880; $300–450.

Milk pan, lead-glazed redware; Cain Pottery, Sullivan County, Tennessee; 10.5 inches in diameter; c. 1840–1860; $450–600.

Milk pan, lead-glazed redware, impressed maker's mark; by Hervey Brooks, Goshen, Connecticut; 17 inches in diameter; c. 1840–1865; $500–650.

Miniature harvest jug with two spouts and handle, lead-glazed redware; Northeastern; 2.5 inches high; c. 1860–1900; $100–175.

Miniature crock, lead-glazed redware speckled in black; Pennsylvania; 2.7 inches high; c. 1850–1870; $80–130.

Miniature bowl, lead-glazed redware decorated in white-and-green slip; Strasburg, Virginia; 3.75 inches in diameter; c. 1860–1890; $360–450.

Miniatures, black manganese–glazed redware, Pennsylvania, c. 1830–1860. Left to right; *pitcher, 3 inches high, $80–110; jug, 2.5 inches high, $65–95; porringer cup, 2 inches high, $75–100.*

Miniatures, unglazed redware. Left to right, *jug, Northeastern, c. 1880–1900, 2.5 inches high, $10–15; jug, New York, dated 1892, 2.5 inches high, $45–60; bean pot, impressed "BOSTON BAKED BEANS," New England, c. 1880–1900, 1.75 inches high, $15–20.*

Miniatures, redware. Left to right; *jug, mustard glazed, Maine, c. 1840–1860, 3 inches high, $150–200; mold, lead glazed, New England, c. 1860–1880, 3.25 inches in diameter, $110–150; pot, black manganese–glazed, Pennsylvania, c. 1830–1860, 2.4 inches high, $60–90.*

Miniature flower pot, unglazed redware; Western Stoneware Company, Monmouth, Illinois; 1.7 inches high; c. 1920–1930; $12–18.

Miniature jug, brown Albany slip-glazed redware; North Carolina; 4 inches high; c. 1900–1920; $50–70.

Miniature jug, unglazed redware, floral painting in oils; New York; 2.75 inches high; c. 1870–1900; $25–35.

Miniature bean pot, unglazed redware, impressed "BOSTON BAKED BEANS"; New York or Massachusetts; 2 inches high; c. 1880–1910; $15–20.

Miniature chamber pot, black manganese glazed redware; Pennsylvania; 2 inches high; c. 1870–1900; $65–85.

Miniature keg or rundlet, black manganese glazed redware; Pennsylvania; 2.2 inches high; c. 1840–1860; $100–150.

Miniature platter, oblong lead-glazed redware decorated with wavy
bands of white slip; Connecticut or Pennsylvania; 3 × 4.5
inches; c. 1840–1860; $400–550.

Miniature butter tub or keeler with upright staved handles, brown
manganese glaze; Pennsylvania; 3 inches in diameter;
c. 1830–1850; $250–350.

Miniature pitcher and bowl set, lead-glazed redware; Northeastern; 3.5 inches high; c. 1830–1870; $300–450 the set.

Miniature pitcher, lead-glazed redware splashed with black; Massachusetts; 2.3 inches high; c. 1840–1870; $160–230.

Miniature shaving mug, straight-sided ale mug form, lead-glazed
redware; New Hampshire; 2.5 inches high; c. 1820–1850;
$225–300.

Miniature jar, cylindrical black manganese glazed redware; New
Hampshire; 2.8 inches high; c. 1830–1860; $100–150.

Miniature pudding pot, sloping sides, black manganese glazed redware; Massachusetts; 1.7 inches high; c. 1850–1880;
$65–95.

Mug, cylindrical with ear handle, impressed maker's mark, redware with a cream glaze; by John Bell, Waynesboro, Pennsylvania; 5 inches high; c. 1840–1860; $550–750.

Mug, lead-glazed earthenware, New York or New Jersey, c. 1830–1860, 5.5 inches high,
$175–250.

Mug, cylindrical with ear handle, sgrafitto-decorated redware, incised floral pattern filled in green on white; Pennsylvania; 6 inches high; c. 1810–1820; $9,000–12,000.

Mug, cylindrical with ear handle, black manganese glazed redware; New England; 6.5 inches high; c. 1820–1860; $160–230.

Mug, cone tapering out toward base, ear handle, lead-glazed redware splashed in brown manganese; Solomon Miller; Adams County, Pennsylvania; 4 inches high; c. 1865–1885; $300–450.

Mustard pot, ovoid with ear handle and matching domed top, redware splashed with green, yellow, and brown; Newburyport, Massachusetts; 3.5 inches high; c. 1800–1830; $500–700.

Paperweight, unglazed redware in the form of a cardinal perched on a molded base, embossed maker's mark; Western Stoneware Company, Monmouth, Illinois; 4.5 inches high; c. 1920–1940; $200–275.

Picture frame, molded in an oval form with floral patterns, redware with cream glaze touched with green and brown; Strasburg, Virginia; 10 inches high; c. 1850–1890; $1,500–2,200.

Pie plate, lead-glazed redware with phrase "Green Back" in white slip; Connecticut; 10 inches in diameter; c. 1840–1870; $5,000–6,000.

Pie plate, lead-glazed redware with phrase "Indian Bitters" in white slip; Connecticut; 11 inches in diameter; c. 1845–1865; $3,800–4,500.

Pie plate, lead-glazed redware with word "Good" in white slip; Connecticut; 10 inches in diameter; c. 1850–1870; $2,500–3,200.

Pie plate, lead-glazed redware with phrase "St. Dionysius" in white slip; Connecticut; 13 inches in diameter; c. 1840–1870; $2,300–2,800.

Pie plate, lead-glazed redware with initials "W.H.D." in white slip; 10.5 inches in diameter; Connecticut; c. 1830–1850; $1,200–1,600.

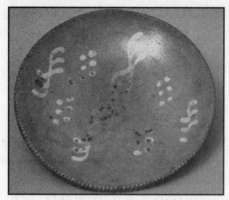

Pie plate, slip-decorated, lead-glazed redware, Pennsylvania, c. 1830–1860, 8.5 inches in diameter, $180–240.

Pie plate, slip-decorated, lead-glazed redware inscribed "CURREN (sic.) PIE," Norwalk, Connecticut, c. 1835–1865, 8 inches in diameter, $500–700.

Pie plate, very rare black manganese slip-decorated; lead-glazed redware, by John B. Gregory, Clinton, New York, 1823, 13.5 inches in diameter; $10,000–12,000.

Pie plate, lead-glazed redware with flowing calligraphic decoration in white slip; Pennsylvania; 13 inches in diameter; c. 1830–1860; $3,500–4,000.

Pie plate, lead-glazed redware with parallel bands of white slip in chainlike configuration, impressed maker's mark; McCully Pottery, Trenton, New Jersey; 9.3 inches in diameter; c. 1815–1855; $1,400–1,800.

Pie plate, lead-glazed redware with bird on branch in white slip; New Jersey or Pennsylvania; 9 inches in diameter; c. 1830–1860; $3,000–3,800.

Pie plate, lead-glazed redware with letters "ABC" in white slip; Connecticut; 10 inches in diameter; c. 1840–1870; $900–1,400.

Pie plate, lead-glazed redware with phrase "Sarah's Dish" in white slip; Connecticut; 10 inches in diameter; c. 1840–1870; $1,300–1,800.

Pie plate, lead-glazed redware, double tulip design in red and green on a white ground with date; Pennsylvania; 11 inches in diameter; 1808; $7,500–9,000.

Slip-decorated, lead-glazed Connecticut redware, c. 1830–1880. Left to right: pie plate, 8 inches in diameter, $165–235; pie plate, 8.5 inches in diameter, $200–275; loaf dish or platter, 12 inches long, $275–375.

Left to right: *redware pie plate slip-decorated in green and white, Pennsylvania, c. 1830–1850, 10.5 inches in diameter, $300–450; lead-glazed redware mold, New England, c. 1840–1870, 4.5 inches in diameter, $55–75; redware preserve jar with brown manganese–slip decoration, New York, c. 1830–1850, 8 inches high, $250–350.*

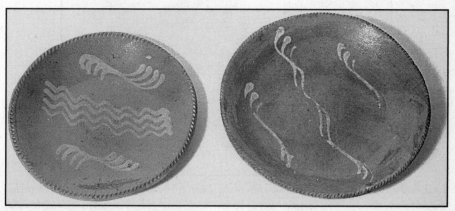

White slip–decorated redware pie plates; New Jersey or Pennsylvania, c. 1840–1870; left, 8 inches diameter, $200–275; right, 10 inches in diameter, $165–235.

Pie plate, lead-glazed redware with six parallel wavy bands of white slip; Pennsylvania or New Jersey; 8.5 inches in diameter; c. 1830–1870; $200–275.

Pie plate, lead-glazed redware, date "1866" in black slip; New Jersey or Pennsylvania; 9 inches in diameter; 1866; $650–850.

Pie plate, lead-glazed redware with so-called "chicken foot" design in white slip; Pennsylvania; 8.5 inches in diameter; c. 1850–1870; $250–350.

Pie plate lead-glazed redware with central circular decoration having hooklike appendages, all in white slip; Huntington, New York; 9 inches in diameter; c. 1830–1860; $500–700.

Pie plate, lead-glazed redware with central tulip motif, border of smaller tulips, all in green, black, and yellow slip, impressed maker's mark; by Justus L. Blaney, Cookstown, Pennsylvania; 10.5 inches in diameter; c. 1825–1854; $4,000–5,500.

Pie plate, lead-glazed redware with name "J. Innes" and date "1867" in white slip, border of white dots; Pennsylvania or New Jersey; 9.5 inches in diameter; 1867; $1,200–1,700.

Pie plate, lead-glazed redware, undecorated; New England or Pennsylvania; 10 inches in diameter; c. 1840–1870; $45–60.

Pipe bowl, molded unglazed redware with ridged body; Ohio; 1.75 inches long; c. 1850–1880; $10–15.

Left to right: *white slip–decorated pie plate, Pennsylvania, c. 1830–1860, 7.5 inches in diameter, $285–365; handled apple butter crock, lead-glazed redware, Pennsylvania, c. 1850–1880, 6 inches high, $45–70; white slip–decorated pie plate, Huntington, New York, 6 inches in diameter, c. 1840–1870, $230–300.*

Plates: left, *lead-glazed redware, Pennsylvania, c. 1840–1870, 7 inches in diameter,* $40–60; right, *lead-glazed redware, New Jersey, c. 1840–1870, 11.5 inches in diameter,* $110–160.

Molded redware pipe bowls: left, *unglazed, Ohio, c. 1850–1870, 2 inches across,* $10–15; right, *gray slip–glazed, Illinois, c. 1850–1880, 2 inches across,* $17–25.

Pipe bowl, molded in shape of man's head, lead-glazed redware; Ohio; 2 inches long; c. 1850–1880; $30–45.

Pipe bowl, molded in the form of a corncob pipe, unglazed redware; Taber Pottery, East Alton, New Hampshire; 1.5 inches high; c. 1864–1872; $25–35.

Pipkin, bean pot form with pouring spout and hollow handle, matching lid, lead-glazed redware speckled with black; New England or New York; 5.5 inches high; c. 1850–1880; $200–250.

Pitcher, lead-glazed redware, yellow splashed with brown, incised maker's mark; by Isaac Goode, Timberville, Virginia; 9.5 inches high; c. 1830–1860; $8,500–9,500.

Pitcher, lead-glazed redware, with impressed maker's mark; by John M. Safford, Monmouth, Maine; 6 inches high; c. 1840–1870; $600–750.

Pitcher, redware covered with a clear orange glaze, impressed maker's mark; Jugtown Pottery, Seagrove, North Carolina; 5.5 inches high; c. 1930–1950; $35–45.

Pitcher, redware slipped in tan and green over white; Strasburg, Virginia; 8.5 inches high; c. 1860–1890; $500–650.

Pipkin, lead-glazed redware, Pennsylvania or Ohio, c. 1860–1880, 5 inches high, $175–250.

Pitcher, manganese-splashed redware, Connecticut, c. 1830–1850, 10.5 inches high, $225–300.

Pitcher (very large) black manganese–glazed redware, Pennsylvania, c. 1850–1870, 15 inches high, $240–290.

Pitchers: Left to right, *lead-glazed redware, New Jersey, c. 1830–1860, 6.5 inches high, $55–85; black manganese–glazed redware, Pennsylvania, c. 1840–1880, 3.5 inches high, $45–65; black manganese–glazed redware, Pennsylvania, c. 1840–1880, 4 inches high, $45–65.*

Pitcher, redware with cream, brown, and green glaze, Pennsylvania, c. 1835–1865, 8 inches high, $300–450.

Pitcher, redware with brown slip glaze, South Carolina, c. 1850–1880, 10 inches high, $70–100.

Pitcher, lead-glazed redware; Northeastern; 5.5 inches high; c. 1850–1870; $65–80.

Pitcher, ovoid black manganese glazed redware, tooled neck; New England or Pennsylvania; 10.5 inches high; c. 1820–1840; $70–100.

Pitcher, ovoid black manganese glazed redware, tooled neck and shoulder, impressed maker's mark; by Darlington Cope, Chester County, Pennsylvania; 11 inches high; c. 1840–1850; $350–500.

Pitcher or creamer with matching top, lead-glazed redware; Mineral Point, Wisconsin; 5 inches high; c. 1855–1875; $235–285.

Pitcher, semi-ovoid form, redware with overall green glaze; Galena, Illinois; 9.5 inches high; c. 1850–1870; $550–750.

Pitcher and washbowl set, applied soap dish and decorative scrollwork, redware glazed in green and brown on white; Strasburg, Virginia; 13 inches high; c. 1860–1890; $3,000–4,000.

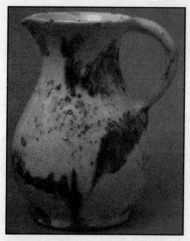

Pitcher, white slip–glazed redware splashed with green and brown, Strasburg area of Virginia, c. 1880–1900, 9 inches high, $700–950.

Pitcher, lead-glazed redware splashed in green and white, New York, c. 1820–1840, 10.5 inches high, $550–750.

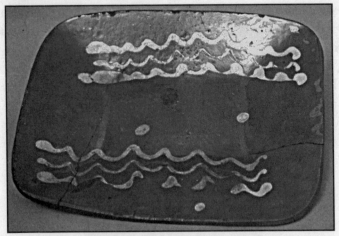

Platter, slip-decorated redware, New Jersey, c. 1830–1850, 8 × 13 inches, $450–600.

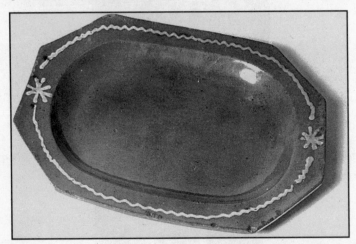

Platter, octagonal, white slip–decorated redware, Massachusetts, c. 1830–1850, 12 × 8 inches, $600–750.

Platter, oblong lead-glazed redware with phrase "Money Wanted" in white slip; Connecticut; 14.5 inches long; c. 1840–1860; $6,900–7,400.

Platter, oblong lead-glazed redware with elaborate overall calligraphic decoration in white slip; Connecticut; 18 inches long; c. 1840–1870; $5,000–6,000.

Platter, oblong lead-glazed redware with wavy border and music-scale-like central calligraphic design, all in white slip; Connecticut; 15 inches long; c. 1840–1870; $2,800–3,200.

Platter, oblong lead-glazed redware with white slip motif consisting of quartered circle with wavy outer border; Huntington, New York; 12.5 inches long; c. 1830–1870; $800–1,100.

Platter, oblong lead-glazed redware with wavy lines alternating with loops, all in white slip; Connecticut; 11.5 inches long; c. 1840–1870; $650–850.

Platter, oblong, octagonal lead-glazed redware; by Carl Mehwaldt, Bergholz, New York; 12 inches long; c. 1860–1880; $200–300.

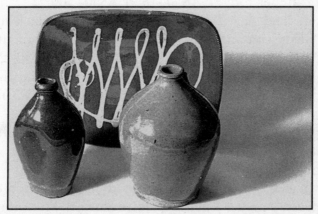

Left to right: *flask, lead-glazed redware, New England, c. 1830–1850, 6 inches high, $100–150; platter, slip-decorated redware, Connecticut, c. 1830–1860, 7 × 10 inches, $550–750; jug, white slip–glazed redware, Maine, c. 1840–1860, 7.5 inches high, $80–120.*

Charger, sgrafitto and slip-decorated redware, Gottfried Aust, Salem, North Carolina, 1773, 18 inches in diameter, $35,000–50,000.

Platter or vegetable dish, oblong with center divider, lead-glazed redware with multiple bands of wavy white slip; Pennsylvania or Connecticut; 18 inches long; c. 1820–1850; $800–1,100.

Platter, ovoid with scalloped and fluted border, sgrafitto-decorated redware with incised branching tulip, verse, and date in green, red, and yellow on white; Pennsylvania; 13 inches long; c. 1800–1830; $16,000–22,000.

Platter, oblong with scalloped edges, lead-glazed redware; Ohio; 12 inches long; c. 1830–1860; $350–500.

Porringer, lead-glazed redware splashed with black manganese, flaring rim and ear-shaped handle; Connecticut or Massachusetts; 3.7 inches high; c. 1820–1850; $230–280.

Porringer, black manganese glazed redware, flaring rim and ear-shaped handle; New Jersey or Pennsylvania; 3.5 inches high; c. 1830–1860; $125–175.

Porringer, lead-glazed redware, flaring rim and ear-shaped handle; by Hervey Brooks, Goshen, Connecticut; 3.3 inches high; c. 1825–1855; $350–450.

Pot, with single handle, rose-colored lead-glazed redware, impressed maker's mark; by John Safford, Monmouth, Maine; 8.5 inches high; c. 1825–1840; $700–850.

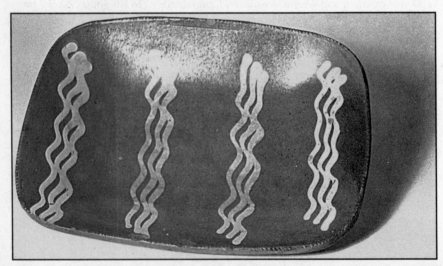

Platter, white slip–decorated redware, Norwalk, Connecticut, c. 1840–1860, 13 × 9 inches, $500–650.

Cup or porringer cup, redware splashed with cream and black glaze, New York, c. 1820–1840, 5 inches in diameter, $265–335.

Pot, brown and cream–splashed redware, Pennsylvania or New Jersey, c. 1830–1860, 8.5 inches high, $180–260.

Wisconsin lead-glazed redware. Left to right: *pot from the Cole Pottery, Whitewater, c. 1845–1855, 10 inches high, $250–350; jug by John Hammett, Belmont, c. 1850–1860, 7.5 inches high, $325–425; jug by John Hammett, Belmont, 4 inches high, $450–600.*

A selection of lead-glazed redware pots, jars, jugs and plates, all by James J. Hansen, Hyrum, Utah, c. 1860–1900, largest crock is 20 inches high, values range $125–700.

Pot, lead-glazed redware, ovoid with ear handles, incised maker's name and date; by Daniel Dry, Berks County, Pennsylvania; 11 inches high; 1856; $300–450.

Pot, with single rope twist handle and matching domed top, redware, sgrafitto-decorated with tulips in red and green on white; Pennsylvania; 8.5 inches high; c. 1790–1810; $7,500–9,500.

Pot, sides sloping outward from bottom, redware lead-glazed only on interior; Buxton, Maine; 7 inches high; c. 1860–1870; $55–75.

Pot, semi-ovoid with two horizontal handles, lead-glazed redware; by James J. Hansen, Hyrum, Utah; 14 inches high; c. 1860–1890; $250–350.

Pot, round with matching high domed top, interior divider, lead-glazed redware encircled with bands of brown-and-white slip; Salem, North Carolina; 6.5 inches high; c. 1800–1830; $1,600–2,200.

Pudding pan, tapering sides, lead-glazed redware; Northeastern; 4 inches high; c. 1830–1880; $55–85.

Pudding pan, tapering sides, lead-glazed redware splashed with brown manganese; Kendrick Pottery, Hollis Center, Maine; 9.5 inches in diameter; c. 1860–1875; $275–350.

Puzzle jug, double handles, false spouts, lead-glazed redware with incised eagle, date, and verse; Pennsylvania; 8.5 inches high; c. 1800–1820; $6,000–8,000.

Ring bottle, doughnut form, lead-glazed redware flecked with black; New England; 11 inches in diameter; c. 1830–1850; $300–400.

Ring flasks: left, *alkaline-glazed redware, Georgia or Alabama, c. 1860–1890, 10.5 inches in diameter, $300–425;* right, *lead-glazed redware, New England, c. 1840–1860, 11.5 inches in diameter, $275–375.*

Ring bottle, doughnut form, black manganese glazed redware; New Jersey or Pennsylvania; 9.5 inches in diameter; c. 1840–1870; $250–325.

Ring bottle, doughnut form mounted on circular base, lead-glazed redware splashed with green and brown; Massachusetts; 7 inches high; c. 1790–1830; $500–750.

Ring bottle, doughnut form mounted on circular base, redware with a green glaze; Salem, North Carolina; 6.5 inches high; c. 1830–1850; $450–650.

Roasting pan, shaped like a jug cut lengthwise, drain at one end, hand lift at other, redware brown-glazed on interior only; Salem, North Carolina; 13 inches long; c. 1850–1875; $275–375.

Salt shaker or caster, molded in form of chicken, green glazed redware; Salem, North Carolina; 3 inches high; c. 1840–1860; $2,000–2,800.

Serving dish, molded, octagonal lead-glazed redware; by Carl Mehwaldt, Bergholz, New York; 8.5 inches long; c. 1860–1880; $300–400.

Shaving mug, ear-shaped handle and two compartments, lead-glazed redware; New England; 4 inches high; c. 1830–1860; $140–190.

Shaving mug, oblong with ear-shaped handle and two compartments, cream glazed redware vertically sponged in brown; Pennsylvania; 4.5 inches high; c. 1840–1870; $275–375.

Shaving mug, straight-sided ale mug form, lead-glazed redware splashed with brown manganese, decorative tooling top and bottom; Massachusetts; 5 inches high; c. 1820–1850; $350–450.

Skimmer, flat perforated bowl with short handle, lead-glazed redware; Pennsylvania; 6 inches in diameter; c. 1820–1850; $300–450.

Soap dish, molded oval form with perforated top, lead-glazed redware splashed with brown to resemble Rockingham ware; by John Bell, Waynesboro, Pennsylvania; 2.5 inches high; c. 1860–1880; $400–550.

Left to right: *lead-glazed food mold, Ohio, c. 1840–1860, 6.5 inches in diameter, $65–95;* right, *stove or table foot rest, lead-glazed redware, Pennsylvania, c. 1840–1880, 4 inches high, $50–65.*

Standing salt or egg cup with pedestal base, lead-glazed redware; Pennsylvania or Virginia; 3.5 inches high; c. 1820–1850; $175–250.

Stove leg support, molded in form of human head, manganese-glazed redware; Pennsylvania; 4 inches high; c. 1850–1880; $225–300.

Stove leg support, cylindrical with shelflike rest, lead-glazed redware with manganese splotching; Pennsylvania; 3.5 inches high; c.1850–1880; $135–185.

Stove leg support, columnar form, unglazed redware; Pennsylvania; 3.2 inches high; c. 1830–1880; $25–35.

Sugar bowl with matching cover, molded redware with acorn finial, tooled and beaded surface, brown-and-green glaze over white, incised name; Pennsylvania; 6 inches high; c. 1850–1870; $1,700–2,500.

Sugar bowl, molded in manner of ironstone china, fluted sides, matching top, lead-glazed redware speckled with black manganese; Pennsylvania; 6 inches high; c. 1860–1890; $250–350.

Sugar bowl, ovoid with small handles, matching top, and coggled banding, black manganese decorated redware; New Jersey; 5.5 inches high; c. 1830–1860; $175–275.

Sugar bowl, ovoid with freestanding vertical handles and matching top, redware, only upper half of body lead-glazed; Plymouth, Massachusetts; 4 inches high; c. 1830–1850; $225–300.

Sugar cone mold, redware glazed only on interior, bullet-shaped; Connecticut; 11 inches long; c. 1830–1860; $175–250.

Teapot, molded black manganese glazed redware with embossed representation of "Rebecca at the Well"; Pennsylvania; 7 inches high; c. 1860–1890; $275–350.

Teapot, black manganese glazed redware, cylindrical body with short spout and ear handle; Ohio; 6.5 inches high; c. 1820–1850; $200–280.

Teapot, squat ovoid body with ear handle, black manganese glazed redware; Massachusetts or New York; 5 inches high; c. 1820–1850; $200–275.

Teapot, lead-glazed redware, bulbous form with matching top; Northeastern; 6 inches high; c. 1820–1850; $225–300.

Tea pot, lead-glazed redware, Connecticut, c. 1830–1860, 3 inches high, $165–245.

Tea pot, black manganese–glazed redware, attributed to John Man, Rahway, New Jersey, c. 1830–1850, 7 inches high, $250–325.

Roof tile, molded unglazed redware, James B. Hamilton, Greensboro, Pennsylvania, patented 1871, 10 inches long, $45–60.

Tile or trivet, lead-glazed redware with sgrafitto tulip in pot flanked by birds and hearts; Pennsylvania; 4 × 6.5 inches; c. 1810–1830; $2,200–2,800.

Tile or trivet, circular unglazed redware; Pennsylvania; 6.5 inches in diameter; c. 1830–1880; $20–35.

Toy rattle, lead-glazed redware in the form of sitting goose; Pennsylvania; 3.5 inches long; c. 1850–1880; $1,800–2,400.

Trap for ants or roaches, cone-shaped, lead-glazed only on interior of sloping rim; Pennsylvania; 4.5 inches high; c. 1840–1880; $40–65.

Umbrella stand, vase-shaped, lead-glazed redware splashed with brown and yellow; Strasburg, Virginia; 17 inches high; c. 1860–1890; $400–550.

Urn, lead-glazed redware with wavy banding in green and orange; Virginia or North Carolina; 15 inches high; c. 1840–1880; $600–850.

Urn, redware with overall floral sgrafitto decoration in yellow, brown, and green, incised date and verse; Pennsylvania; 13 inches high; 1788; $8,000–13,000.

Vase, with two freestanding handles, redware covered with green, brown, and white glaze, impressed "STRASBURG"; Strasburg area of Virginia; 10.5 inches high; c. 1860–1890; $1,200–1,800.

Vase, baluster-shaped unglazed redware with later floral painting in oils; Maine; 12 inches high; c. 1870–1900; $55–85.

Vase, ovoid lead-glazed redware covered with green slip, incised name and date; attributed to Andrew Miller, Philadelphia, Pennsylvania; 9 inches high; c. 1785–1800; $3,000–4,000.

Vase, concave cylinder, lead-glazed redware splashed in cream and green, impressed maker's mark; by Solomon Bell, Strasburg, Virginia; 8.5 inches high; c. 1840–1870; $3,000–3,800.

Vase, in the form of a fan with five holders and pedestal base, slip-decorated redware with applied decoration in green and white; Charles Headman, Bucks County, Pennsylvania; 10 inches high; c. 1845–1850; $6,500–8,000.

Wall pocket, demilune front, flat back with loop-form hanger, applied flowers, redware covered with a cream glaze splashed with green; Strasburg, Virginia; 8.5 inches high; c. 1860–1890; $900–1,200.

Washbasin, circular with hole for drainpipe, redware with brown slip on interior only; Salem, North Carolina; 10.5 inches in diameter; c. 1860–1880; $200–280.

Washboard (rare child's size), molded black manganese–splashed redware in a wooden frame, Pennsylvania or Ohio, c. 1880–1900, 6 inches square, $500–650.

Wash bowl, interior lead-glazed, Midwestern, c. 1840–1870, 12 inches in diameter, $165–245.

Water cooler, lead-glazed redware, barrel-shaped with holes to fill and empty; New England; 12 inches high; c. 1810–1840; $200–300.

Water cooler, barrel-shaped, lead-glazed redware splashed with green and brown, applied figures of man and lions, matching top; attributed to Bell Pottery, Strasburg, Virginia; 16.5 inches high; c. 1840–1860; $8,000–11,000.

Whistle in the form of a bird, lead-glazed redware with swirled white slip; Pennsylvania; 4 inches high; c. 1830–1870; $800–1,200.

Whistle in the form of a pig, lead-glazed redware; Carl Mehwaldt, Bergholz, New York; 4.5 inches long; c. 1860–1880; $550–750.

MAJOLICA

The term *majolica* is applied to molded earthenwares
which are glazed in a variety of bright colors and
typically take naturalistic forms such as shell-shaped
oyster plates, leaflike serving dishes, and pitchers
festooned with flowers or even cast to resemble fish or
birds. The clay body may be redware or, as was usually
the case in this country, a coarse white earthenware.
Known in Europe as faience, this fragile ware originated
in the Near East and was later widely produced in Italy,
Spain, and France, being first made in the United States
around 1850.

Though currently one of our most collectible

earthenwares, majolica was produced by only a few American potteries. Nevertheless, those who seek them can find native examples. The foremost producer of marked ware was the firm of Griffen, Smith & Hill of Phoenixville, Pennsylvania (c. 1882–1889). For several years this firm supplied majolica tablewares to the Atlantic and Pacific Tea Company (A&P), which used them as promotional premiums. As a result, vast quantities came on the market and much remains. Harder to find are the products of such firms as Baltimore's Chesapeake Pottery; the Mayer Pottery Manufacturing Company, Trenton, New Jersey; the Hampshire Pottery, Keene, New Hampshire; Morrison & Carr of New York City; and George Morley & Sons of East Liverpool, Ohio.

Pricing has little to do with origin. Most collectors seek rare, large, or spectacular examples regardless of nationality. While common wares such as leaf-form serving dishes or small pitchers may bring modest prices, a large animal-form tureen or covered cake plate can cost in excess of a thousand dollars.

A substantial variety of majolica forms are available to the collector. Common items such as cuspidors, soap dishes, flower pots, pitchers, plates, and bowls are readily found. Harder to come by are oblong trays, fruit and cake plates, spooners, covered butter and cheese dishes, and complete tea sets.

Since the ware is so fragile and so often damaged, hidden repairs can be a problem. Any potentially costly purchase should be examined for restoration under a black light, and a warranty as to condition should be obtained from the seller. Collectors should also note that majolica continues to be made today, principally in Portugal and Italy. Since some of the forms produced duplicate earlier examples, there is the possibility of confusion. Always look for crazing in the glaze and wear at points of normal contact. These should distinguish the older from the new.

As with other areas of American ceramics, marked examples will bring higher prices than comparable unmarked ones. Also, since a few catalogs produced by American majolica manufacturers have survived, it may sometimes be possible to identify certain unmarked pieces by reference to these. Bear in mind, though, that molds were often carried from factory to factory, so that very similar forms might be made over a period of time at widely distant locations.

Basket, molded and hand-formed polychrome-glazed white earthenware with embossed leaves and flowers; John L. Rue Pottery Company, Matawan, New Jersey; 7 inches in diameter; c. 1881–1894; $200–275.

Basket, molded polychrome-glazed white earthenware with embossed basket-weave body and rustic strap handle; J.S. Taft & Company, Keene, New Hamsphire; 6.5 inches high; c. 1880–1900; $150–225.

Basket, molded oval body with twisted handle and four stub feet, polychrome-glazed white earthenware with embossed begonia design; Griffen, Smith & Hill, Phoenixville, Pennsylvania; 6 inches high; c. 1882–1889; $125–175.

Berry bowl, molded polychrome-glazed white earthenware in cauliflower pattern, impressed maker's mark; Griffen, Smith & Hill, Phoenixville, Pennsylvania; 5 inches in diameter; c. 1882–1889; $150–225.

Figurine, molded polychrome-glazed majolica, Midwestern, c. 1910–1930, 5 inches high, $75–100.

Berry tray, molded three-piece set including leaf-form tray into which fit small sugar bowl and creamer, all polychrome white earthenware with embossed leaf designs; Griffen, Smith & Hill, Phoenixville, Pennsylvania; 9 inches long; c. 1882–1889; $800–1,100.

Bowl, molded polychrome-glazed white earthenware in black berry pattern, stamped maker's mark; Chesapeake Pottery Company, Baltimore, Maryland; 7.5 inches in diameter; c. 1882–1890; $165–235.

Bowl, shallow, molded polychrome-glazed white earthenware with embossed rose pattern; Griffen, Smith & Hill, Phoenixville, Pennsylvania; 8 inches in diameter; c. 1882–1892; $180–250.

Butter pat, molded petunia form, polychrome-glazed white earthenware, impressed maker's mark; Griffen, Smith & Hill, Phoenixville, Pennsylvania; 3.5 inches in diameter; c. 1882–1889; $175–200.

Butter pat, molded leaf form, polychrome-glazed white earthenware; Maryland; 3 inches in diameter; c. 1870–1890; $70–95.

Butter dish, covered, oblong molded polychrome-glazed white earthenware with embossed representation of cow and matching cover; Pennsylvania or Ohio; 6 inches long; c. 1880–1900; $200–275.

Cake stand, molded pedestal form with maple leaf motifs, polychrome-glazed white earthenware, impressed maker's mark; Griffen, Smith & Hill, Phoenixville, Pennsylvania; 10.5 inches in diameter; c. 1882–1889; $275–400.

Cake tray, oblong, molded with inset handles, polychrome-glazed white earthenware, embossed oak leaf pattern; New Jersey or Pennsylvania; 9.5 inches long; c. 1880–1900; $125–175.

Celery holder, molded in the form of palm leaves with foliated rim, polychrome-glazed white earthenware; New Jersey or Pennsylvania; 7.5 inches high; c. 1880–1900; $225–300.

Celery holder, molded in form of ear of corn with husks, polychrome-glazed white earthenware; Maryland or Pennsylvania; 6.5 inches high; c. 1870–1890; $185–265.

Molded majolica with hand-formed details, Faience Manufacturing Company, Greenpoint, New York c. 1880–1882; left, *box in blue, pink and white, 3 inches high, $400–500;* right, *vase in pink and blue, 8 inches high, $900–1,200.*

Cheese box, molded circular vessel resting on separate tray, top crowned with swan, polychrome-glazed white earthenware in lily pattern; Griffen, Smith & Hill, Phoenixville, Pennsylvania; 6.5 inches high; c. 1882–1889; $425–550.

Cigar box, molded polychrome-glazed white earthenware with embossed shell pattern and cover crowned with shells, impressed maker's mark, Griffen, Smith & Hill, Phoenixville, Pennsylvania; 8.5 inches high; c. 1882–1889; $275–375.

Coffeepot, molded octagonal polychrome-glazed white earthenware, impressed maker's mark; Bennett Pottery, Baltimore, Maryland; 10.5 inches high; c. 1860–1870; $400–550.

Cup and saucer, molded polychrome-glazed white earthenware with embossed floral patterns, stamped maker's mark; Willets Manufacturing Company, Trenton, New Jersey; cup, 4 inches high; c. 1880–1890; $135–185.

Cup and saucer, molded polychrome-glazed white earthenware with embossed oak leaf design; Griffen, Smith & Hill, Phoenixville, Pennsylvania; cup, 3.7 inches high; c. 1882–1889; $150–200.

Cuspidor, molded bulbous form, polychrome-glazed white earthenware with embossed floral patterns, paper label; Bennett Pottery, Baltimore, Maryland; 6 inches high; c. 1894–1900; $95–125.

Cuspidor, molded square form, polychrome-glazed white earthenware with embossed floral pattern; Ohio; 8.5 inches square; c. 1880–1900; $80–110.

Flower pot, molded polychrome-glazed white earthenware with embossed forest scene; New Jersey or Pennsylvania; 7 inches high; c. 1880–1910; $85–135.

Flower pot, molded polychrome-glazed white earthenware with attached saucer and embossed floral patterns; Ohio; 8 inches high; c. 1880–1910; $70–95.

Flower pot, molded polychrome-glazed white earthenware with embossed head of Indian; Ohio; 7.5 inches high; c. 1890–1920; $100–150.

Fruit bowl, oblong molded polychrome-glazed white earthenware with embossed grapes and leaves, impressed maker's mark; Hampshire Pottery, Keene, New Hampshire; 12 inches long; c. 1900–1910; $250–350.

Jar with matching cover, molded polychrome-glazed white earthenware with embossed floral patterns; New York City Pottery, New York, New York; 7.5 inches high; c. 1856–1876; $350–500.

Leaf-form serving dish, polychrome-glazed white earthenware, impressed maker's mark; Griffen, Smith & Hill, Phoenixville, Pennsylvania; 7.5 inches long; c. 1882–1889; $65–85.

Molasses jug, molded polychrome-glazed white earthenware with embossed bamboo motif, pewter top, impressed maker's mark; Griffen, Smith & Hill, Phoenixville, Pennsylvania; 8 inches high; c. 1882–1892; $275–350.

Mug, polychrome-glazed white earthenware with embossed leaf patterns; Willets Manufacturing Company, Trenton, New Jersey; 5 inches high; c. 1880–1890; $95–120.

Mug, molded polychrome-glazed white earthenware with embossed lily pattern; Pennsylvania; 4.7 inches high; c. 1880–1900; $65–85.

Pitcher, molded blue-glazed white earthenware body covered with embossed representations of fish and shellfish, impressed maker's mark; Bennett Pottery, Baltimore, Maryland; 9 inches high; c. 1853–1875; $650–850.

Pitcher, molded polychrome-glazed white earthenware in strawberry pattern, stamped maker's mark; Chesapeake Pottery Company, Baltimore, Maryland; 10 inches high; c. 1882–1895; $150–225.

Pitcher, molded ovoid form with embossed anchor and chain, polychrome-glazed white earthenware; John L. Rue Pottery Company, Matawan, New Jersey; 8 inches high; c. 1881–1894; $275–350.

Pitcher, molded in the form of an owl, polychrome-glazed white earthenware; George Morley & Company, Wellsville, Ohio; 10 inches high; c. 1879–1890; $1,000–1,400.

Pitcher, molded polychrome-glazed white earthenware with embossed bust of President Garfield; Pennsylvania or Ohio; 9.5 inches high; c. 1880–1885; $400–550.

Molded polychrome-glazed majolica: left, *bud vase, Chesapeake Pottery, Baltimore, Maryland, c. 1880–1890, 4 inches high, $50–75;* right, *creamer, Griffen, Smith & Hill, Phoenixville, Pennsylvania, c. 1882–1889, 3.5 inches high, $65–85.*

Pitcher, molded polychrome-glazed white earthenware with embossed figures of boys playing baseball; Griffen, Smith & Hill, Phoenixville, Pennsylvania; 8.5 inches high; c. 1882–1889; $650–950.

Plate, molded polychrome-glazed white earthenware in maple leaf pattern, impressed maker's mark; Griffen, Smith & Hill, Phoenixville, Pennsylvania; 10 inches in diameter; c. 1882–1889; $110–140.

Plate, molded polychrome-glazed white earthenware in morning-glory pattern with unusual red ground, impressed maker's mark; Griffen, Smith & Hill, Phoenixville, Pennsylvania; 10 inches in diameter; c. 1882–1889; $300–375.

Plate, molded polychrome-glazed white earthenware in black berry pattern, stamped maker's mark; Chesapeake Pottery Company, Baltimore, Maryland; 9.5 inches in diameter; c. 1882–1895; $80–110.

Plate, molded polychrome-glazed white earthenware in daisy pattern; Ohio; 8 inches in diameter; c. 1880–1910; $60–85.

Platter, molded polychrome-glazed white earthenware in grape leaf pattern, impressed maker's mark; Griffen, Smith &

Plate in form of leaf, molded polychrome-glazed majolica, Griffen, Smith & Hill, Phoenixville, Pennsylvania, c. 1882–1889, 9 inches long, $50–65.

Hill, Phoenixville, Pennsylvania; 11 inches long; c. 1882–1889; $275–350.

Platter, molded polychrome-glazed white earthenware with embossed fish and shellfish; New York City Pottery, New York, New York; 13 inches long; c. 1856–1876; $650–800.

Salad bowl, molded pedestal form, polychrome-glazed white earthenware with embossed lily pad pattern, impressed maker's mark; Griffen, Smith & Hill, Phoenixville, Pennsylvania; 10.5 inches in diameter; c. 1882–1889; $650–850.

Salt and pepper shakers, molded baluster forms with pewter tops, polychrome-glazed white earthenware with embossed floral patterns; Griffen, Smith & Hill, Phoenixville, Pennsylvania; 5.5 inches high; c. 1882–1889; $300–375 the pair.

Sardine box, molded oval receptacle resting on separate tray, polychrome-glazed fluted white earthenware body with finial or lift in form of small leaves; Griffen, Smith & Hill, Phoenixville, Pennsylvania; 3.7 inches high; c. 1882–1889; $400–575.

Saucer, molded polychrome-glazed white earthenware in cauliflower pattern, impressed maker's mark; Griffen, Smith & Hill, Phoenixville, Pennsylvania; 6 inches in diameter; c. 1882–1889; $125–150.

Serving dish, molded in oblong leaf form, polychrome-glazed white earthenware; J. S. Taft & Company, Keene, New Hampshire; 9 inches long; c. 1880–1890; $75–125.

Shaving mug, molded polychrome-glazed white earthenware in lily pattern, impressed maker's mark; Griffen, Smith & Hill, Phoenixville, Pennsylvania; 5 inches high; c. 1882–1889; $300–400.

Shaving mug, molded polychrome-glazed white earthenware with embossed figures of birds and animals; Pennsylvania or Ohio; 5 inches high; c. 1880–1910; $200–280.

Soap dish, molded polychrome-glazed white earthenware with embossed maple leaf pattern and matching cover; Pennsylvania; 4.5 inches in diameter; c. 1880–1890; $230–290.

Soap dish, molded oblong hanging form with raised hanging hole in back, polychrome-glazed white earthenware; New Jersey or Pennsylvania; 5 inches long; c. 1880–1910; $100–150.

Spice tray, molded in form of four conjoined leaves with central lift handle, polychrome-glazed white earthenware, impressed maker's mark; Griffen, Smith & Hill, Phoenixville, Pennsylvania; 7 inches across; c. 1882–1889; $450–600.

Spooner or spoon holder, molded polychrome-glazed white earthenware in strawberry pattern, stamped maker's mark; Chesapeake Pottery Company, Baltimore, Maryland; 6 inches high; c. 1882–1890; $100–135.

Stove tile, molded circular form with embossed classical head, white earthenware covered with yellow glaze, impressed maker's mark; John L. Rue Pottery Company, Matawan, New Jersey; 4 inches in diameter; c. 1881–1894; $175–225.

Sugar bowl, molded octagonal form with matching cover, polychrome-glazed white earthenware with embossed birds; Willets Manufacturing Company, Trenton, New Jersey; 4.7 inches high; c. 1880–1890; $215–265.

Sugar bowl, molded majolica-glazed in scarlet and white, Chesapeake Pottery, Baltimore, Maryland, c. 1880–1890, 5 inches high, $60–80.

Sugar bowl, molded oval form with matching cover, polychrome-glazed white earthenware with embossed bamboo design; New Jersey or Pennsylvania; 5 inches high; c. 1880–1900; $135–185.

Syrup jug or pitcher, molded polychrome-glazed white earthenware in sunflower pattern, impressed maker's mark; Griffen, Smith & Hill, Phoenixville, Pennsylvania; 6.5 inches high; c. 1882–1889; $250–350.

Teapot, molded in the "Rebecca at the Well" form, polychrome-glazed white earthenware; Edwin Bennett, Baltimore, Maryland; 8.5 inches high; c. 1925–1935; $90–120.

Teapot, molded polychrome-glazed earthenware in the form of a cauliflower; New York City Pottery, New York, New York; 6.5 inches high; c. 1856–1876; $700–950.

Teapot, molded polychrome-glazed white earthenware in bamboo pattern, impressed maker's mark; J.S. Taft & Company, Keene, New Hampshire; 5 inches high; c. 1880–1900; $200–300.

Teapot, polychrome-glazed majolica, George Ohr, Biloxi, Mississippi, c. 1895–1905, 8 inches high, $1,500–2,000.

Tea set, molded three-piece polychrome-glazed white earthenware (teapot, creamer, and sugar bowl) in bamboo pattern, impressed maker's mark; Griffen, Smith & Hill, Phoenixville, Pennsylvania; 4 to 7 inches high; c. 1882–1889; $550–700.

Trivet, molded polychrome-glazed white earthenware with embossed wickerwork design; New Jersey or Pennsylvania; 5.5 inches in diameter; c. 1880–1900; $55–80.

Tureen, molded polychrome-glazed white earthenware in turnip form with matching cover; New York City Pottery, New York, New York; 10 inches long; c. 1856–1876; $800–1,200.

Vase, flattened canteen form, molded polychrome-glazed white earthenware decorated with floral sprays, printed maker's mark; Chesapeake Pottery, Baltimore, Maryland; 8 inches high; c. 1880–1890; $200–275.

Vase, molded polychrome-glazed white earthenware in grapevine pattern with lizard-form handles; Bennett Pottery, Baltimore, Maryland; 23 inches high; c. 1856; $2,000–2,500.

Vase, molded cylindrical form with embossed floral pattern, polychrome-glazed white earthenware; J.S. Taft & Company, Keene, New Hampshire; 8 inches high; c. 1880–1890; $160–220.

Jardiniere, molded polychrome-glazed majolica, Maryland or Pennsylvania, c. 1880–1900, 8 inches high, $70–100.

Vase, molded majolica with hand-formed details, red and green, Midwestern, c. 1890–1910, 11 inches high, $400–600.

Vase, hand-formed and wheel-thrown majolica in pink, green and white by Wheatley Pottery Company, Cincinnati, Ohio, c. 1880–1883, $1,500–2,000.

YELLOWWARE

Yellowware is one of the most common and inexpensive of American ceramics. Like redware, it takes its name from the color to which the clay fires, a pale yellow to near-brown hue. Baked at a high temperature and given a clear alkaline glaze, the ware is durable enough that it has long been favored for cooking and baking utensils. Indeed, many collectors associate the term almost exclusively with mixing bowls and pie plates. However, yellowware has been produced in many different forms, including such unexpected items as book-shaped whiskey bottles, snuff jars, baskets, candlesticks, washboards, and even bird baths.

Some confusion may arise from the fact that both spongeware and Rockingham pottery, discussed elsewhere in this guide, may be made of yellow firing clay. Thus, they are technically yellowware. However, collectors have long described both on the basis of their decorative glazing rather than their ceramic bodies, and we shall continue to do so.

Yellowware was originally developed in England during the 1780s as a by-product of attempts to achieve a much-desired white earthenware. While there is evidence that it was manufactured in New York State in the 1790s and in Philadelphia before 1810, the first successful domestic manufacturer was David Henderson of Jersey City, New Jersey, active from 1828. However, suitable clay was widely available, and other factories soon appeared: William Lewis in Louisville, Kentucky, in 1829; Jabez Vodrey at Troy, Indiana, in 1839; James Bennett in East Liverpool, Ohio, in 1840; and Christopher Webber Fenton, active at Bennington, Vermont, from 1844.

Examples from many of the earlier firms are known, though the majority of collectible yellowware dates from a much later period—c. 1890–1940, when large factories in New Jersey, Ohio, and Minnesota turned out vast quantities of inexpensive cookware. Much of this pottery is maker-marked, so it is particularly appealing to collectors who are also attracted by the embossed decoration on the molded pieces and by the colorful slip banding on bowls and storage pieces. Another nice aspect of this ware is the fact that bowls, nappies, and other pieces were often made in nesting sizes ranging from as little as 3 inches to as much as 18 inches in diameter. Few collectors can resist the temptation to complete a "nest."

Yellowware also attracts the "crossover" collector interested in advertising memorabilia, since many twentieth-century pieces bear stenciled advertising logos and were used to promote various products such as butter, baked goods, and even clothing.

Most yellowware is relatively inexpensive, and there are no problems with reproductions. It should be noted, though, that mixing bowls continue to be made, so not all that are available are very old. Particularly common are pale yellow examples banded in light blue, pink, and white that date to the 1950–1970 period.

Also, English yellowware is often indistinguishable from American examples, though the former may be more finely shaped and decorated. Most collectors are glad to have both.

YELLOWWARE PRICES

Baking dish, molded yellowware, rectangular with sloping sides, stamped maker's mark, "Yellow Rock"; Philadelphia, Pennsylvania; 12 inches long; c. 1880–1900; $165–215.

Baking dish, molded yellowware, oval with outward sloping sides, stamped maker's mark; J.E. Jeffords & Company, Philadelphia, Pennsylvania; 9 inches long; c. 1870–1890; $85–135.

Baking dish, molded yellowware, American Pottery Company, Jersey City, New Jersey, c. 1833–1845; 8.5 × 12 inches, $225–300.

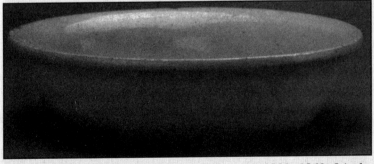

Baking dish, oval form, molded yellowware, New Jersey, c. 1830–1860, 8 inches long, $70–100.

Bank, molded yellowware in form of a pear with penny slot; New Jersey or Pennsylvania; 5 inches high; c. 1860–1890; $225–275.

Bank, molded yellowware in form of a barrel; New Jersey or Pennsylvania; 4 inches high; c. 1860–1890; $160–220.

Basket, molded yellowware with loop handle and vertical ribbing; Midwestern; 5.5 inches high; c. 1910–1940; $40–65.

Basket, molded yellowware with loop handle and overall floral embossing; New Jersey; 6.5 inches high; c. 1890–1920; $70–95.

Batter bowl, molded yellowware with pouring spout, embossed floral designs; New Jersey or Ohio; 9.5 inches in diameter; c. 1890–1920; $70–95.

Batter bowl, molded yellowware with pouring spout, scalloped band below rim, and fluted sides; Midwestern; 10 inches in diameter; c. 1900–1930; $80–110.

Batter bowl, molded yellowware with pouring spout, broad band of white slip within which are sponged spots of blue mocha-like decoration; Ohio; 10 inches in diameter; c. 1870–1900; $300–375.

Batter bowl, molded yellowware with pouring spout and large handle, decorated with bands of white-and-brown slip; Ohio or Illinois; 9 inches in diameter; c. 1920–1935; $70–95.

Banks, molded yellowware, New Jersey or Pennsylvania, c. 1860–1890; left, *barrel form, 4 inches high, $160–220;* right, *pear form, 5 inches high, $225–275.*

Batter bowl, molded yellowware with embossed decoration, New Jersey or Ohio, c. 1900–1920, 13 inches in diameter, $60–90.

Batter bowl, molded yellowware, New Jersey or Ohio, c. 1880–1920, 10 inches in diameter, $65–85.

Batter bowls, molded yellowware; left, Ohio, c. 1900–1920, 6.5 inches in diameter, $55–75; right, rare handled form, Ohio or Illinois, c. 1920–1935, $80–110.

Beakers, molded yellowware, Pennsylvania or Ohio, c. 1870–1910; left, *6.5 inches high,* $70–90; right, *4 inches high, $70–95.*

Beaker, molded cylindrical yellowware body tapering out from foot; New Jersey or Midwestern; 5.5 inches high; c. 1870–1910; $55–75.

Beaker, yellowware with matching flat cover, cylindrical body tapers out slightly from foot; Pennsylvania or Ohio; 4 inches high; c. 1870–1900; $70–95.

Bean pot, molded yellowware with two loop handles, fluted lower body, and band of white slip between two of brown, matching cover, Red Wing Union Stoneware Company, Red Wing, Minnesota; 5.5 inches high; c. 1906–1936; $80–120.

Bean pot, bulbous molded yellowware body with two loop handles, matching flat cover; Midwestern; 6.5 inches high; c. 1900–1930; $45–65.

Beater jar, molded yellowware with fluted sides below band of white slip between two of brown; Red Wing Potteries, Red Wing, Minnesota; 5 inches high; c. 1936–1967; $70–95.

Bedpan, molded yellowware, round doughnut form with straight drain tube; Midwestern; 16.5 inches long; c. 1870–1890; $30–55.

Bedpan, molded yellowware, round doughnut form with upcurved drain tube and wedge-shaped foot; New Jersey or Midwestern; 17 inches long; c. 1880–1920; $20–40.

Bowl, molded yellowware with embossed sawtooth rim above grape and grape leaf pattern body; Red Wing Union Stoneware Company, Red Wing, Minnesota; 6.5 inches in diameter; c. 1906–1936; $55–70.

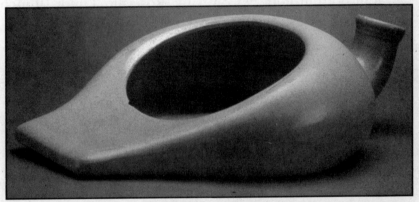

Bed pan, molded yellowware, New Jersey or Ohio, c. 1880–1910, 15 inches long, $20–35.

Bowl, molded yellowware, Illinois or Minnesota, c. 1910–1930, 11 inches in diameter, $40–60.

Bowl, molded yellowware with printed maker's mark; Pacific Clay Manufacturing Company, Los Angeles, California; 9 inches in diameter; c. 1880–1930; $55–85.

Bowl, molded yellowware with three narrow bands of white slip; Midwestern; 4 to 13 inches in diameter; c. 1880–1930; $25–45; set of seven to ten matching bowls, $300–550.

Bowl, molded yellowware with embossed shell design and bands of red-and-blue slip, impressed maker's mark; Robinson, Ransbottom Pottery Company, Roseville, Ohio; 10 inches in diameter; c. 1950–1970; $15–25.

Bowls, molded yellowware, New Jersey or Ohio, c. 1860–1930; left, rare divided serving bowl, 9 inches long, $175–225; right, paneled, 7 inches across, $45–55.

Bowls, molded yellowware serving or baking bowls, New Jersey or Pennsylvania, c. 1870–1900. Left to right, J.E. Jeffords & Company, Philadelphia, 10 inches long, $75–95; baker, 8 inches long, $55–70; scalloped rim, 10.5 inches long, $110–140.

Bowls, molded yellowware glazed in red, green, and black, Pacific Clay Manufacturing Company, Riverside, California, c. 1890–1910, 8 inches in diameter, $45–65 each.

Bowls, molded yellowware with mocha type decoration, Ohio, c. 1870–1900: left, *green on white, 8 inches in diameter, $145–185;* right, *batter bowl in blue on white, 9.5 inches in diameter, $275–350.*

Bowl, molded yellowware covered serving bowl banded in brown and white, Ohio or Minnesota, c. 1910–1930, $65–90.

Bowls, molded yellowware banded in blue, Illinois or Minnesota, c. 1920–1940, 5 to 8 inches in diameter, $30–45 each; custard cup, 3 inches high, $20–25.

Bowls, molded yellowware banded in white slip, Ohio or Minnesota, c. 1910–1930: nest of five matching bowls, 4 to 9 inches in diameter, $225–325.

Bowl, molded yellowware with broad band of white slip within which are mocha-like seaweed patterns in blue; Ohio; 8.5 inches in diameter; c. 1870–1900; $200–275.

Bowl, molded yellowware with broad band of white slip within which are sponged spots of mocha-like green; New Jersey or Ohio; 10 inches in diameter; c. 1860–1890; $175–250.

Bowl, molded yellowware with embossed representations of child watering flowers in front of house; Midwestern; 6 inches in diameter; c. 1930–1945; $40–60.

Bowl, yellowware with slightly everted rim and incised band around lower body; Midwestern; 8.5 inches in diameter; c. 1880–1910; $65–95.

Bowl, molded yellowware with entire body covered with embossed floral motifs; Ohio; 11 inches in diameter; c. 1900–1920; $65–90.

Bulb vase, ovoid molded yellowware vessel with openings for shoots in sides; New Jersey or Midwestern; 7.5 inches high; c. 1910–1940; $65–95.

Butter storage container, molded yellowware in the form of an elongated melon with loop handle on top; East Liverpool, Ohio; 7.5 inches long; c. 1910–1930; $275–375.

Candlestick, yellowware, tubular form mounted on dish with free-standing loop handle; New Jersey or Pennsylvania; 3 inches high; c. 1850–1875; $200–280.

Casserole, molded yellowware with matching top and stubby hand lifts, fluted body with band of white slip between two of brown, printed maker's mark; Red Wing Union Stoneware Company, Red Wing, Minnesota; 8.5 inches in diameter; c. 1906–1936; $95–135.

Candlestick, yellowware, New Jersey or Pennsylvania, c. 1850–1875, 4.5 inches in diameter (extremely rare), $200–280.

Casserole, molded blue-banded yellowware, Minnesota or Ohio, c. 1930–1945, 10 inches in diameter, $100–125.

Chamber pots, molded yellowware banded in brown and white, New Jersey or Ohio, c. 1880–1920: left, full size, 10 inches in diameter, $60–80; miniature, 2.5 inches in diameter, $50–75; miniature with blue mocha type decoration, 3 inches in diameter, $125–155.

Casserole, molded yellowware with matching domed top, each decorated with band of blue slip between two of white; Midwestern; 10 inches in diameter; c. 1930–1945; $80–125.

Chamber pot, yellowware, mug form with ear-shaped handle; New Jersey or Maryland; 5 inches high; c. 1850–1870; $45–65.

Chamber pot, molded yellowware, mug form with matching cover, both decorated with band of white slip within two of brown; D.E. McNichol Pottery Company, East Liverpool, Ohio; 6.5 inches high; c. 1895–1925; $80–120.

Chamber pot, molded yellowware with ear-shaped handle and fluted body; New Jersey or Midwestern; 4.7 inches high; c. 1900–1930; $55–85.

Churn, yellowware with matching top, wooden dasher; Midwestern; 16.5 inches high; c. 1860–1880; $250–350.

Coffeepot, molded yellowware, two pieces with matching top and interior strainer; Midwestern; 11 inches high; c. 1920–1940; $150–225.

Coffeepot, molded yellowware, elaborately embossed ovoid vessel with handle in form of man's body and spout in shape of sea serpent, impressed maker's mark; D. & J. Henderson, Jersey City, New Jersey; 12 inches high; c. 1829–1833; $3,000–4,000.

Colander, yellowware in form of bowl with turned foot, perforated sides; New Jersey; 11 inches in diameter c. 1840–1860; $110–150.

Colander, molded yellowware in form of bowl, lower half perforated, upper half decorated with wide band of white slip; Ohio; 10.5 inches in diameter; c. 1870–1900; $275–350.

Colanders, molded yellowware: left, with blue and white banding, Ohio, c. 1860–1880, 12 inches in diameter, $200–275; right: *Midwestern, c. 1900–1920, 10 inches in diameter, $150–200.*

Colander, molded yellowware banded in blue and white, Ohio, c. 1890–1910, 12 inches in diameter, $230–280.

Colander, yellowware in form of pie plate or deep dish, bottom only perforated; impressed 1861 patent date; Maryland; 10 inches in diameter; c. 1861–1885; $300–375.

Colander, molded yellowware in form of bowl, lower half perforated, upper half with band of white slip decorated with blue mocha-like sponging; New Jersey or Ohio; 11 inches in diameter; c. 1860–1880; $450–550.

Cream pot, semi-ovoid yellowware (similar to typical stoneware form); New Jersey; 9 inches high; c. 1860–1890; $140–180.

Crock, molded straight-sided form with embossed banding and freestanding handles, slightly domed top; Maryland or New Jersey; 6.5 inches high; c. 1870–1900; $165–245.

Crock, molded yellowware banded in brown and white, New Jersey or Ohio, c. 1890–1910, 8 inches high, $100–130.

Molded yellowware: Left to right, *crock, English, c. 1880–1910, 6 inches in diameter, $65–85; eating bowl, Illinois, c. 1910–1930, 5.5 inches in diameter, $40–55; keeler, Ohio or Illinois, c. 1890–1910, 8 inches in diameter (rare), $220–270.*

Crocks, molded yellowware, Ohio or Illinois, c. 1900–1930. Left to right, 9 inches high, $55–75; banded in white stamped "BUTTER," 4 inches high, $90–120; banded in blue, 5 inches high, $65–90.

Crock, molded yellowware banded in blue and white, Ohio, c. 1880–1900, 5 inches high, $75–100.

Crock, molded straight-sided form decorated with broad band of white slip, matching top; Ohio; 5 inches high; c. 1870–1910; $125–175.

Crock, molded straight-sided form decorated with broad band of white slip within two narrower bands and printed words "BUTTER," "SUGAR," "LARD," etc., matching flat cover; Midwestern; 4.7 inches high; c. 1900–1920; $150–200.

Crock, molded straight-sided yellowware with concentric bands of brown-and-white slip, matching flat top; Midwestern; 5 inches high; c. 1910–1940; $90–140.

Crock, molded straight-sided yellowware with broad band of white slip decorated with blue mocha-like sponging, matching cover, Ohio; 3.5 inches high; c. 1860–1880; $235–315.

Crock, molded straight-sided yellowware cylinder with matching flat cover; Midwestern; 9 inches high; c. 1920–1930; $35–55.

Crocks, molded yellowware with mocha type decoration, English, c. 1860–1890; left, *earthworm pattern, 7 inches in diameter, $265–325;* right, *blue on white, 5.5 inches in diameter, $285–355.*

Cookie crock, molded yellowware, New Jersey or Ohio, c. 1935–1950, 10 inches high, $40–60.

Cup, molded yellowware, Midwestern, c. 1920–1940, 3.5 inches high, $65–85.

Cuspidor, molded yellowware, Bennett Pottery, East Liverpool, Ohio, c. 1841–1844, 8 inches across, $150–225.

Cup, yellowware with flaring rim and applied ear-shaped handle; Ohio; 3.5 inches high; c. 1850–1880; $170–230.

Cuspidor, molded yellowware, octagonal; Ohio; 8 inches wide; c. 1840–1860; $85–135.

Cuspidor, molded yellowware, octagonal with embossed floral patterns and maker's mark; Salt & Mear, East Liverpool, Ohio; 7.5 inches wide; c. 1842–1850; $300–450.

Custard cup, molded yellowware, tapering cone shape; Bennington, Vermont; 3 inches high; c. 1847–1858; $40–55.

Custard cup, molded yellowware with embossed Gothic arch design; Midwestern; 3 inches high; c. 1900–1920; $40–55.

Custard cup, molded yellowware with slightly rolled rim; Maryland or Pennsylvania; 2.5 inches high; c. 1850–1880; $20–30.

Custard cup, molded yellowware decorated with three blue slip bands; Midwestern; 2.3 inches high; c. 1880–1920; $25–35.

Molded yellowware, Midwestern, c. 1880–1920. Left to right: *custard cup banded in brown, 3 inches high, $15–20; blue mocha decorated mixing bowl, 9 inches in diameter, $170–240; rolling pin with wooden handles, 15 inches long, $250–350.*

Custard cups, molded yellowware, c. 1890–1920. Left to right: *Bristol glazed interior, Jeffords Pottery, Philadelphia, 3 inches high, $20–25; blue slip-banded, Ohio, 3 inches high, $25–35; United States Pottery, Bennington, Vermont, c. 1849–1858, 3.25 inches high, $40–60.*

Custard cup, molded yellowware with Gothic Revival–style panels, Ohio, c. 1880–1900, 3 inches high, $25–30.

Molded yellowware, California, c. 1890–1930. Left to right: custard cup, Sacramento, 3 inches high, $40–55; mixing bowl sponged in green, Elsinore, 12 inches in diameter, $200–240; mixing bowl, Bauer Pottery, Los Angeles, 10 inches in diameter, $110–140.

Creamer, molded yellowware in the form of a cow, United States Pottery Company, Bennington, Vermont, c. 1849–1858 (very rare), $600–800.

Footwarmer, molded yellowware, New Jersey or Ohio, c. 1870–1900, 12 inches across, $55–70.

Figurine, molded and modeled yellowware mantel decoration, standing poodle holding basket of flowers in mouth; Bennington, Vermont; 9 inches long; c. 1847–1858; $4,000–5,000.

Figurine, molded yellowware sitting dachsund, Midwestern; 5 inches long; c. 1900–1930; $80–120.

Figurine, creamer in form of standing cow, molded yellowware, United States Pottery Company, Bennington, Vermont; 5.5 inches long; c. 1848–1858; $600–800.

Figurine, molded yellowware, pitcher in form of head and truncated body of President Herbert Hoover; Syracuse, New York; 5.5 inches high; c. 1928–1932; $85–145.

Flask, molded yellowware in the form of man holding fiddle and bow; New York or New Jersey; 8 inches high; c. 1870–1890; $350–500.

Flask, flattened ovoid molded yellowware embossed on each side with American eagle and flags; East Liverpool, Ohio; 8 inches high; c. 1840–1850; $800–1,200.

Foot warmer, molded yellowware, wedge-shaped with pierced brackets at sides for wire bale handle, impressed maker's mark; American Pottery Company, Jersey City, New Jersey; 10.5 inches wide; c. 1838–1845; $250–350.

Foot warmer, molded yellowware, tubular form with knob at each end and flat bottom; Midwestern; 11 inches long; c. 1860–1930; $55–75.

Funnel, molded yellowware with graduated foot to fit jars of various sizes; D.E. McNichol Pottery Company, East Liverpool, Ohio; 4 inches high; c. 1895–1925; $80–120.

Molded yellowware, Ohio, c. 1885–1925. Left to right: *pitcher, 8 inches high, Globe Pottery, East Liverpool, 8 inches high, $55–70; honey pot, 5 inches high, $25–35; rolling pin, 15 inches long, $185–245; fruit jar funnel, McNichol Pottery, East Liverpool, 4.5 inches across, $80–120.*

Honey pot, molded yellowware, ovoid with matching flat cover; impressed Roycraft Industries, East Aurora, New York, but made in Ohio; 5 inches high; c. 1900–1915; $25–35.

Inkwell, molded yellowware in form of reclining whippet dog; East Liverpool, Ohio; 5 inches long; c. 1860–1880; $1,200–1,800.

Jar, molded yellowware with matching flat top and body tapering out to shoulder, in to rim, stamped advertising logo; Red Wing Potteries, Red Wing, Minnesota; 7.5 inches high; c. 1936–1967; $70–95.

Jar, cylindrical molded yellowware with matching cover, both decorated with bands of brown-and-white slip; Ohio; 5 inches high; c. 1880–1910; $185–265.

Jar, molded yellowware with inset base having embossed swirling pattern, cylindrical body with band of white slip stenciled

Preserve jar, yellowware, Trule Stevens, Omaha, Nebraska, c. 1860–1870, 14 inches high (exceedingly rare), $800–1,200.

Spice canister set, molded yellowware banded in blue slip, Red Wing, Minnesota,
c. 1925–1945, 4 to 6.5 inches high, $220–300/the partial set of four.

Milk pan, Vermont or Ohio, c. 1850–1870, 11 inches in diameter, $150–225.

in black, "NUTMEG," "GINGER," etc., matching top;
Midwestern; 4.5 inches high; c. 1890–1910; $110–140.
Jug, molded yellowware with straight sides and cone-shaped shoul-
der; Midwestern; 10.5 inches high; c. 1915–1925; $45–65.

Keeler, molded yellowware nappylike form with two upstanding
pierced handles, decorated with two bands of brown slip;
Ohio or Illinois; 8 inches in diameter; c. 1890–1910;
$200–275.

Milk pan, yellowware with everted rim, impressed maker's mark;
United States Pottery Company, Bennington, Vermont; 12
inches in diameter; c. 1849–1858; $500–650.

Milk pan, molded yellowware with slightly everted rim; D.E. McNichol Pottery Company, East Liverpool, Ohio; 12. 5 inches in diameter; c. 1892–1915; $145–195.

Miniature, molded yellowware jug, straight-sided with two bands in blue and white, ink-stamped maker's mark; Minnesota Stoneware Company, Red Wing, Minnesota; 3.2 inches high; c. 1883–1906; $350–500.

Miniature, yellowware jug, slightly ovoid; Bennington, Vermont; 2.5 inches high; c. 1850–1860; $175–255.

Miniature, molded yellowware covered serving dish, sides taper in toward bottom, decorated with bands of blue-and-white slip, matching flat cover; Midwestern; 1.75 inches high; c. 1910–1930; $85–135.

Miniature plate, yellowware; New Jersey or Ohio; 3.5 inches in diameter; c. 1870–1910; $70–90.

Miniature bean pot, molded yellowware with matching flat cover, single handle; New Jersey or Ohio; 3.5 inches high; c. 1870–1890; $140–190.

Miniature, heart-shaped yellowware mold, fluted interior, stamped maker's mark; Philadelphia, Pennsylvania; 3 inches across; c. 1870–1900; $65–105.

Molded yellowware, Pennsylvania and New Jersey, c. 1870–1900. Left to right, *food mold, 7 inches in diameter, $60–80; miniature vase, 3 inches high, $25–35; serving bowl, 9 inches in diameter, $80–110; miniature food mold, 4 inches long, $40–60.*

Miniature jug, molded yellowware, Bennington, Vermont, c. 1870–1890, 2 inches high, $35–50.

Miniature or candy molds; molded yellowware, Philadelphia, Pennsylvania, c. 1900–1930, 2.5 to 4 inches long, $35–55 apiece.

Miniatures in molded yellowware, Ohio or New Jersey, c. 1870–1910. Left to right: *plate, 3.5 inches in diameter, $40–55; skillet, 2.5 inches in diameter, $55–75; bean pot, 3.5 inches high, $60–80.*

Miniature, round shell-shaped yellowware mold, fluted interior, stamped maker's mark; Philadelphia, Pennsylvania; 2.5 inches in diameter; c. 1870–1900; $55–85.

Miniature, molded yellowware helmet-shaped creamer; Midwestern; 2 inches high; c. 1870–1900; $135–185.

Miniature skillet, yellowware; New Jersey or Ohio; 2.5 inches in diameter; c. 1870–1900; $130–175.

Miniature, molded yellowware custard cup, tapering straight sides and rolled rim; Midwestern; 1.5 inches high; c. 1870–1910; $55–85.

Miniature, yellowware crock, straight sides with ear handles; Bennington, Vermont; 2.5 inches high; c. 1850–1860; $275–350.

Miniature chamber pot, molded yellowware decorated with wide band of white slip; New Jersey or Ohio; 1.8 inches high; c. 1860–1910; $75–125.

Miniature pitcher and bowl set, molded yellowware decorated with blue mocha-like sponging against a broad white slip band; English; 3 inches high; c. 1860–1910; $650–850 the set.

Molded yellowware banded in brown and white, Ohio c. 1880–1910. Left to right: *mug, 3.5 inches high, $60–80; miniature chamber pot, 2.5 inches high, $40–60; mug, 4 inches high, $70–90.*

Molded yellowware, Ohio, c. 1870–1900: left, *food mold, 5 inches in diameter, $50–75; serving bowl, 8 inches in diameter, $45–65.*

Miniature sugar bowl with small lift handles; molded yellowware with matching cover, both with ribbed surface; East Liverpool, Ohio; 3 inches high; c. 1890–1920; $225–300.

Mold, molded yellowware oblong, octagonal food mold with fluted sides and sheaf of wheat intaglio design in bottom; Swan Hill Pottery, South Amboy, New Jersey; 7 inches long; c. 1860–1890; $75–100.

Mold, molded yellowware round food mold with bunch of

Food molds, molded yellowware, Maryland or Ohio, c. 1880–1920. Left to right, *so-called Turk's Cap form, 7 inches in diameter, $55–75; octagonal with grape pattern, 8.5 inches long, $45–60; rare rabbit pattern, 8 inches long, $160–210.*

grapes intaglio design in bottom; Arsenal Pottery, Trenton, New Jersey; 4 inches in diameter; c. 1860–1875; $90–120.

Mold, molded yellowware octagonal form with Gothic ribbing on interior and intaglio design of asparagus on bottom; Mid-western; 6 inches long; c. 1880–1920; $65–95.

Mold, molded yellowware Turk's cap type with swirled rib interior; Maryland or New Jersey; 9 inches in diameter; c. 1860–1890; $80–120.

Mold, molded yellowware; bowl-like form with fluted sides and pinwheel bottom; New Jersey or Ohio; 5.5 inches in diameter; c. 1860–1890; $55–85.

Mold, molded oblong yellowware form with interior in shape of crouching rabbit; New Jersey or Pennsylvania; 8.5 inches long; c. 1890–1910; $160–210.

Mold, molded yellowware in the form of a fish with detailed head, tail, and scales; Midwestern; 11.5 inches long; c. 1890–1920; $200–285.

Mug, molded straight-sided yellowware vessel embossed "HAPPY DAYS ARE HERE AGAIN"; Red Wing Union Stoneware

Molded yellowware, Midwestern, c. 1880–1920. Left to right: *mug banded in white, 4 inches high, $65–85; pitcher, 9 inches high, $75–95; miniature mold, 3 inches in diameter, $45–60.*

Mug, molded yellowware with brown glaze and advertising, Cincinnati, Ohio, c. 1870–1890, 7 inches high, $135–185.

Mugs, molded yellowware, banded in blue, brown and white, England or Ohio, c. 1880–1910, 4 to 6 inches high, $75–135 apiece.

Mugs, molded yellowware: left, *English, c. 1890–1910, 6 inches high, $65–85;* right, *Minnesota or Illinois, c. 1920–1940, 7 inches high, $25–35.*

Company, Red Wing, Minnesota; 5 inches high; c. 1933–1940; $55–75.

Mug, molded straight-sided yellowware with two broad concentric bands of white slip; New Jersey or Ohio; 4 inches high; c. 1870–1900; $80–120.

Mug, molded straight-sided yellowware with six narrow concentric bands of white slip; New Jersey or Ohio; 4.3 inches high; c. 1870–1900; $65–95.

Mug, molded straight-sided yellowware with broad band of white slip decorated with blue mocha-like sponging; Ohio; 3.5 inches high; c. 1860–1880; $165–235.

Mug, molded yellowware in the form of a man's head and hat; New Jersey or Maryland; 4.5 inches high; c. 1880–1920; $225–300.

Mug, molded yellowware with embossed tavern scene touched with orange slip; Midwestern; 7 inches high; c. 1920–1940; $15–25.

Mustard pot, mug-shaped molded yellowware vessel decorated with blue mocha-like sponging on a wide band and having ear handle and matching flat cover; New Jersey or England; 3 inches high; c. 1850–1880; $225–350.

Mustard pot, yellowware with pewter cover, bulbous body with straight neck and ear handle; New Jersey or Midwestern; 4 inches high; c. 1880–1910; $175–245.

Nappy or deep dish, molded yellowware; Vermont, New Jersey, or Ohio; 5 to 12 inches in diameter; c. 1840–1910; $35–95; in nesting sets of six to eight, $450–650.

Mustard pots, molded yellowware banded in blue, brown and white slip, England, c. 1870–1900, 4 to 4.5 inches high, $140–180 apiece.

Nappies or baking dishes, molded yellowware, New Jersey or Ohio, c. 1850–1900: a nest of nine measuring 4 to 13 inches in diameter, $500–650/set.

Nappy or baking dish, molded yellowware with fluted sides and band of white slip between two of brown, stamped grocer's mark; Red Wing Potteries, Red Wing, Minnesota; 8.5 inches in diameter; c. 1936–1967; $65–85.

Nappy or baking dish, square molded yellowware; New Jersey or Ohio; 7 inches across; c. 1860–1890; $65–95; in nesting sets of three to five, $300–450.

Pepper pot or shaker, baluster-shaped molded yellowware shaker decorated with band of white slip sponged in blue mocha-like designs, perforated dome; English; 3.5 inches high; c. 1840–1920; $275–375.

Pie plate, drape-molded yellowware, impressed maker's mark; Congress Pottery, South Amboy, New Jersey; 10 inches in diameter; c. 1849–1854; $225–325.

Pie plate, molded yellowware with fluted sides and band of white slip between two of brown, stamped maker's mark; Red

Pie plate, molded yellowware, New Jersey or Vermont, c. 1850–1880, 9 inches in diameter, $50–70.

Wing Potteries, Red Wing, Minnesota; 9 inches in diameter; c. 1936–1967; $85–125.

Pie plate, molded yellowware with stamped maker's mark; J.E. Jeffords & Company, Philadelphia, Pennsylvania; 8.5 inches in diameter; c. 1870–1900; $75–125.

Pie plate, molded yellowware, back embossed with hearts, triangles, or roundels; Pennsylvania, Maryland, or Ohio; 8 to 11 inches in diameter; c. 1850–1890; $90–140.

Pie plates, molded yellowware; Eastern and Midwestern; 7 to 12 inches in diameter; c. 1850–1920; $30–110; nesting sets of six to eight plates, $350–500.

Pipkin, molded yellowware, bulbous ribbed body with ear handle and pouring spout, matching domed top; Bennington, Vermont; 8 inches high; c. 1847–1858; $200–275.

Pipkin, molded yellowware, bulbous ribbed body with ear handle and matching domed top, no spout, impressed maker's mark; J.E. Jeffords & Company, Philadelphia, Pennsylvania; 6.5 inches high; c. 1865–1885; $185–255.

Pipkin or bean baker, yellowware, New England or Pennsylvania, c. 1850–1890, 7 inches high (rare), $175–225.

Pitcher, molded yellowware with overall relief decoration of acorns and leaves, foliate handle, impressed maker's mark; D. & J. Henderson, Jersey City, New Jersey; 8.5 inches high; c. 1829–1833; $2,000–2,800.

Pitcher, molded yellowware with embossed roses within paneled reserves below floral cartouches; American Pottery Manufacturing Company, Jersey City, New Jersey; 7 inches high; c. 1838–1845; $1,800–2,600.

Pitcher, molded yellowware with embossed figures of firemen and fire pumper wagon, hound-form handle, impressed maker's mark; Congress Pottery, South Amboy, New Jersey; 8.5 inches high; c. 1849–1854; $2,200–3,000.

Pitcher, molded yellowware in the so-called "Cascade" pattern with embossed floral designs, rustic handle, impressed maker's mark; Peoria Pottery, Peoria, Illinois; 9 inches high; c. 1863–1873; $900–1,200.

Pitcher, yellowware, Massachusetts or New York, c. 1850–1870, 6.5 inches high, $55–75.

Pitchers, molded yellowware banded in blue, white and brown, Ohio or New Jersey, c. 1900–1940, 5 to 9 inches high, $35–75 each.

Pitchers, molded yellowware with embossed decoration, Ohio or Illinois, c. 1910–1940: left, barrel form, 8 inches high, $55–75; center, bark-like surface, 7.5 inches high, $50–70; right, floral, 9 inches high, $55–75.

Pitcher, molded yellowware, pear-shaped with relief decoration of grapes and vine, forked handle, impressed maker's mark; Swan Hill Pottery, South Amboy, New Jersey; 9.5 inches high; c. 1860–1870; $450–600.

Pitcher, molded yellowware hexagonal form with embossed floral patterns and impressed mark; Norton & Fenton, Bennington, Vermont; 6.3 inches high; c. 1844–1847; $1,500–2,000.

Pitcher, molded yellowware in barrel form with six encircling bands against barklike background; Red Wing Union Stoneware Company, Red Wing, Minnesota; 7.5 inches high; c. 1906–1936; $70–95.

Pitcher, cone-shaped molded yellowware vessel with sharply angled handle, impressed maker's mark; Globe Pottery Company, East Liverpool, Ohio; 8.5 inches high; c. 1880–1890; $90–130.

Pitcher, molded yellowware with vertical body and tapering shoulder, incised bands about body, stamped maker's mark; Philadelphia, Pennsylvania; 6 inches high; c. 1860–1890; $110–160.

Pitcher, molded yellowware body embossed in form of walnut or squash; Midwestern; 5.5 inches high; c. 1870–1910; $85–135.

Pitcher, molded yellowware with two broad bands of white slip, top and bottom, each edged in brown slip; New Jersey or Ohio; 7 inches high; c. 1860–1880; $265–345.

Pitcher with hound handle, molded yellowware, American Pottery Company, Jersey City, New Jersey, c. 1833–1845, 10 inches high (possibly unique), $2,500–3,000.

Pitcher, molded yellowware in the form of bust of President Herbert Hoover, Syracuse China Company, Syracuse, New York, c. 1928–1932, 6 inches high, $90–130.

Plates, molded yellowware: left, with scenes of American West, English, c. 1915–1930, 7 inches across, $80–110; right, New Jersey, c. 1855–1875, 7 inches in diameter (rare), $100–150.

Pitcher, molded yellowware with broad band of white slip decorated with blue mocha-like designs, several thin bands of white slip above and below; East Liverpool, Ohio; 6.5 inches high; c. 1865–1895; $300–400.

Plate, drape-molded yellowware; New Jersey; 7 inches in diameter; c. 1855–1875; $140–190.

Plate, molded yellowware, square with scalloped border and embossed Western scenes; England; 7 inches across; c. 1915–1930; $85–135.

Platter, molded yellowware, elongated octagonal, impressed maker's mark; James Bennett & Brothers, East Liverpool, Ohio; 14 inches long; c. 1840–1844; $250–350.

Platter, molded oval form; New Jersey or Midwestern; 12.5 inches long; c. 1860–1890; $135–185.

Porringer cup, yellowware, ovoid body with flaring rim and ear handle; New Jersey or Pennsylvania; 3.5 inches high; c. 1850–1870; $150–225.

Preserve jar, molded yellowware, octagonal with low shoulder and gentle taper to top, inset rim for tin cover; Ohio or Maryland; 6 inches high; c. 1880–1900; $60–75.

Crock, molded yellowware banded in brown and white, Minnesota or Ohio, c. 1920–1940, 6.5 inches high, $120–160.

*Preserve jar, molded yellowware, New Jersey or Maryland, c. 1850–1870, 7 inches high,
$65–95.*

Preserve jar, molded yellowware, barrel-shaped with embossed
    banding at top, bottom, and waist, inset rim for tin cover;
    New Jersey; 6.5 inches high; c. 1900–1915; $70–95.

Preserve jar, molded yellowware, embossed geometric "stairstep"
    pattern and raised ribbing at waist, inset rim for tin cover;
    Midwestern; 6 inches high; c. 1900–1920; $65–85.

Preserve jar, molded cylindrical yellowware form with stepped
    shoulder and matching flat cover impressed with maker's
    mark; Edwin Bennett, Baltimore, Maryland; 7 inches high;
    c. 1858–1865; $135–185.

Price list, printed paper; Vodrey Pottery, East Liverpool, Ohio;
    c. 1860–1865; $250–325.

Price list, printed paper; John Goodwin's Eagle Pottery, East Liver-
    pool, Ohio; c. 1850–1860; $350–450.

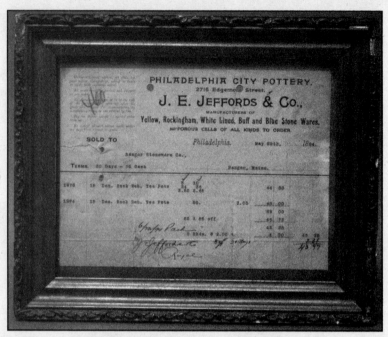

Bill head, printed paper, J.E. Jeffords & Company, Philadelphia yellowware manufacturers, 1894, 6 × 8 inches, $150–200.

Price list, illustrated printed paper; C.C. Thompson & Company, East Liverpool, Ohio; c. 1870–1886; $200–275.

Price list, printed paper; Swan Hill Pottery, South Amboy, New Jersey; c. 1852–1855; $350–450.

Price list, printed paper, illustrated; Morton Pottery Company, Morton, Illinois; c. 1930–1940; $135–185.

Pudding dish, molded ten-sided vessel with green stenciled floral decoration; Morton Pottery Company, Morton, Illinois; 4.5 inches in diameter; c. 1920–1940; $45–65.

Rolling pin, molded yellowware cylinder with two turned wooden handles; New Jersey or Midwestern; overall length 12 inches; c. 1870–1910; $250–350.

Salt, molded yellowware pedestal-based open salt decorated with three thin bands of white slip; New Jersey or England; 2.5 inches high; c. 1840–1860; $120–170.

Salt box, hanging, molded yellowware demilune form with vertically ribbed body and three bands of blue slip, wooden
cover; Minnesota; 6 inches high; c. 1925–1945; $80–125.

Salt shaker, baluster-form molded yellowware shaker decorated
with broad band of white slip edged in blue, perforated
dome; England; 4 inches high; c. 1840–1920; $200–275.

Serving dish, molded yellowware with embossed leaf decoration
and close-set handles, matching domed cover with turnip
finial; New Jersey or Ohio; 6.5 inches in diameter;
c. 1870–1900; $225–325.

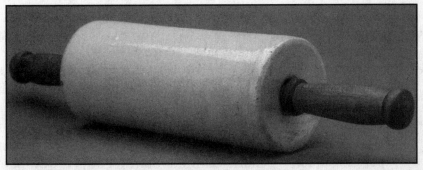

*Rolling pin, molded yellowware with turned wooden handles, New Jersey or Ohio,
c. 1870–1900, 15 inches long, $250–350.*

*Salt-and-pepper shakers: molded yellowware banded in blue, brown and white, some with
mocha type decoration in blue and green, English, c. 1870–1910, 3 to 5 inches high;
salts, $150–250 apiece; pepper casters, $175–275 apiece.*

Serving dish, molded yellowware with concentric bands of brown-and-white slip, slightly domed cover sits within broad inset collar; Midwestern; 4.3 inches high; c. 1920–1950; $65–95.

Serving dish, molded yellowware, octagonal; New Jersey, Pennsylvania, or Ohio; 12.5 inches long; c. 1840–1860; $200–285.

Serving dish, molded yellowware, oval with slightly flaring rim; New Jersey or Midwestern; 9 inches long; c. 1870–1910; $80–110.

Serving dish, molded yellowware, oval with lightly embossed scalloped border; New Jersey or Ohio; 10.5 inches long; c. 1880–1910; $135–185.

Serving dish, molded yellowware, oval with center divider; New Jersey or Ohio; 9 inches long; c. 1860–1890; $150–225.

Serving dish, molded yellowware, twelve-sided with stenciled florets in red and blue; Morton Pottery Company, Morton, Illinois; 6.5 inches in diameter; c. 1920–1940; $55–75.

Snuff jar, molded yellowware in form of squatting man holding pitcher and glass, cover in form of broad-brimmed hat, impressed maker's mark; United States Pottery Company,

Molded European yellowware, France or Austria, c. 1880–1920. Left to right: *cigarette and match holder, 7 inches long, $30–45; covered beetle form box, 5.5 inches long, $45–60; cigarette and match holder, 7.5 inches long, $35–50.*

oneware, brown glazed and blue
·corated preserve jars from Missouri,
1860–1900, 7" to 11" high, $60–90 apiece; blue
corated example, $150–225.

Redware preserve jar with brown slip
glaze, Alabama, c. 1870–1900,
7" high, $60–85.

·dware pie plate, lead-glazed and
·p decorated "Apple Pie," Norwalk,
·nnecticut, c. 1830–1870, 9" in
·ameter; $600–750.

Redware doorstop, molded lion painted white,
Ohio, c. 1850–1880, 8" long; $450–600.

Yellowware mixing bowl, molded with pink and blue slip banding, Red Wing Union Stoneware Company, Red Wing, Minnesota, c. 1920–1935, 9.5" in diameter; $35–45.

Yellowware crock, molded with blue a[nd] white banding, Ohio, c. 1900–19[ ] 6" high; $70–90.

Rockingham crock, molded yellowware w[ith] brown Rockingham glaze, Massachuse[tts] c. 1860–1890, 7.5" in diameter; $90–130[.]

Rockingham miniatures, molded yellowware with brown Rockingham glaze, New Jersey or Ohio, c. 1880–1910. *Left to right:* covered crock, 3" high, $25–35; churn, 3.25" high, $40–55; covered pot, 2.5" high, $35–45.

White earthenware druggist's jar, molded with wood and tin cover, New York or New Jersey, c. 1860–1880, 7.5" high; $45–55.

...nt enamelware cuspidor, molded yel-...ware glazed in brown, green, and blue, ...w Jersey or Ohio, c. 1855–1885, 8.5" in ...ameter; $75–100.

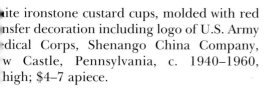

...ite ironstone custard cups, molded with red ...nsfer decoration including logo of U.S. Army ...dical Corps, Shenango China Company, ...w Castle, Pennsylvania, c. 1940–1960, ...high; $4–7 apiece.

White ironstone plates, molded with blue transfer decoration, Sterling China Company, Wellsville, Ohio, c. 1920–1940, 10" in diameter; $15–25 apiece.

White earthenware plate, molded with po[ly]chrome transfer decoration, Harker Potte[ry] Company, East Liverpool, Ohio, c. 1890–19[00], 7" in diameter; $25–35.

White ironstone, molded with blue transfer of fouled anchor, probably U.S. Navy issue, Ohio or New Jersey, c. 1930–1950; demitasse cups, 2" high, $5–7 apiece; bowl, 9.5" in diameter, $20–25.

Bisque porcelain miniature jug, New England or New Jersey, c. 1860–1880, 1.8" high; $35–50.

Sewer tile pitcher, dark brown glaze, wheel-turned and hand-shaped with applied frogs, New York or Ohio, c. 1880–1910, 9" high; $140–190.

Rockingham–glazed yellowware doorstop molded in form of sitting spaniel dog, Ohio, c. 1850–1880, 9" high; $300–400.

Stoneware pitcher, molded and brown glazed in "pseudo-Rockingham" manner, Caire Pottery, Poughkeepsie, New York, c. 1842–1852, 10" high; $750–950.

Stoneware flask with incised blue filled decoration, New York or New Jersey, 1860, 7" high; $1,700–2,500.

Stoneware jar decorated in blue, Keller Pottery, New Albany, Indiana, c. 1860–1865, 10.5" high; $200–275.

Stoneware churn with rare decoration, a man's profile, Hart Pottery, Fulton, New York, c. 1840–1876, 26" high; $5,500–7,000.

Stoneware jar, brown alkaline-slip glaze decorated in white slip, Edgefield, North Carolina, c. 1850–1855, 9" high; $300–450.

Stoneware pot with incised, blue-filled bird decoration, Albany, New York, c. 1800–1801, 11" high; $2,500–3,500.

Stoneware churn, salt-glazed, John S. Perry, Putnam County, Indiana, c. 1831–1864, 25" high; $125–200.

Stoneware crock, unusual blue slip decoration of log cabin, Seymour & Bosworth, Hartford, Connecticut, c. 1871–1890, 14.5" high; $3,000–4,000.

Stoneware pitcher, Bristol glaze with green-slip decoration and inscription, Gas City, Indiana, 1897, 9.5" high; $800–1,400.

Redware preserve jar, molded hexagonal form with embossed classical figures, lead glaze splashed with white, Pennsylvania, c. 1860–1880, 8" high; $300–450.

Redware bedpan, black manganese-splashed lead glaze, Norwalk, Connecticut, c. 1840–1860, 10" in diameter; $40–60.

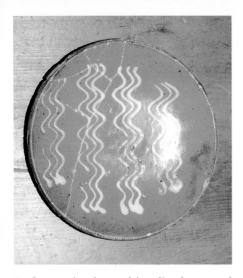

Redware pie plate, white-slip decorated lead glaze, New England, c. 1840–1860, 11" in diameter; $275–350.

Rockingham-glazed yellowware tea pot w[ith] pewter fittings, Massachusetts, c. 1870–187[?] 8" high; $250–350.

Molded yellowware kitchen accessories, New Jersey and Ohio, c. 1860–1900, 3–10" high, prices range from $20–30 for the custard cup to $225–300 for the colander.

Left, *soap dish, molded yellowware, Knowles, Taylor & Knowles, East Liverpool, Ohio, c. 1860–1890, 4.5 inches in diameter, $150–225;* right, *porringer cup, New Jersey or Pennsylvania, c. 1850–1870, 3.5 inches in diameter, $120–150.*

Tea pot, molded yellowware banded in blue and white with blue mocha type decoration, England, c. 1860–1890, 4 inches high, $300–400.

Bennington, Vermont; 5.5 inches high; c. 1849–1858; $3,500–4,500.

Snuff jar, molded yellowware, beaker-shaped with bands of leaves above and below waist, matching cover; Eagle Pottery, Perth Amboy, New Jersey; 7 inches high; c. 1858–1865; $165–245.

Soap dish, molded yellowware, round with perforated top and drain hole in side; Knowles, Taylor & Knowles, East Liverpool, Ohio; 4.5 inches in diameter; c. 1860–1890; $150–225.

Teapot, molded yellowware with overall "basket weave" embossing, matching domed top, stamped maker's mark; J.E. Jeffords & Company, Philadelphia, Pennsylvania; 8 inches high; c. 1870–1890; $245–335.

Tea pot, molded yellowware, Swan Hill or Bay View Potteries, South Amboy, New Jersey, c. 1870–1890, 6.5 inches high, $250–350.

Tea pot, molded yellowware, C.C. Thompson Pottery, East Liverpool, Ohio, c. 1890–1915, 7 inches high, $165–235.

Toby pitcher, molded yellowware vessel in form of man's head and shoulders with conical hat forming spout and rim; Bay View Pottery, South Amboy, New Jersey; 5 inches high; c. 1895–1905; $150–225.

Trivet, yellowware disk; Midwestern; 6 inches in diameter; c. 1870–1920; $20–35.

Umbrella stand, molded yellowware with embossed floral banding and fluted sides; New Jersey; 33 inches high; c. 1930–1945; $65–85.

Vase, molded yellowware, semi-ovoid with paneled sides and collar-form neck above sloping shoulder; New Jersey; 7.5 inches high; c. 1920–1940; $55–75.

Washboard, molded yellowware with horizontal ribbing, set in wooden frame; Midwestern; 8 × 12 inches; c. 1880–1910; $400–600.

Keg or rundlet, molded yellowware with brown glaze, New Jersey or Ohio, c. 1850–1870, 6 inches high (rare), $175–225.

ROCKINGHAM AND FLINT-GLAZED WARES

A great deal of confusion exists regarding these wares, in terms of both history and method of manufacture. In both cases the name of the ceramic relates to the method of glazing rather than the clay type. American—and later, English—Rockingham ware was cast from a yellow firing clay, but when the first examples were produced in England during the late eighteenth century on the estate of Lord Rockingham (hence the name), the clay body was white earthenware. By 1800 yellowware had become the preferred medium, continuing so until Rockingham went out of production around 1900.

Postcard, lithographed printed cardboard, view of Bennett yellowware and Rockingham pottery, East Liverpool, Ohio, c. 1910–1920, 3.5 × 5.5 inches, $40–60.

The Rockingham finish was a rich brown iron-based glaze that was spattered or dripped onto the surface of an unfired piece as it rotated on the potter's wheel, resulting in a streaky, spotted surface that was then given a clear alkaline glaze. The unpredictable result should not be confused with later brown glazed spongeware, which was applied with a shaped device in a definite pattern. The Rockingham technique often left large areas of the yellow body visible, somewhat resembling in appearance the shell of the common land turtle. As a consequence, the ware was often described as having a "tortoiseshell" glaze.

The term "Bennington Ware" is also sometimes applied to Rockingham glazed vessels, reflecting the fact that large quantities were produced at the United States Pottery Company located in that Vermont town. This term is an unfortunate misnomer, though, since the bulk of the ordinary ware, such as pie plates, bowls, and teapots, was made elsewhere, chiefly in New Jersey, Maryland, and the Midwest. However, a much higher percentage of the Bennington product was marked, leading to the impression that this community dominated the field.

An interesting but uncommon variation was the use of cobalt-blue rather than brown glaze. Such pieces mimic brown Rockingham in both form and finish, and some have suggested the rather obvious term "Blue Rockingham" for a glaze which clearly has its origin in English spatterware decoration. There is some indication that most of this ware was made in Ohio and New Jersey.

Flint enamel glaze was developed in the mid-nineteenth century, one version having been patented by the potter Jonathan Fenton of Bennington in 1849. To achieve this finish, a piece of yellowware was first given a coating of clear glaze. While this was still wet, various powdered metallic glazes were sprinkled over it. A subsequent firing produced brilliant streaks of green, blue, orange, and white. Since brown manganese was also often added to the mixture, this ware may be confused with Rockingham. Flint enamelware was made in great variety, especially at Bennington, but in a relatively limited quantity. Consequently, it is uncommon today.

Rockingham and flint enamelware were made in many different forms, primarily for use in the kitchen and dining room. While bowls and pie plates are most often seen today, many other objects were produced, including candlesticks, mantel decorations, pitchers, coffee and tea pots, sugar bowls, cake molds, serving dishes, vases, water coolers, and even such unlikely items as picture frames and doorknobs.

The term *Rockingham* was also applied by nineteenth-century pottery owners to a third type of ware. This was a cast stoneware body entirely covered with a dark brown manganese or Albany slip glaze. This pseudo-Rockingham can be distinguished from the real thing by the fact that the body is stoneware, not yellowware, and has a uniform overall glaze as opposed to the streaky Rockingham finish. Pseudo-Rockingham was made primarily in three forms—pitchers, teapots, and flower pots.

The Rockingham market is a small but active one, with rare pieces bringing four-figure prices and even ordinary pie plates often selling for $100–200. Marked examples are fairly uncommon and will always sell for substantially more. Flint enamel commands even higher prices. A flint enamel candlestick will frequently bring twice as much as the same form in plain Rockingham. On the other hand, pseudo-Rockingham stoneware finds little favor with collectors. Unless an example is maker-marked or in some other way unusual, it is not likely to even break the $100 barrier.

ROCKINGHAM AND FLINT-GLAZED WARES PRICES

Ale jug, molded yellowware with overall pseudo-Rockingham glaze, elongated spout with built-in strainer, embossed floral decoration, matching cover; McNichol Pottery Company, East Liverpool, Ohio; 10.5 inches high; c. 1870–1890; $225–300.

Ale jug or pitcher, molded Rockingham glazed yellowware with embossed floral patterns, spout with built-in strainer, impressed maker's mark; Salamander Works, Woodbridge, New Jersey; 11.3 inches high; c. 1840–1855; $1,600–2,300.

Ale jug or pitcher, molded Rockingham glazed yellowware, forked handle, embossed grapes and vines motif, impressed maker's mark; Hanks & Fish, South Amboy, New Jersey; 8 inches high; c. 1850–1852; $1,750–2,500.

Bank, molded globe-shaped form with coin slot and bulbous finial, flint-enamel glazed yellowware; Eastern or Midwestern; 4 inches high; c. 1850–1880; $90–130.

Bank, molded head of Uncle Sam, coin slot in hat, Rockingham glazed yellowware; United States Pottery Company, Bennington, Vermont; 4.5 inches high; c. 1847–1855; $175–250.

Batter bowl, molded flint-enamel glazed yellowware, tapering sides and large pouring spout, impressed maker's mark; United States Pottery Company, Bennington, Vermont; 10 inches in diameter; c. 1849–1858; $300–400.

Batter bowl, molded Rockingham glazed yellowware, small pouring spout; Midwestern; 11 inches in diameter; c. 1860–1900; $90–120.

Beaker or tumbler, molded Rockingham glazed yellowware, cylindrical widening toward the top; United States Pottery Company, Bennington, Vermont; 3.2 inches high; c. 1844–1858; $300–400.

Bedpan, molded Rockingham glazed yellowware, flattened foot, upturned spout; Eastern or Midwestern; 16 inches long; c. 1850–1890; $65–85.

Bottle, in form of cloaked and top-hatted "Uncle Toby" holding pitcher, molded Rockingham glazed yellowware; United States Pottery Company, Bennington, Vermont; 10.5 inches high; c. 1849–1858; $550–700.

Bowl, molded Rockingham glazed yellowware; Northeastern or Midwestern; 10.5 inches in diameter; c. 1850–1900; $65–115; in nesting sets of four to seven, 5 to 12 inches in diameter, $275–550.

Bed pan, Rockingham-glazed yellowware, Ohio, c. 1860–1890, 15 inches long, $70–95.

Bowl, molded Rockingham-glazed yellowware, Ohio, c. 1860–1890, 9 inches in diameter, $100–150.

Bowl, Rockingham-glazed yellowware, Ohio or Maryland, c. 1850–1870, 7 inches in diameter, $135–175.

Bowl, molded Rockingham-glazed yellowware, Ohio or Illinois, c. 1880–1900, 5.5 inches in diameter, $55–70.

Bowl, molded oval serving vessel, Rockingham-glazed yellowware, East Liverpool, Ohio, c. 1850–1870, 6.5 inches long, $65–85.

Bowl and pitcher set, molded flint-enamel glazed yellowware, Gothic style in embossed diamond pattern, impressed maker's mark; United States Pottery Company, Bennington, Vermont; bowl, 13 inches in diameter; pitcher, 10.5 inches high; c. 1849–1858; $1,300–1,900.

Candlestick, molded Rockingham glazed yellowware, columnar form with flaring base, decorative rings, and rolled rim; United States Pottery Company, Bennington, Vermont; 9 inches high; c. 1849–1858; $175–225; matching set of two, $450–600.

Candlestick, molded flint-enamel glazed yellowware, trumpet-form shaft with flaring base and rolled rim; United States Pottery Company, Bennington, Vermont; 7.8 inches high; c. 1849–1858; $200–275; matching set of two, $600–750.

Candlesticks (pair), molded Rockingham-glazed yellowware, United States Pottery Company, Bennington, Vermont, c. 1849–1858, each 9.5 inches high, $400–600/pair.

Chamber pot, molded flint-glazed yellowware, United States Pottery Company, Bennington, Vermont, c. 1849–1858, 9 inches high, $300–400.

Chamber pot, bowl-shaped molded Rockingham glazed yellowware with single vertical handle; Ohio; 5.5 inches high; c. 1860–1890; $85–135.

Chamber pot, molded Rockingham glazed yellowware, Gothic form with matching domed cover, impressed maker's mark; United States Pottery Company, Bennington, Vermont; 9 inches high; c. 1849–1858; $300–400.

Chamber stick, molded Rockingham glazed yellowware, short bulblike shaft on saucer base with vertical loop handle; United States Pottery Company, Bennington, Vermont; 3.5 inches high; c. 1849–1858; $300–450.

Coffeepot, molded flint-enamel glazed yellowware in Gothic style with octagonal body and domed cover, impressed maker's mark; United States Pottery Company, Bennington, Vermont; 12.3 inches high; c. 1849–1858; $1,700–2,200.

Croup kettle or invalid's inhaler, molded Rockingham glazed yellowware, baluster form with several orifices; United States Pottery Company, Bennington, Vermont; 7.3 inches high; c. 1849–1858; $350–500.

Curtain tieback, molded Rockingham or flint-enamel glazed yellowware, faceted ten-sided form with inset metal screw; United States Pottery Company, Bennington, Vermont; 3 inches high; c. 1849–1858; $95–175.

Cuspidor, molded flint-enamel glazed yellowware, impressed maker's mark; United States Pottery Company, Bennington, Vermont; 8 inches in diameter; c. 1849–1858; $350–500.

Coffeepot, molded flint enamel–glazed yellowware, United States Pottery Company, Bennington, Vermont, c. 1849–1858, 8 inches high, $500–650.

Cuspidor, molded shell form, Rockingham-glazed yellowware, Maryland or Ohio, c. 1850–1880, 10 inches in diameter, $65–105.

Cuspidor, molded blue-and-brown Rockingham glazed yellowware, embossed date and maker's mark; Etruria Works, East Liverpool, Ohio; 7.5 inches in diameter; 1852; $1,300–1,800.

Cuspidor, molded stoneware with pseudo-Rockingham glaze, embossed floral decoration and impressed date and maker's mark; Pliny Thayer, Lansingburgh, New York; 7.5 inches in diameter; 1852; $300–450.

Cuspidor, molded stoneware covered with overall pseudo-Rockingham glaze; New York; 8.5 inches in diameter; c. 1860–1880; $35–45.

Cuspidor, Rockingham glazed yellowware with embossed shells, impressed maker's mark; Boston Earthenware Manufacturing Company, Boston, Massachusetts; 8.5 inches in diameter; c. 1855–1875; $275–350.

Cuspidor, molded Rockingham glazed yellowware, octagonal sides, round top and embossed floral decoration, impressed maker's mark; Peoria Pottery, Peoria, Illinois; 8.5 inches in diameter; c. 1863–1875; $275–375.

Cuspidor, molded Rockingham glazed yellowware, octagonal, embossed angels and cherubs; South Amboy, New Jersey; 8.5 inches long; c. 1850–1880; $200–280.

Custard cup, molded Rockingham glazed yellowware; Eastern or Midwestern; 2.5 inches high; c. 1870–1910; $20–30.

Custard cup, molded stoneware with a pseudo-Rockingham glaze, Northeastern; 2.2 inches high; c. 1880–1910; $5–10.

Doorknobs, molded Rockingham glazed yellowware; Eastern or Midwestern; 1.5 to 2.5 inches in diameter; c. 1850–1890; $3–9 each; in flint enamel, $25–40 each.

Figurine, molded recumbent lion, yellowware with a blue Rockingham glaze; Ohio; 6.5 inches long; c. 1845–1875; $750–1,000.

Figurine, molded recumbent lion, Rockingham glazed yellowware; Ohio; 9.5 inches long; c. 1845–1885; $550–750.

Left to right: *molded Rockingham-glazed yellowware, Ohio, c. 1850–1870; nappy or utility bowl, 6 inches in diameter, $65–85; custard cup, 3 inches high, $20–30; nappy, 10 inches in diameter, $85–115.*

Door knobs, molded Rockingham-glazed yellowware, New Jersey or Ohio, c. 1850–1900, 2 to 3 inches in diameter, $15–25 apiece.

Figural piece, molded Rockingham-glazed yellowware lion, United States Pottery Company, Bennington, Vermont, c. 1849–1858, 11.5 inches long, $2,500–3,500.

Figurine, molded sitting poodle, yellowware with a blue Rockingham glaze; Ohio; 8 inches high; c. 1850–1880; $1,000–1,400.

Figurine, molded sitting poodle, yellowware with flint enamel glaze; Ohio; 7 inches high; c. 1860–1880; $600–850.

Figurine, molded sitting poodle on platform with shell decoration, yellowware with Rockingham glaze; Midwestern; 7.5 inches high; c. 1860–1890; $400–575.

Figurine, molded sitting poodle, stoneware with brown pseudo-Rockingham glaze; northeastern United States; 6.5 inches high; c. 1850–1870; $250–350.

Figurine, Rockingham glazed yellowware, molded sitting poodle, incised name and date; Swan Hill Pottery, South Amboy, New Jersey; 8 inches high; 1872; $800–1,100.

Figurine, molded standing poodle holding basket in mouth, flint-enamel glazed yellowware with porcelain basket; United States Pottery Company, Bennington, Vermont; 9 inches high; c. 1849–1858; $2,500–3,000.

Figurals, pair of molded Rockingham-glazed yellowware bookends in form of spaniels, Maryland or Ohio, c. 1860–1890, each 5.5 inches high, $300–450/set.

Paperweight in form of crouching Spaniel, molded Rockingham-glazed yellowware, United States Pottery Company, Bennington, Vermont, c. 1849–1858, 5 inches long, $250–350.

Figural piece, molded Rockingham-glazed dog holding porcelain basket, United States Pottery Company, Bennington, Vermont, c. 1849–1858, 10 inches long, $2,500–3,000.

Figurine, molded roosting owl, yellowware with Rockingham glaze in blue and brown, impressed advertiser's logo; Cincinnati, Ohio; 9 inches high; c. 1860–1870; $3,400–4,100.

Figurine, molded standing lion with orb under foot, flint-enamel glazed yellowware, coleslaw mane, impressed maker's mark; United States Pottery Company, Bennington, Vermont; 9 inches high; c. 1849–1858; $3,000–3,700.

Figurine, recumbent cow, molded Rockingham glazed yellowware; Abraham Cadmus' Congress Pottery, South Amboy, New Jersey; 10 inches long; c. 1848–1854; $2,000–2,800.

Figurine, recumbent cow with tree stump in background, molded flint-enamel glazed yellowware; United States Pottery Company, Bennington, Vermont; 10 inches long; c. 1849–1858; $2,500–3,200.

Figurine, creamer in the shape of a standing cow, molded Rockingham glazed yellowware; J.E. Jeffords & Company, Philadelphia, Pennsylvania; 5 inches long; c. 1870–1890; $175–255.

Figural, cow mantelpiece decoration, molded Rockingham-glazed yellowware, United States Pottery Company, Bennington, Vermont, c. 1849–1858, 10 inches long, $2,500–3,200.

Cow creamer, molded Rockingham-glazed yellowware, Ohio, c. 1860–1880, 6.25 inches long, $175–245.

Stove or window rest, molded Rockingham-glazed yellowware, New Jersey or Maryland, c. 1850–1870, 4.5 inches high, $110–140.

Toby bottles, molded Rockingham-glazed yellowware, United States Pottery Company, Bennington, Vermont, c. 1849–1858: left, *9 inches high, $600–850;* right, *10 inches high, $500–750.*

Figurine, creamer in the form of a standing cow, molded flint-enamel glazed yellowware; United States Pottery Company, Bennington, Vermont, 7 inches long; c. 1849–1858; $400–550.

Figurine, recumbent stag with tree stump in background, molded flint-enamel glazed yellowware; United States Pottery Company, Bennington, Vermont; 10.8 inches long; c. 1849–1858; $3,500–4,500.

Figurine, pitcher in the form of a bust, head to hips, of "Uncle Toby," molded stoneware with pseudo-Rockingham glaze, impressed maker's mark; American Pottery Company, Jersey City, New Jersey; 10.5 inches high; c. 1833–1845; $2,100–2,900.

Figurine, pitcher in the form of a bust, head to waist, of Ben Franklin in cloak, extended hand holds glass, molded Rockingham glazed yellowware; United States Pottery Company, Bennington, Vermont; 5.7 inches high; c. 1849–1858; $200–275.

Toby pitcher, molded flint enamel–glazed yellowware, Maryland or New Jersey, c. 1860–1880, 8 inches high, $285–355.

Toby pitchers, molded Rockingham-glazed yellowware: left, Bennington, Vermont reproduction, c. 1960–1970, 6 inches high, $20–30; right, United States Pottery Company, Bennington, Vermont, c. 1849–1858, 5.75 inches high, $200–300.

Figurine, woman seated on wall reading book, Staffordshire type in molded stoneware with a pseudo-Rockingham glaze; Lyons Pottery, Lyons, New York; 9 inches high; c. 1840–1870; $350–500.

Flask, molded Rockingham glazed yellowware, flattened ovoid embossed with eagle and flag; 6.5 inches high; East Liverpool, Ohio; c. 1850–1860; $700–900.

Flask, molded Rockingham glazed yellowware, flattened ovoid embossed with figures of men drinking at table; United States Pottery Company, Bennington, Vermont; 6 inches high; c. 1849–1858; $900–1,300.

Flask, in the form of a book, molded Rockingham glazed yellowware; Midwestern; 7 inches high; c. 1860–1880; $950–1,250.

Flask, in the form of a book, molded Rockingham glazed yellowware; William Young & Company, Trenton, New Jersey; 4.7 inches high; c. 1857–1879; $1,000–1,500.

Flask, in the form of a book, molded stoneware with blue-and-brown Rockingham glaze; Midwestern; 5.5 inches high; c. 1850–1870; $300–400.

Flask, in the form of a book, molded flint-enamel glazed yellowware, embossed "HERMIT'S COMPANION"; United

Book form whiskey flasks, molded Rockingham-glazed yellowware: left, 6 inches high; right, 8 inches high, United States Pottery Company, Bennington, Vermont, c. 1849–1858, $300–550 each.

States Pottery Company, Bennington, Vermont; 11 inches high; c. 1849–1858; $750–950.

Flask, in the form of a shoe, molded Rockingham glazed yellowware; Vermont, New Jersey, or the Midwest; 5 inches high; c. 1850–1880; $125–175.

Flower pot, molded stoneware with pseudo-Rockingham glaze, embossed swag and tassel design below rim; New England or New York; 5.5 inches high; c. 1850–1880; $55–85.

Flower pot or jardiniere, molded Rockingham glazed yellowware, two-piece pedestal base with embossed leaf pattern; United States Pottery Company, Bennington, Vermont; 12 inches high; c. 1847–1858; $145–195.

Flower pot, molded Rockingham-glazed yellowware, New England or New Jersey, c. 1860–1900, 16 inches high, $175–250.

Flower pot, hanging type, molded Rockingham-glazed yellowware, New Jersey or Ohio, c. 1860–1890, 7 inches in diameter, $60–85.

Food mold, molded flint-enamel glazed yellowware, tray form with twelve swirled depressions for cupcakes; Ohio; 12 inches long; c. 1860–1880; $1,000–1,400.

Food mold, flint-enamel glazed yellowware, fluted Turk's cap form; United States Pottery Company, Bennington, Vermont; 8 inches in diameter; c. 1849–1858; $200–250.

Footbath, molded flint-enamel glazed yellowware, oblong ribbed body with foliated handles, impressed maker's mark; United States Pottery Company, Bennington, Vermont; 20 inches long; c. 1849–1858; $950–1,350.

Foot warmer, molded demilune form with filling spout, Rockingham glazed yellowware; John L. Rue Pottery Company, Matawan, New Jersey; 12.5 inches long; c. 1881–1894; $250–350.

Foot warmer, molded Rockingham glazed yellowware, sausage or tube form with flattened body and knob at each end; United States Pottery Company, Bennington, Vermont; 12.5 inches long; c. 1847–1858; $200–275.

Mold, flint enamel–glazed molded yellowware, Vermont or Ohio, c. 1850–1870, 7 inches in diameter, $300–450.

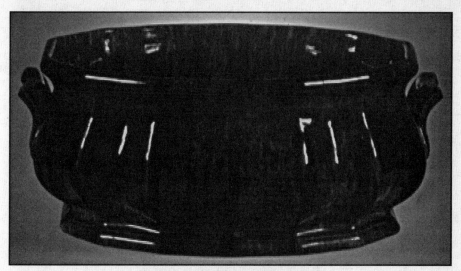

Footbath, molded flint enamel–glazed yellowware, United States Pottery Company, Bennington, Vermont, c. 1849–1858, 19 inches long, $900–1,400.

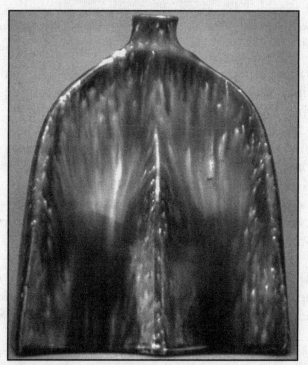

Footwarmer, molded Rockingham-glazed yellowware, Ohio, c. 1850–1870, 12 inches long, $165–245.

Goblet, Rockingham-glazed yellowware, United States Pottery Company, Bennington, Vermont, c. 1849–1858, 5 inches high, $250–325.

Goblet, molded Rockingham glazed yellowware with pedestal base, United States Pottery Company, Bennington, Vermont; 5.7 inches high; c. 1844–1858; $275–375.

Inkwell, molded dome-shaped Rockingham glazed yellowware; United States Pottery Company, Bennington, Vermont; 3.7 inches high; c. 1853–1858; $275–350.

Inkwell, molded, six-sided baluster form, flint-enamel glazed yellowware; United States Pottery Company, Bennington, Vermont; 3 inches high; c. 1849–1858; $450–600.

Lamp, slab-thrown stoneware fluid lamp in form of log cabin with loop handle and chimney, brass burner, pseudo-Rockingham glaze; Ohio; 5 inches long; c. 1870–1890; $500–700.

Milk pan, molded Rockingham glazed yellowware, rolled rim; Vermont or Midwestern; 14.5 inches in diameter; c. 1850–1870; $150–225.

Ink stand/desk set, rare molded Rockingham-glazed yellowware, United States Pottery Company, Bennington, Vermont, c. 1849–1858, 15 inches high, $4,000–6,000.

Inkwell in form of lion, molded Rockingham-glazed yellowware, Vermont or Ohio, c. 1850–1870, 4.5 inches long, $250–350.

Miniature cuspidor, molded Rockingham glazed yellowware; Eastern or Midwestern; 2 inches in diameter; c. 1850–1880; $80–130.

Miniature flower pot with scalloped rim, molded Rockingham glazed yellowware; Eastern or Midwestern; 2.3 inches high; c. 1850–1890; $150–225.

Miniature footed goblet, molded flint-enamel glazed yellowware; United States Pottery, Bennington, Vermont; 2.5 inches high; c. 1849–1858; $200–300.

Miniature bowl and pitcher set, molded Rockingham glazed yellowware; United States Pottery Company, Bennington, Vermont; pitcher, 2.8 inches high; bowl, 3.5 inches in diameter; c. 1849–1858; $350–450.

Mug, molded Rockingham glazed yellowware with embossed figure of sitting man holding glass and jug; Swan Hill Pottery, South Amboy, New Jersey; 4 inches high; c. 1850–1875; $400–550.

Miniature pitcher and bowl set, molded Rockingham-glazed yellowware, Ohio, c. 1860–1880, bowl diameter 3.75 inches, $250–350.

Mug, molded Rockingham-glazed yellowware, Ohio, c. 1860–1880, 4.25 inches high, $75–95.

Mugs, molded Rockingham-glazed yellowware, both Illinois or Minnesota, c. 1910–1930; left, 5 inches high, $25–35; right, 4.7 inches high, $15–20.

Mug, molded Rockingham glazed yellowware, straight-sided with ear handle and shaped base; United States Pottery Company, Bennington, Vermont; 4 inches high; c. 1844–1858; $100–150.

Mug, molded Rockingham glazed yellowware, straight paneled sides with ear handle; Ohio; 4.5 inches high; c. 1850–1880; $80–120.

Nappy or baking dish, molded Rockingham glazed yellowware; New Jersey, Vermont, or Midwestern; 7 inches in diameter; c. 1850–1880; $80–110; in sets of five to seven, 5 to 11 inches in diameter, $550–850.

Paperweight, molded flint-enamel glazed yellowware, recumbent spaniel atop a pillowlike base, impressed maker's mark; United States Pottery Company, Bennington, Vermont; 3 inches high; c. 1849–1858; $400–525.

Picture frame, molded stoneware with pseudo-Rockingham glaze, oval with embossed floral patterns; Mogadore, Ohio; 10 inches high; c. 1865–1885; $235–285.

Picture frame, molded flint-enamel glazed yellowware, oblong with scalloped edge; United States Pottery Company, Bennington, Vermont; 12 inches high; c. 1849–1858; $350–450.

Left to right: *molded Rockingham-glazed yellowware, New Jersey or Ohio, c. 1850–1870; nappy, 5 inches in diameter, $75–85; paneled mixing bowl, 9 inches in diameter, $80–110; creamer, 4 inches high, $60–80.*

Frame, for painting or photograph, flint enamel–glazed yellowware, United States Pottery Company, Bennington, Vermont, c. 1849–1858, 9 inches across, $275–375.

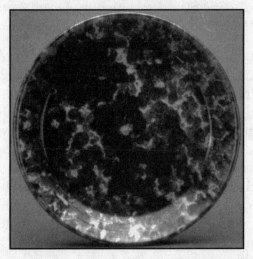

Pie plate, Rockingham-glazed yellowware, Ohio, c. 1860–1900, 9 inches in diameter, $80–110.

Picture frame, oval molded Rockingham glazed yellowware; Ohio; 7 inches high; c. 1860–1880; $200–300.

Pie plate, molded Rockingham glazed yellowware; Northeastern or Midwestern; 9 inches in diameter; c. 1860–1900; $85–115; in nests of four to six, 7 to 12 inches in diameter, $350–600.

Pipkin (cooking pot), Rockingham-glazed yellowware, United States Pottery Company, Bennington, Vermont, c. 1849–1858, 8.5 inches high, $350–500.

Pipkin or "milk boiler," molded Rockingham glazed yellowware, semi-ovoid body with spout and ear handle; Ohio; 5.5 inches high; c. 1870–1890; $115–155.

Pipkin, molded Rockingham glazed yellowware with ribbed ovoid body; spout and ear handle, matching cover, impressed maker's mark; United States Pottery Company, Bennington, Vermont; 7.5 inches high; c. 1849–1858; $375–475.

Pipkin, molded flint-enamel glazed yellowware, ribbed ovoid body with long curving hollow handle, matching cover, impressed maker's mark; United States Pottery Company, Bennington, Vermont; 7 inches high; c. 1849–1858; $550–700.

Pitcher, molded Rockingham glazed yellowware with embossed grapes and leaves, rustic handle, and impressed maker's mark; Swan Hill Pottery, South Amboy, New Jersey; 8.5 inches high; c. 1850–1875; $750–950.

Pitcher, molded Rockingham glazed yellowware, hound handle and embossed hunting scenes, impressed maker's mark; American Pottery Company, Jersey City, New Jersey; 9 inches high; c. 1833–1845; $1,500–2,200.

Pitchers, molded Rockingham-glazed yellowware: left, *Baltimore, Maryland, c. 1860–1880, 6 inches high, $80–100;* right, *Midwestern, c. 1860–1900, 4 inches high, $45–60.*

Pitcher, molded Rockingham-glazed yellowware, East Liverpool, Ohio, c. 1850–1870, 9.5 inches high, $200–250.

Pitcher, molded stoneware with pseudo-Rockingham glaze, embossed representations of hanging game birds and rabbits, impressed maker's mark; Sidney Risley, Norwich, Connecticut; 8 inches high; c. 1850–1875; $550–850.

Pitcher, molded Rockingham glazed yellowware, semi-ovoid body with beaded handle and owner's name in applied porcelain letters; Alfred Hall & Sons, Perth Amboy, New Jersey; 9 inches high; c. 1866–1876; $850–1,250.

Pitcher, molded stoneware with pseudo-Rockingham glaze, semi-ovoid body with embossed leaf pattern below spout and under handle; New York; 8.5 inches high; c. 1870–1910; $55–70.

Pitcher, molded blue Rockingham glazed white earthenware, scalloped rim, ovoid body; New Jersey or Ohio; 8 inches high; c. 1880–1900; $225–300.

Pitcher, molded Rockingham glazed yellowware with embossed floral decoration; William H. Farrar, Geddes, New York; 10.5 inches high; c. 1857–1868; $300–450.

Pitcher, molded stoneware with pseudo-Rockingham glaze, hound handle and embossed hunting scenes, impressed date and maker's mark; Nichols & Alford, Burlington, Vermont; 8.3 inches high; 1854; $600–750.

Pitcher, molded Rockingham-glazed yellowware, Trenton, New Jersey, c. 1860–1880, 7 inches high, $65–90.

Pitchers, molded Rockingham-glazed yellowware with hound handles: left, Ohio, c. 1860–1880, 10.5 inches high, $225–300; right, Maryland, c. 1850–1875, 9 inches high, $250–325.

Group of molded Rockingham glazed yellowware pitchers all made at the Bennett Pottery, Baltimore, Maryland, c. 1855–1885; 8 to 11 inches high, $225–475 apiece.

Pitcher, molded stoneware with pseudo-Rockingham glaze, faceted body with embossed classic decorative motifs, impressed maker's mark; J.T. Winslow, Portland, Maine; 10 inches high; c. 1850–1870; $150–235.

Pitcher, molded Rockingham glazed yellowware with embossed roses, impressed maker's mark; Peoria Pottery, Peoria, Illinois; 9.5 inches high; c. 1863–1875; $400–550.

Pitcher, molded Rockingham glazed yellowware, hound handle and embossed hunting scenes, impressed maker's mark; Harker, Taylor & Company, East Liverpool, Ohio; 10 inches high; c. 1847–1850; $500–700.

Pitcher, molded Rockingham glazed yellowware, octagonal body, helmet-form spout, impressed maker's mark; Otto V. Lewis, Greenwich, New York; 7.5 inches high; c. 1849–1852; $800–1,200.

Plate, molded blue Rockingham glazed white earthenware, maker's stamp; Burford Brothers, East Liverpool, Ohio; 7.2 inches in diameter; c. 1880–1900; $250–350.

Relish dish, molded leaf form, Rockingham glazed yellowware; United States Pottery Company, Bennington, Vermont; 10 inches long; c. 1849–1858; $175–225.

Ring flask, molded stoneware with pseudo-Rockingham glaze, embossed floral decoration; Indiana; 6 inches in diameter; c. 1870–1880; $300–400.

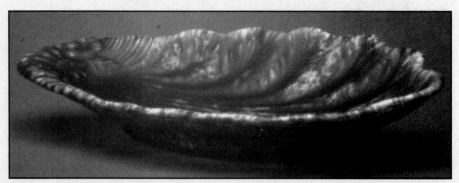

Relish dish, molded Rockingham-glazed yellowware, United States Pottery Company, Bennington, Vermont, c. 1849–1858, 9.5 inches long, $175–225.

Baker or serving bowl, molded, oval Rockingham-glazed yellowware, Ohio, c. 1850–1880, 9 inches long; $65–85.

Serving dish or oval baker, molded Rockingham glazed yellowware; New Jersey, Vermont, or Midwestern; 8.5 inches long; c. 1840–1890; $75–95; in sets of five to seven, 6 to 9 inches long, $500–700.

Serving dish or oval baker, molded flint-enamel glazed yellowware, impressed maker's mark; United States Pottery Company, Bennington, Vermont; 12 inches long; c. 1849–1858; $225–300.

Serving dish or octagonal baker, molded flint-enamel glazed yellowware, impressed maker's mark; United States Pottery Company, Bennington, Vermont; 11.5 inches long; c. 1849–1858; $275–350.

Shaving mug, molded Rockingham glazed yellowware with embossed figure of seated man holding jug and glass, interior soap shelf, impressed maker's mark; Edwin & William Bennett, Baltimore, Maryland; 4.5 inches high; c. 1846–1848; $800–1,200.

Shaving mug, molded Rockingham glazed yellowware with embossed figure of boy in hat; Abraham Miller, Philadelphia, Pennsylvania; 4.4 inches high; c. 1845–1850; $550–750.

Snuff jar, in form of seated "Uncle Toby" holding pitcher and glass, molded Rockingham glazed yellowware, impressed maker's mark; United States Pottery Company, Bennington, Vermont; 4.3 inches high; c. 1849–1858; $450–600.

Soap dish, molded Rockingham glazed yellowware, oblong with ridged interior platform; McNichol Pottery Company, East Liverpool, Ohio; 5 inches long; c. 1880–1910; $70–95.

Snuff jar, molded Rockingham-glazed yellowware, top in form of hat, United States Pottery Company, Bennington, Vermont, c. 1849–1858, 4.5 inches high, $450–650.

Soap dishes, molded Rockingham-glazed yellowware, Ohio or Maryland, c. 1850–1900: left, oval, 5 inches long, $55–75; right, oblong, 5.5 inches long, $65–85.

Soap dishes, molded Rockingham-glazed yellowware: left, *New York, c. 1870–1900, 5 inches long, $45–60;* right, *New Jersey, 3.75 inches in diameter, $75–95.*

Left to right: *molded Rockingham-glazed yellowware, New Jersey or Ohio, c. 1850–1870; oblong soap dish, 5.5 inches long, $45–60; mug, 4.5 inches high, $70–95; oval soap dish, 5 inches long, $40–55.*

Soap dish, molded Rockingham glazed yellowware, round with perforated interior soap platform; United States Pottery Company, Bennington, Vermont; 4 inches in diameter; c. 1847–1858; $95–135.

Sugar bowl, molded flint-enamel glazed yellowware covered bowl in Gothic style with ribbed body, impressed maker's mark; United States Pottery Company, Bennington, Vermont; 7 inches high; c. 1849–1858; $550–750.

Sugar bowl, molded Flint Enamel–glazed yellowware, United States Pottery Company, Bennington, Vermont, c. 1849–1858, 7 inches high, $550–750.

Tea pot, molded Rockingham-glazed yellowware in the "Rebecca at the Well" pattern, Baltimore, Maryland, c. 1860–1900, 8.5 inches high, $65–85.

Teapot, molded yellowware in the "Rebecca at the Well" pattern with flint enamel glaze, embossed maker's mark; Southern Porcelain Company, Kaolin, South Carolina; 7.5 inches high; c. 1856–1863; $550–750.

Teapot, molded Rockingham glazed yellowware in the "Rebecca at the Well" pattern, impressed maker's mark; Edwin Bennett, Baltimore, Maryland, 7.5 inches high; c. 1850–1870; $250–375.

Teapot, molded stoneware in the "Rebecca at the Well" pattern with pseudo-Rockingham glaze; New York; 7 inches high; c. 1870–1890; $55–75.

Teapot, molded stoneware with pseudo-Rockingham glaze, rounded body with beading about handle spout and rim, matching domed top; New York or Massachusetts; 6.5 inches high; c. 1870–1900; $45–60.

Teapot, molded yellowware with flint enamel glaze, octagonal body in the Gothic style with domed cover; United States

Tea pot, molded Flint Enamel–glazed yellowware, United States Pottery Company, Bennington, Vermont, c. 1849–1858, 8 inches high, $550–750.

Crock, molded oval form, Rockingham-glazed yellowware, Maryland, c. 1850–1870, 7 inches long, $135–185.

Pottery Company, Bennington, Vermont; 9 inches high; c. 1844–1858; $650–800.

Tobacco jar, molded stoneware with pseudo-Rockingham glaze, decorative reeding and geometric decoration, impressed maker's mark, matching cover; Ballard & Brothers, Burlington, Vermont; 10.5 inches high; c. 1856–1867; $125–175.

Tobacco jar, molded Rockingham glazed yellowware, octagonal body, foliated stub handles, domed top; United States Pottery Company, Bennington, Vermont; 8.5 inches high; c. 1847–1858; $450–600.

Tobacco jar, molded flint-enamel glazed yellowware, octagonal body with embossed Gothic arch design and shaped stub handles, impressed maker's mark; United States Pottery Company, Bennington, Vermont; 11.5 inches high; c. 1847–1858; $750–1,000.

Crock, molded Rockingham-glazed yellowware, Illinois or Minnesota, c. 1910–1930, 6 inches in diameter, $60–85.

Tobacco humidor, molded Rockingham-glazed yellowware, United States Pottery Company, Bennington, Vermont, c. 1849–1858, 11 inches high, $300–400.

Toilet box, molded Flint Enamel–glazed yellowware, United States Pottery Company, Bennington, Vermont, c. 1849–1858, 8 inches long, $325–400.

Toilet box, molded flint-enamel glazed yellowware, oblong, vertically ribbed body with matching domed cover; United States Pottery Company, Bennington, Vermont; 7.5 inches long; c. 1849–1858; $325–400.

Vase, molded flint-enamel glazed yellowware with octagonal base and faceted tulip-form body, lobbed rim; United States Pottery Company, Bennington, Vermont; 9 inches high; c. 1849–1858; $250–325.

Washboard, Rockingham glazed yellowware with wooden frame; Ohio 8 × 12 inches; c. 1870–1900; $450–600.

Washboard, Rockingham glazed yellowware with wooden frame, impressed maker's mark; United States Pottery Company, Bennington, Vermont; 10 × 10.5 inches; c. 1849–1858; $650–900.

Water cooler, molded Rockingham blazed yellowware with reeded pedestal-form body and matching domed cover, spigot hole, impressed maker's mark; Fenton's Works, Bennington, Vermont; 27 inches high; c. 1845–1847; $2,500–3,200.

Vase or spoon holder, molded Rockingham-glazed yellowware, United States Pottery Company, Bennington, Vermont, c. 1849–1858, 10 inches high, $250–350.

Water cooler, molded Rockingham-glazed yellowware, United States Pottery Company, Bennington, Vermont, c. 1849–1858, 17 inches high, $600–850.

SPONGEWARE

The term *spongeware* is applied to a large group of mostly late-nineteenth- and twentieth-century utility vessels which are decorated under the glaze with patterned or irregular blotches of color—usually blue, brown, yellow, green, or red. Since in many cases this decoration appears to have been applied with a sponge or some other soft material cut in the form of a circle, triangle, or "T," collectors have adopted the word "spongeware," just as they have applied fanciful names like "chicken wire" to certain recurrent decorative patterns found on this ware. Of course, none of these terms were used by those who made the pottery;

indeed, the only word they seem to have had for it was "mottled."

Spongeware may be distinguished from the usually earlier Rockingham by the fact that color on the latter appears to have been spattered or dripped on and covers most of the body without a discernible pattern. Spongeware, on the other hand, generally shows a conscious design and larger undecorated areas.

Compared with such pioneer ceramics as redware, stoneware, and even yellowware, spongeware is of rather recent vintage. It appears to have developed in the 1860s and 1870s, when certain large Maryland, New Jersey, and Ohio potteries began to apply blue sponging to dishes and other tableware made of white earthenware. These early examples are relatively uncommon. However, by 1890 Midwestern factories began to sponge both stoneware and yellowware bodies. Such pieces are generally heavy, molded kitchen and storage wares like mixing bowls, crocks, jars, pitcher and bowl sets, water coolers, and jugs, though miniatures and other unusual things may be found. Miniatures, in fact, represent the high end of this field, with rare examples selling in the $500 range.

Desirability and price in this field have little to do with age. A rare form like a 1930s "sponge band" salt shaker will bring far more than a common bowl made a half century before. Nor does it matter greatly to most collectors that the ceramic body is stoneware or yellowware.

The yellowware body was sponged and then covered with a clear alkaline-based glaze. After 1900, fancier pieces such as tureens and creamers might also be decorated with overglaze gilding. Stoneware, on the other hand, was usually first given an overall coating of white Bristol slip, then decoratively sponged, after which it was fired with either an alkaline or a salt glaze. Either type might be sponged in several colors such as red and blue on white or green and brown on yellow, though two-color wares are most common.

Collector interest in spongeware is largely a thing of the past two decades and, for many, is focused on the blue-on-white pitchers and bowls that, like blue-and-white quilts, became during the 1980s a symbol of the popular "country look." As a result of this trendy collecting, blue sponged pitchers from the 1920s have commanded prices in the $200–400 range, yet most spongeware in different hues remains rather inexpensive and relatively common, making this area an ideal one for the beginning collector. Moreover, though the number of forms is relatively limited, the decoration is remarkably varied. It would be possible, for example, to put together an interesting and diversified collection encompassing dozens of distinctly different pitchers or bowls.

This is also very much an area of "crossover" collecting, since many pieces of spongeware bear stenciled advertising logos reflecting the fact that they were given away to promote sales. As a consequence, collectors of advertising memorabilia compete with ceramics collectors in this field.

Spongeware is also frequently marked by a manufacturer such as the Western Stoneware Company of Illinois or Red Wing Potteries of Red Wing, Minnesota; so collectors may also hope to identify much of it either though marks or through existing sales catalogs. The latter are a great collecting tool seldom available to the enthusiast for earlier ceramics like redware or stoneware.

The only real problem with spongeware is reproductions. Capitalizing on the craze for blue-and-white pieces, several firms have produced a line of "look-alikes" based on original molds. Mostly pitchers and bowls, these are often extremely well done. Some examples in the market today have been worn and even chipped in order to create the appearance of age. When offered in a gift shop as repros, these pieces will sell in the $30 range, about a tenth of what they might bring if old. So any blue-and-white pitcher or large bowl that is in good condition and being sold for $75–125 should be looked at very closely. It may just not be right.

SPONGEWARE PRICES

Baking dish, molded with overlapping banded form, stoneware
     covered with white Bristol slip and sponged in blue and red;
     Red Wing, Minnesota; 9 inches in diameter; c. 1920–1935;
     $100–150.
Baking dish, molded with broad rim, stoneware covered with white

Baking dish, molded Bristol-glazed stoneware sponged in blue, Illinois or Minnesota, c. 1900–1920, 12 inches in diameter; $225–275.

Molded Bristol-glazed stoneware, Illinois or Minnesota, c. 1900–1925. Left to right; *custard cup sponged in blue, 3 inches high, $45–60; baking dish sponged in green and brown, 10 inches in diameter, $75–100; mixing bowl sponged in red and blue, 7 inches in diameter, $100–140.*

Molded Bristol-glazed stoneware sponged in blue, Red Wing Minnesota, c. 1910–1930. Left to right: *pitcher, 8 inches high, $160–210; baking dish, 9 inches in diameter, $135–175; pitcher, 7 inches high, $175–245.*

Bristol slip and sponged in green-and-brown circles; Illinois; 8 inches in diameter; c. 1900–1925; $85–135.

Baking dish, molded with broad rim and wire bale handle, stoneware, salt-glazed and sponged in brown; Ohio; 8.5 inches in diameter; c. 1900–1930; $75–110.

Bank, molded in the form of a standing pig, yellowware sponged with blue and pink; Ohio; 5.5 inches long; c. 1890–1920; $45–65.

Bank, molded in form of miniature center-spout jug with wire bale handle, stoneware covered with white Bristol slip, sponged and banded in blue; Illinois or Minnesota; 3 inches high; c. 1885–1905; $250–350.

Bank in form of miniature jug, Bristol-glazed stoneware sponged in blue, Western Stoneware Company, Monmouth, Illinois, c. 1890–1910, 4 inches high; $225–325.

Banks, molded Bristol-glazed stoneware and yellowware in form of pigs sponged in blue, green and brown, Midwestern, c. 1900–1930, 3.5 to 5 inches long; $65–135 apiece.

Batter bowl, molded with fluted sides, pouring spout, and wire bale handle, yellowware decorated with band of red sponging within two blue lines; Red Wing Union Stoneware Company, Red Wing, Minnesota; 8.5 inches in diameter; c. 1906–1936; $225–300.

Bean pot, molded with two handles, fluted body, and matching lid, yellowware sponged in red and blue, stenciled maker's mark; Red Wing Union Stoneware Company, Red Wing, Minnesota; 5 inches high; c. 1930–1936; $165–235.

Bean pot, molded with single handle and matching lid, lower body fluted, yellowware sponged in green and brown; Ohio or Minnesota; 4.7 inches high; c. 1910–1940; $125–165.

Left: *casserole, molded Bristol-glazed stoneware sponged in blue and brown, Minnesota, 7.5 inches in diameter, c. 1915–1935, $135–175;* right: *covered bean pot, molded yellowware sponged in green and brown, Ohio, c. 1910–1930, 6 inches high, $80–110.*

Molded yellowware sponged in brown, Red Wing, Minnesota, c. 1910–1930: left, *bean pot, 6.5 inches high, $110–140;* right, *baking dish, 8.5 inches in diameter, $75–95.*

Molded white earthenware sponged in blue, Maryland or Pennsylvania, c. 1880–1910. Left to right: cereal bowl, 6 inches in diameter, $80–110; beater or serving bowl, 5 inches high, $115–145; nappy or baking bowl, 9 inches in diameter, $200–250.

Left to right: *soup bowl, molded white earthenware sponged in blue, Ott & Brewer, Trenton, New Jersey, c. 1870–1885, 9 inches in diameter, $150–210; bowls, Bristol-glazed stoneware sponged in blue, Midwestern, c. 1910–1935, 4 to 6 inches in diameter, $55–85 each.*

Beater jar, molded with embossed clover leaf pattern, yellowware sponged with green and orange; Red Wing Union Stoneware Company, Red Wing, Minnesota; 6 inches high; c. 1906–1936; $90–120.

Bowl, molded stoneware, interior covered with white Bristol slip, exterior sponged in blue and brown over white; Western Stoneware Company, Monmouth, Illinois; 8 inches in diameter; c. 1910–1935; $55–75.

Bowl, molded yellowware sponged with vertical bands of brown; New Jersey; 7 inches in diameter; c. 1910–1930; $40–55.

Bowl, molded with everted lip, yellowware sponged in the "chicken wire" pattern in green and brown; Ohio; 9 inches in diameter; c. 1900–1930; $65–85.

Bowl, molded with horizontal overlapping ridges, yellowware sponged with green and brown; Midwestern; 8 inches in diameter; c. 1900–1940; $50–75.

Bowl, molded with fluted sides and wide rim, yellowware sponged in blue and brown; Minnesota or Ohio; 8 inches in diameter; c. 1925–1935; $70–95.

Bowls, molded yellowware sponged in green and brown, New Jersey or Maryland, c. 1880–1910, 5 to 8 inches in diameter; $50–125.

Molded Bristol-glazed stoneware sponged in blue, Minnesota or Illinois, c. 1910–1930. Left to right: serving bowl, 7.5 inches in diameter, $80–110; serving bowl, 5 inches in diameter, $65–95; mixing bowl, 9 inches in diameter, $100–140.

Bowls, molded Bristol-glazed stoneware with advertising, sponged in red and blue, Red Wing Union Stoneware Company, Red Wing, Minnesota, c. 1910–1930: left, *10 inches in diameter, $140–200;* right, *8 inches in diameter, $125–175.*

Bowls, molded yellowware sponged in brown, Midwestern, c. 1910–1930, 9 to 10 inches in diameter; $60–75.

Bowls, molded yellowware and Bristol-glazed stoneware sponged in green, Ohio, c. 1880–1910, 6 to 10 inches in diameter; $70–110.

Bowl, molded Bristol-glazed stoneware sponged in blue, Illinois or Minnesota, c. 1910–1940, 10 inches in diameter; $125–165.

Bowl, molded with heavy rim, stoneware sponged in red and green and salt-glazed; Ohio; 7.5 inches in diameter; c. 1900–1920; $85–125.

Bowl, molded with matching flat lid having inset lift knob, embossed circles and banding, stoneware sponged in blue and brown and salt-glazed; Red Wing, Minnesota; 5.5 inches high; c. 1900–1920; $135–185.

Bowl, stoneware covered with a white Bristol slip and having bands of blue sponging around rim and base; Ohio; 4 inches in diameter; c. 1910–1925; $75–125.

Bread-and-butter or salad plate, white earthenware sponged in blue; Midwestern; 6 inches in diameter; c. 1860–1900; $70–95.

Cake stand, molded disklike form with vertically fluted sides, yellowware decorated with red sponging within blue lines, stenciled maker's mark; Red Wing Union Stoneware Com-

Bowl, molded Bristol-glazed stoneware sponged in blue, Minnesota or Illinois, c. 1900–1920, 9.5 inches in diameter; $140–200.

Bowl, molded yellowware sponged in brown and green, Red Wing Union Stoneware Company, Red Wing, Minnesota, c. 1915–1935, 7.5 inches in diameter; $65–85.

pany, Red Wing, Minnesota; 2.5 inches high; c. 1906–1936; $400–550.

Candlestick, tubular holder mounted on disklike base with vertical loop handle, yellowware sponged with brown; Midwestern; 4.5 inches high; c. 1860–1890; $200–300.

Casserole, bowl-like form with matching domed top, salt-glazed stoneware sponged in blue and brown; New Jersey; 6.5 inches high; c. 1890–1910; $200–250.

Casserole, molded stoneware with fluted sides and broad rim, stoneware covered with white Bristol slip and sponged in blue sawtooth pattern; Akron, Ohio; 8.5 inches in diameter; c. 1890–1920; $65–95.

Casserole, molded with stubby handles and matching top having inset lift, yellowware sponged in red and blue; Red Wing, Minnesota; 8 inches in diameter; c. 1920–1935; $165–245.

Chamber pot with cover, molded in bulbous ironstone form, stoneware covered with white Bristol slip and sponged in

Casserole, molded Bristol-glazed stoneware sponged in blue and having matching cover, Illinois or Minnesota, c. 1910–1930, 10 inches in diameter; $250–325.

red; Red Wing Union Stoneware Company, Red Wing, Minnesota; 7.5 inches high; c. 1906–1936; $70–95.

Covered dish, molded in the form of hen on nest (similar to pressed glass examples), impressed maker's mark, stoneware covered with white Bristol slip and sponged in blue; Monmouth Pottery Company, Monmouth, Illinois; 6 inches long; c. 1893–1906; $600–850.

Creamer, molded with ridged body, yellowware sponged with green and brown; Ohio; 4 inches high; c. 1910–1930; $60–85.

Creamer, bulbous body with decorative rings, stoneware covered with white Bristol slip sponged in blue; Lowell Pottery, Tonica, Illinois; 3.5 inches high; c. 1895–1915; $275–350.

Cookie crock, molded with fluted sides and matching top, yellowware decorated with bands of red sponging within blue lines, stenciled "Cookies" and maker's mark; Red Wing Union Stoneware Company, Red Wing, Minnesota; 7 inches in diameter; c. 1906–1936; $300–400.

Crock, molded with matching cover, embossed birds and vegetation, yellowware sponged with brown; New Jersey; 6 inches high; c. 1890–1910; $65–95.

Molded yellowware sponged in green, Minnesota or Illinois, c. 1910–1930. Left to right: *creamer 4.5 inches high, $55–75; mixing bowl, 8 inches in diameter, $45–65; pitcher, 10 inches high, $70–100.*

Molded yellowware sponged in brown, Ohio or New Jersey, c. 1880–1910. Left to right: covered crock, 6 inches high, $85–115; pie plate, 9 inches in diameter, $55–70; mug, 4 inches high, $80–110.

Molded Bristol-glazed stoneware sponged in blue, Red Wing, Minnesota, c. 1900–1915. Left to right: crock, 6 inches high, $70–90; bowl, 8 inches in diameter, $75–100; bowl, 6 inches in diameter, $50–70.

Crock, molded with matching cover, stoneware covered with a
  white Bristol slip and sponged in blue; Red Wing, Minnesota; 6 inches high; c. 1910–1920; $150–200.
Cup and saucer, molded yellowware sponged in blue; New Jersey
  or Ohio; cup 3.5 inches high; c. 1900–1920; $200–275.
Cup and saucer, handleless type, white earthenware, rim of saucer
  and upper body of cup sponged in purple; Maryland or
  New Jersey; cup 4 inches high; c. 1865–1885; $250–325.

Cups and saucers: molded white earthenware sponged in blue, Pennsylvania or Ohio, c. 1870–1900: left, *mush cup/saucer, 4.25 inches high, $200–250/set;* center and right, *3 inches high, $135–195/set.*

Cuspidor, molded Bristol-glazed stoneware sponged in blue, Midwestern, c. 1900–1930, 8 inches in diameter; $75–95.

Cup and saucer, molded white earthenware sponged in blue, impressed maker's mark; Burford Brothers, East Liverpool, Ohio; cup 3.5 inches high; c. 1880–1905; $300–400.

Cuspidor, molded with narrow waist and flaring lip, stoneware covered with white Bristol slip and sponged in blue; Red

Wing Union Stoneware Company, Red Wing, Minnesota; 10 inches in diameter; c. 1906–1936; $150–200.

Custard cup, stoneware covered with white Bristol slip and sponged in blue; New Jersey; 3.2 inches high; c. 1900–1920; $35–45.

Custard cup, yellowware sponged in brown; New Jersey or Midwestern; 3 inches high; c. 1880–1920; $15–25.

Molded Bristol-glazed stoneware sponged in blue. Left to right: *cuspidor, Minnesota, c. 1900–1920, 6 inches in diameter, $65–85; pitcher, Ohio or Illinois, c. 1890–1920, 7 inches high, $125–175; plate, New Jersey, c. 1870–1890, $70–90.*

Molded Bristol-glazed stoneware sponged in blue, Minnesota or Illinois, c. 1910–1930: left, *woman's cuspidor, 5 inches in diameter, $75–95;* right, *mixing bowl, 9.5 inches in diameter, $135–185.*

Custard cups, molded yellowware sponged in green and brown, New Jersey or Ohio, c. 1900–1920, 2.5 to 3 inches high; $10–20.

Custard cup, yellowware sponged in white; Midwestern; 3 inches high; c. 1880–1910; $20–30.

Fat lamp, cup form with ear handle and saucer base, white earthenware sponged in blue; Pennsylvania; 5 inches high; c. 1860–1880; $350–450.

Figurine, molded standing pig, stoneware covered with white Bristol slip and sponged in brown; Ruckel Pottery, White Hall, Illinois; 4 inches long; c. 1915–1935; $180–260.

Figurine, molded standing pig, yellowware sponged in blue; Ohio or Illinois; 3.5 inches long; c. 1900–1930; $55–75.

Hot-water bottle, demilune form with flat bottom, stoneware sponged in blue and yellow; Midwestern; 11 inches long; c. 1890–1920; $200–275.

Inkwell, molded triangular form, blue sponging on white earthenware; New Jersey; 2.5 × 2.5 inches; c. 1860–1880; $250–325.

Jar for refrigerator storage, molded with fluted sides and matching top, yellowware decorated with a band of red sponging within blue lines, stenciled maker's mark; Red Wing Union Stoneware Company, Red Wing, Minnesota; 5 inches high; c. 1906–1936; $200–275.

Jardiniere or flower pot, bowl shape with everted rim, stoneware covered with white Bristol slip and both banded and sponged in blue; Crooksville, Ohio; 20 inches in diameter; c. 1885–1895; $225–300.

Jardiniere or flower pot, bowl shape with sloping shoulder, stoneware covered with white Bristol slip and sponged in blue; New Jersey; 8 inches in diameter; c. 1900–1920; $140–190.

Jug, molded with top spout and wire bale handle, stoneware covered with white Bristol slip and sponged in pale blue, stenciled advertising logo; Minnesota Stoneware Company, Red Wing, Minnesota; 8.5 inches high; c. 1883–1906; $350–450.

Jug, molded with cylindrical body and sloping shoulder, yellowware sponged in green and brown; Ohio or Minnesota; 10 inches high; c. 1890–1920; $125–175.

Jugs, molded yellowware sponged in green, Red Wing Union Stoneware Company, Red Wing, Minnesota, c. 1910–1930; $70–110 each.

Juicer or reamer, molded with fluted central shaft yellowware decorated with band of red sponging within blue lines, stenciled maker's mark; Red Wing Union Stoneware Company, Red Wing, Minnesota; 4 inches high; c. 1906–1936; $250–350.

Milk pan, molded with wide rim glazed in blue, lower stoneware body covered with white Bristol slip sponged in blue and brown, impressed maker's mark; Western Stoneware Company, Monmouth, Illinois; 10 inches in diameter; c. 1906–1930; $200–275.

Miniature jug, molded, straight-sided with rounded shoulder, impressed maker's mark, stoneware covered with white Bristol slip and sponged in blue with various designs including the Maltese cross; Fort Dodge Stoneware Company, Fort Dodge, Iowa; 3 inches high; c. 1892–1906; $450–600.

Miniature jug, stoneware covered with white Bristol slip and sponged in blue; Red Wing Union Stoneware Company, Red Wing, Minnesota; 2.75 inches high; c. 1906–1936; $275–350.

Miniature water cooler, semi-ovoid form, stenciled maker's mark, stoneware covered with white Bristol slip and sponged in blue; Monmouth Pottery Company, Monmouth, Illinois; 4 inches high; c. 1893–1906; $400–500.

Miniature sadiron, molded yellowware sponged in light brown; New Jersey or Ohio; 4 inches long; c. 1880–1910; $100–150.

Miniature doll cradle, molded and modeled yellowware sponged in loops of brown; Ohio; 4.5 inches long; c. 1880–1910; $135–185.

Miniature pitcher, molded white earthenware sponged in red and blue; Maryland or New Jersey; 3 inches high; c. 1870–1890; $150–200.

Miniature cup and saucer, molded white earthenware sponged in red and blue; Maryland or New Jersey; 2 inches high; c. 1870–1890; $225–300.

Mug, straight-sided with ear handle, white earthenware sponged with tight bands of blue; Maryland; 4 inches high; c. 1870–1890; $140–180.

Mug, molded yellowware sponged in green, Minnesota or Illinois, c. 1910–1930, 4 inches high; $60–80.

Mug, soda fountain, molded yellowware sponged in red and blue, Maryland or Ohio, c. 1890–1930, 7 inches high; $100–130.

Mug, molded barrel shape with embossed bands, yellowware sponged in brown; New Jersey or Ohio; 5 inches high; c. 1910–1930; $50–70.

Mug, molded straight-sided with ear handle, yellowware with two bands of red sponging within blue lines, impressed maker's mark; Red Wing Union Stoneware Company, Red Wing, Minnesota; 5 inches high; c. 1894–1906; $200–275.

Nappy or baking dish with tapering sides, yellowware sponged in brown; Ohio; 6 inches in diameter; c. 1890–1910; $60–85.

Pap boat or infant feeder, boat-shaped, molded and modeled white earthenware sponged in blue; Pennsylvania; 6.2 inches long; c. 1830–1850; $450–550.

Pipkin, molded squat pitcherlike form with matching flat top, stoneware covered with white Bristol slip and sponged in red and blue, impressed maker's mark; Red Wing Union

Deep dish or nappy, white earthenware sponged in rare combination of blue and yellow, New Jersey or Maryland, c. 1850–1870, 10 inches in diameter; $250–350.

Nappies or baking dishes, "nest" or set of matching molded yellowware sponged in brown, Midwestern, c. 1870–1910, 5.5 to 9.5 inches in diameter; $200–250 for set of four.

Molded yellowware nappies or baking dishes sponged in brown, all Ohio, c. 1900–1910. Left to right: 3 inches in diameter, $70–95; 6 inches in diameter, $45–65; 4 inches in diameter, $55–75.

Pottery Company, Red Wing, Minnesota; 6 inches high; c. 1883–1906; $225–300.

Pipkin, molded squat pitcherlike form lacking top, stoneware covered with white Bristol slip and sponged in blue "chicken wire" pattern; Ohio or Minnesota; 4 inches high; c. 1910–1930; $175–250.

Pitcher, molded tapering cylinder, stoneware covered with white Bristol slip and sponged in blue; by Frederick Ohmann, Lyons, New York; 8 inches high; c. 1897–1898; $350–450.

Molded yellowware sponged in brown and yellow, Minnesota or Illinois, c. 1910–1930.
Left to right; pitcher 6.5 inches high, $65–85; serving bowl, 8 inches in diameter,
$40–60; pitcher, 11 inches high, $70–90.

Pitcher, molded Bristol-glazed stoneware sponged in blue, Minnesota, c. 1900–1920,
9 inches high; $250–325.

Pitcher, molded tapering cylinder, stoneware covered with white Bristol slip and a pattern of blue sponged, Z-shaped devices; Midwestern; 8.5 inches high; c. 1900–1930; $275–350.

Pitcher, bulbous, molded in the ironstone form, yellowware randomly sponged in green; Croxall Pottery, East Liverpool, Ohio; 7.5 inches high; c. 1890–1910; $130–180.

Printed mark on base of molded Bristol-glazed and blue sponged stoneware pitcher. A maker's mark enhances the value of any piece.

Pitchers, all Midwestern, c. 1900–1920. Left to right: *molded yellowware sponged in green, 7 inches high, $70–90; molded yellowware sponged in green and brown, 10 inches high, $110–150; molded Bristol-glazed stoneware sponged in blue, 7.5 inches high, $150–225.*

Pitchers, molded white earthenware sponged in blue, Pennsylvania, c. 1880–1910; left, *by Griffin, Smith & Hill, Phoenixville, 7 inches high, $200–275;* center, *9 inches high, $160–220;* right, *6.5 inches high, $150–210.*

Pitchers, all Midwestern, c. 1900–1910: left, *molded blue slipped stoneware sponged in blue, 8 inches high, $125–175;* center, *molded yellowware sponged in brown, 9 inches high, $65–85; molded green slipped stoneware sponged in green, 8 inches high, $115–155.*

Pitcher, bulbous, molded with rough barklike surface, stoneware sponged in blue over brown; Midwestern; 7 inches high; c. 1890–1920; $90–140.

Pitcher, bulbous, stoneware covered with a white Bristol slip, sponged-blue, X-shaped pattern on each side; Byrd Pottery, Tyler, Texas; 8.5 inches high; c. 1920–1935; $200–280.

Pitcher and washbowl set, molded stoneware covered with white Bristol slip and sponged in blue; Ohio; 9 inches high; c. 1890–1910; $400–550.

Plate, molded white earthenware sponged in blue, impressed maker's mark; International Pottery Company, Trenton, New Jersey, 10 inches in diameter; c. 1860–1868; $300–400.

Pitcher and bowl set, molded Bristol-glazed stoneware sponged and banded in blue, Ohio, c. 1860–1880, 12 inches high; $450–600.

Saucers, molded white earthenware sponged in blue, Maryland or New Jersey, c. 1850–1870, 5 to 6 inches in diameter; $70–95.

Plates, molded white earthenware sponged in blue, New Jersey, c. 1860–1890, 7 to 9 inches; $80–130 apiece.

Plate, molded white earthenware sponged in blue; New Jersey; 7 inches in diameter; c. 1870–1890; $80–110.

Platter, molded, oblong with scalloped border, white earthenware sponged in blue; Ohio; 8 inches long; c. 1870–1890; $165–235.

Platter, molded oval white earthenware sponged in blue; New Jersey or Maryland; 11 inches long; c. 1860–1890; $185–255.

Salt and pepper shakers, molded with vertical fluting, yellowware decorated with bands of red sponging within blue lines, stamped maker's mark; Red Wing Union Stoneware Company, Red Wing, Minnesota; 4 inches high; c. 1906–1936; $200–275 the set.

Salt box, hanging type, molded with fluted body, yellowware with horizontal bands of red sponging on top and upper body, stamped date and advertising logo; Red Wing Union Stoneware Company, Red Wing, Minnesota; 7 inches high; 1934; $300–400.

Serving dish, molded, oval with matching dome-topped lid, yellowware sponged in green and gilt-decorated; Ohio; 7.5 inches long; c. 1910–1920; $75–110.

Serving dish with cover, molded yellowware sponged in green, Illinois or Ohio, c. 1900–1920, 10 inches long; $110–150.

Serving dish, molded white earthenware sponged in blue, scalloped rim, New Jersey, c. 1850–1880, 8.5 inches long; $200–275.

Molded white earthenware sponged in blue. Left to right: *serving dish, Bennett Pottery, Baltimore, Maryland, c. 1890–1900, 8 inches square, $175–245; baking dish, Trenton, New Jersey, c. 1880–1890, $140–180; oval baking or serving dish, Bennett Pottery, Baltimore, Maryland, c. 1890–1900, 7 inches long, $150–225.*

Slop jar, molded yellowware sponged in green, Illinois or Minnesota, c. 1900–1940, 10 inches high; $80–110.

Serving dish, molded rectangular white earthenware vessel sponged in blue; Trenton, New Jersey; 10 inches long; c. 1880–1900; $200–280.

Slop jar or combinette, molded semi-ovoid form with wire bale handle and matching top, stoneware covered with white

Bristol slip and sponged in red; Red Wing Union Stoneware Company, Red Wing, Minnesota; 12 inches high; c. 1906–1936; $110–170.

Slop jar or combinette, molded with embossed floral pattern below rim, small ear handles, yellowware sponged in green; Ohio or Minnesota; 16 inches high; c. 1900–1930; $85–135.

Soap dish, molded octagonal white earthenware vessel sponged in blue; Ohio; 4.5 inches long; c. 1900–1920; $70–90.

Soap dish, molded circular form with inner perforated platform, yellowware sponged with green and gilded; Ohio or Minnesota; 5 inches in diameter; c. 1915–1935; $45–65.

Stew pot, molded, with pouring spout and wire bale handle, yellowware sponged in green; Ohio or Minnesota; 4.5 inches in diameter; c. 1910–1930; $70–95.

Sugar bowl, molded with domed top and shallow ring handles, white earthenware with bands of chainlike sponging in blue; New Jersey or Maryland; 4.5 inches high; c. 1865–1880; $235–285.

Sugar bowl or storage jar, molded with embossed and gilded

Left to right: *soap dish, molded white earthenware sponged in blue, Ohio, c. 1900–1920, 4 inches long, $70–90; bean pot, Bristol-glazed stoneware sponged in blue, Ohio, c. 1890–1910, 7 inches high, $110–150; fat lamp, Pennsylvania, c. 1860–1880, 5.5 inches high, $300–450.*

Molded yellowware sponged in green, Ohio, c. 1900–1930. Left to right: *covered serving dish, 5 inches high, $75–95; mixing bowl, 8 inches in diameter, $45–60; sugar jar, 6 inches high, $80–110.*

Molded white earthenware sponged in blue, Maryland or Pennsylvania, c. 1870–1900. Left to right: *gravy boat, 7 inches long, $120–150; sugar bowl, 6 inches high, $225–275; creamer, 5 inches high, $135–185.*

"SUGAR," matching top, yellowware sponged in green; Ohio; 5 inches high; c. 1920–1940; $80–120.

Teapot, molded, bulbous form with domed top and shaped handle, yellowware sponged in green and brown; Ohio; 5 inches high; c. 1910–1930; $140–190.

Teapot, molded elongated form with slightly domed top, stoneware covered with white Bristol slip and sponged in green; Midwestern; 6.5 inches high; c. 1900–1930; $125–175.

Toothbrush holder, molded cylinder tapering out slightly at top
and bottom, yellowware sponged with green and gilded;
Ohio or Minnesota; 6 inches high; c. 1900–1930; $60–85.
Trivet, molded disklike, slightly concave form, white earthenware
sponged in blue; New Jersey; 7.5 inches in diameter;
c. 1890–1910; $50–75.

*Toilet or dresser set, molded yellowware sponged in green with applied gilding, Illinois,
c. 1900–1940, 3 to 10 inches high; $250–350/set.*

Molded spongeware. Left to right: *rare white earthenware trivet sponged in red and
blue, New Jersey or Maryland, c. 1890–1910, 6 inches in diameter, $80–110; yellowware
teapot sponged in brown, Ohio, c. 1890–1915, 5.5 inches high, $75–100; stew pot,
yellowware sponged in green, Ohio, c. 1900–1920, $60–85.*

Trivet, molded disklike form with raised rim, yellowware sponged in red and blue; Maryland or New Jersey; 6 inches in diameter; c. 1870–1900; $45–60.

Umbrella stand, molded cylindrical form, stoneware covered with white Bristol slip and sponged in red and blue; Red Wing Union Stoneware Company, Red Wing, Minnesota; 18 inches high; c. 1906–1936; $375–450.

Vase, molded baluster form, white earthenware, clear-glazed and sponged in blue, stenciled maker's mark; Stangl Pottery, Trenton, New Jersey; 10 inches high; c. 1950–1960; $55–85.

Washboard, molded in rectangular ribbed form, yellowware sponged in blue, wooden frame; Midwestern; 11 × 8.5 inches; c. 1880–1910; $350–500.

Water cooler, barrel form, stoneware covered with white Bristol slip and sponged in blue; by Frederick Ohmann, Lyons, New York; 13 inches high; c. 1897–1898; $300–450.

Molded white earthenware sponged in blue; left, vase, New Jersey, c. 1900–1910, 8 inches in diameter, $70–100; handled vase, New Jersey, c. 1930–1940, 9 inches high, $55–75.

Vase (two part), molded white earthenware sponged in blue, Stangl Pottery, Trenton, New Jersey, c. 1950–1965, 10 inches high, $35–45.

Left to right: *molded white earthenware vase sponged in blue, Stangl Pottery, Trenton, New Jersey, c. 1850–1960, 10 inches high, $30–40; molded yellowware pitcher sponged in blue, Robinson, Ransbottom Pottery, Roseville, Ohio, c. 1920–1930, 9.5 inches high, $60–80; molded harvest jug, Bristol-slipped stoneware sponged in blue, Akron, Ohio, c. 1900–1910, 7 inches high, $130–180.*

Washboard, molded yellowware sponged in brown, in a wooden frame, Ohio, c. 1880–1890, 10 × 17 inches; $275–375.

Water cooler, molded Bristol-glazed stoneware sponged in blue, Western Stoneware Company, Monmouth, Illinois, c. 1910–1920, 14 inches high; $250–325.

Water cooler, molded, straight-sided, matching domed top, stenciled maker's mark, stoneware covered with white Bristol
slip and heavily sponged with blue; Monmouth Pottery
Company, Monmouth, Illinois; 14 inches high;
c. 1893–1906; $600–750.

*Watercooler, molded Bristol-glazed stoneware sponged in blue, Monmouth Pottery Com-
pany, Monmouth, Illinois, c. 1893–1906, 33 inches high, $400–550.*

*Keg, molded yellowware sponged in brown, Ohio, c. 1900–1910, 7 inches long;
$120–160.*

Water cooler, molded, straight-sided, with matching domed top, stenciled capacity, and maker's marks, stoneware covered with white Bristol slip and sponged in blue; Western Stoneware Company, Monmouth, Illinois; 11 inches high; c. 1906–1920; $350–450.

Watercooler, Bristol-glazed stoneware sponged in blue, Ohio or Illinois, c. 1890–1920, 16 inches high; $275–350.

PORCELAIN

Porcelain differs greatly in composition from other
American ceramics, and the knowledgeable collector
must be able to distinguish its various forms. In the first
place, unlike stoneware or yellowware, porcelain is not
made from naturally occurring clays but is an artificial
compound composed of various ingredients. Hard paste
or true porcelain is made from kaolin, a white clay, and
feldspar, a mineral. Ground together and fired at a
high temperature, these produce a white, translucent,
resonant, and extremely hard body. The addition of
bone ash to these materials produces a ware known as
bone china, which is not as white or as hard as true

porcelain but is less costly to produce. A third form is the so-called soft paste or artificial porcelain, which combines kaolin or other clays with glass to produce a substitute for true porcelain. It should also be noted that variations such as Belleek (an extremely thin, off-white ware) are not different porcelain bodies but, rather, reflect different techniques in manufacture.

Regardless of its composition, porcelain assumes many forms and various decorations. Unglazed or bisque ware is often referred to as Parian porcelain and, due to its resemblance to marble, was particularly favored by American craftsmen for the manufacture of statuary. Not all such ware was left in the pure white state. In many cases the ceramic batch was stained blue, green, or pink, which experts usually no longer consider true Parian.

Most porcelain is glazed with a clear lead- or glass-based material. Decoration, usually hand-painted, is of two types: underglaze and overglaze; the former is painted onto the ceramic body prior to its being glazed, the latter after, in which case a second firing at a lower temperature is used to "fix" the decoration. While the majority of porcelain is cast in molds, turned wares are sometimes produced, and many pieces are decorated with hand-modeled details such as sprigs of leaves and berries.

As one might suspect, ware as complex as this was expensive to manufacture. The difficulty in obtaining trained workmen, proper materials, and financial backing sufficient to compete against European imports doomed most early American porcelain factories. As a consequence, pre-1850 examples are rare; it was not until the last quarter of the nineteenth century that a viable domestic manufactory was established.

It is probably a consequence of all this that porcelain collecting has never assumed the importance here that it holds in England and Europe. Most Americans collect what they can readily find: stoneware, Rockingham, or yellowware. Porcelain is generally left to a few well-heeled enthusiasts capable of paying prices that regularly run to five figures for early-nineteenth-century examples.

Moreover, American pieces are often hard to distinguish from those made abroad. Many nineteenth-century examples were made in molds brought here by foreign workmen or so closely patterned on these as to be recognizable only by the most knowledgeable. For example, most of the numerous Parian figurines produced at the United States Pottery Company in Bennington, Vermont (c. 1847–1858), are based on English prototypes.

Given this problem, as well as the fact that relatively few examples of pre-1850 American porcelain have survived, it is understandable that there are not that many active collectors. Yet this is a field where great finds can still be made, precisely because so few dealers or collectors know much about it. Not so many years ago, an extremely rare and valuable Bonnin and Morris (Philadelphia, c. 1769–1772) sweetmeat dish was plucked from a house sale for pennies; and in 1993, a Parian sculptural group modeled at the Union Porcelain Works in Brooklyn, New York, by the famous craftsman Carl Muller brought $15,000 at auction, after having been purchased in upstate New York for a mere $500. There are still bargains to be found!

The serious collector of American porcelain will not only be familiar with the history of wares produced by our industry but will also have some knowledge of English and European examples so as to distinguish them. And since much ware was marked, a good guide to this field, such as Kovel's *Dictionary of Marks: Pottery and Porcelain,* is essential.

Fakes are not a problem so far, though the fact that most ware was molded makes this an ever-present possibility. The major difficulty is with unmarked foreign examples, which dealers, because of lack of knowledge or cupidity, attribute to American manufacturers. The more the collector knows, the less likely he or she is to be misled in this manner.

PORCELAIN PRICES

Basket, molded soft paste or artificial porcelain, scalloped and pierced sides, embossed floral decoration touched in blue; Bonnin and Morris, Philadelphia, Pennsylvania; 8 inches in diameter, c. 1769–1782; $25,000–35,000.

Basket, Parian porcelain, hand-shaped latticework with applied flowers and leaves; United States Pottery Company, Ben-

Bank, molded porcelain, United States Pottery Company, Bennington, Vermont, c. 1849–1858, 7 inches high; $300–375.

nington, Vermont; 7.5 inches in diameter; c. 1847–1858; $1,000–1,500.

Basket, molded and hand-worked Belleek porcelain, oval basket-work form with applied polychrome-glazed floral border; Ott & Brewer, Trenton, New Jersey; 9 inches long; c. 1885–1892; $1,200–1,700.

Basket, Belleek porcelain, hand-formed openwork basketry with applied polychrome-glazed flowers; Walter Scott Lenox, Trenton, New Jersey; 6 inches in diameter; c. 1890–1900; $1,000–1,500.

Bonbon dish, molded leaf-form porcelain vessel with applied leaves and buds, polychrome-glazed, stamped maker's mark; Ceramic Art Company, Trenton, New Jersey; 11.5 inches long; c. 1890–1905; $400–600.

Bonbon dish, molded Belleek porcelain in the form of a swan, polychrome-glazed highlights, impressed mark; Ceramic

Art Company, Trenton, New Jersey; 5 inches high; c. 1890–1895; $700–1,100.

Bonbon dish, molded Belleek porcelain in shell form, clear glaze, impressed maker's mark; Knowles, Taylor & Knowles, East Liverpool, Ohio; 5 inches in diameter; c. 1880–1889; $650–850.

Bone dish, molded porcelain in a curvilinear form decorated in blue and gold, stamped maker's mark; Edwin Bennett Pottery Company, Baltimore, Maryland; 7 inches long; c. 1890–1910; $60–85.

Bouillon cup, molded artificial or soft paste porcelain, decorated in blue and gold, stamped maker's mark; Ceramic Art Company, Trenton, New Jersey; 2 inches high; c. 1896–1905; $175–250.

Bowl, molded bulbous Belleek porcelain vessel with two open handles and stub feet, embossed floral decoration, impressed maker's mark; Wheeling Pottery Company, Wheeling, West Virginia; 4 inches high; c. 1896–1905; $150–225.

Bowl, molded Belleek porcelain with scalloped rim and embossed "fish scale" design, hand-painted thistle decoration; Ott & Brewer, Trenton, New Jersey; 8.5 inches in diameter; c. 1885–1892; $700–950.

Bowl, molded Belleek porcelain, four-lobed form with scalloped rim and stub feet; Knowles, Taylor & Knowles, East Liverpool, Ohio; 7.5 inches long; c. 1880–1889; $350–450.

Bowl, molded Parian porcelain with embossed pond lily decoration, matching top with lily finial; United States Pottery Company, Bennington, Vermont; 4 inches high; c. 1847–1858; $550–750.

Bowl, molded Belleek porcelain with gilded dragon-form handle and embossed, gilded daisy motifs, stamped maker's mark; Willets Manufacturing Company, Trenton, New Jersey; 5.5 inches high; c. 1879–1890; $300–400.

Bread plate, molded oval porcelain dish with openwork handles, black transfer busts of President Grover Cleveland and Vice President Thurman, embossed "GIVE US THIS DAY/OUR

DAILY BREAD"; New Jersey; 11 inches long; c. 1888;
$200–300.

Cake plate, molded polychrome-glazed porcelain with gilded blue
    floral decoration and scalloped rim; Onondaga Pottery
    Company, Syracuse, New York; 10 inches in diameter;
    c. 1888–1910; $55–75.
Cake plate, molded porcelain with gold striping; United States
    Pottery Company, Bennington, Vermont; 10 inches long;
    c. 1850–1858; $125–175.
Candlestick, molded artificial or soft paste porcelain, baluster
    form modeled on period brass examples; New York or New
    Jersey; 9.5 inches high; c. 1850–1870; $450–600.
Coffeepot, molded porcelain gilded and decorated in blue,
    stamped maker's mark; Lenox, Incorporated, Trenton,
    New Jersey; 9.5 inches high; c. 1900–1915; $150–225.

*Coffeepot, molded porcelain with gilded details, Maryland or New Jersey, c. 1850–1900,
9.5 inches high; $155–215.*

Chocolate pot, molded bone china porcelain, tapering cylindrical body with embossed floral patterns and polychrome-glazed floral decoration, matching cover, stamped maker's mark; Knowles, Taylor & Knowles, East Liverpool, Ohio; 9 inches high; c. 1890–1905; $250–350.

Chocolate set: pot, creamer, and covered sugar; molded Belleek porcelain with dragon-form handles and gilded, embossed thistle decoration; Willets Manufacturing Company, Trenton, New Jersey; pot, 8.5 inches high; c. 1879–1890; $1,000–1,300 the set.

Cologne bottle, molded blue-and-white porcelain with applied grape and leaf decoration, fluted base and neck, matching domed top; United States Pottery Company, Bennington, Vermont; 7 inches high; c. 1850–1858; $165–245.

Cologne bottle, molded Parian porcelain with bulbous body and long, tapering neck, embossed basketwork design; United States Pottery Company, Bennington, Vermont; 3.5 inches high; c. 1847–1858; $60–85.

Commemorative plate, molded porcelain with gilded blue border, central transfer print of President William McKinley (1843–1901); Knowles, Taylor & Knowles, East Liverpool, Ohio; 10 inches in diameter; c. 1901–1905; $150–250.

Commemorative creamer, molded porcelain with bulbous paneled body, gilded rim and handle; polychrome transfer print of President William McKinley on one side, American flag on other; New Jersey or Ohio; 5.5 inches high; c. 1897–1901; $125–175.

Commemorative pin tray, molded porcelain with transfer-printed bust of President William Howard Taft, oblong with scalloped rim; Onondaga Pottery Company, Syracuse, New York; 6 inches long; c. 1909–1913; $60–80.

Compote, molded, footed vessel with border decoration of hand-shaped and applied grapes and leaves; United States Pottery Company, Bennington, Vermont; 6.5 inches in diameter; c. 1847–1858; $350–500.

Creamer, molded porcelain, gilded and polychrome-glazed, cylindrical form decorated with embossed rushes, handle in

Creamer, molded porcelain with blue slip decoration, United States Pottery Company, Bennington, Vermont, c. 1849–1858, 3.5 inches high; $70–90.

form of crossed rushes, stamped maker's mark; Willets Manufacturing Company, Trenton, New Jersey; 5 inches high; c. 1885–1895; $400–500.

Creamer, molded Parian porcelain with embossed vine and flower pattern set in panels; Christopher Webber Fenton, Bennington, Vermont; 5 inches high; c. 1847–1848; $400–650.

Cup and saucer, molded artificial or soft paste porcelain, paneled reserves decorated with gilded and polychrome-glazed flowers; Charles Cartlidge & Company, Brooklyn, New York; 4 inches high; c. 1844–1856; $300–450 the set.

Cup and saucer, molded porcelain, cup handle in the form of Liberty, embossed classical figures in white against a blue ground with gilding; Union Porcelain Works, Brooklyn, New York; 4.5 inches high; c. 1876; $700–850.

Cup and saucer, molded Belleek porcelain, ribbed pattern simulating seashells, cup with two handles cast to resemble coral sprigs, stamped maker's mark; Willets Manufacturing Company, Trenton, New Jersey; 2.5 inches high; c. 1890–1905; $200–300.

Cup and saucer, molded porcelain with gilded decoration; United
States Pottery Company, Bennington, Vermont; 3 inches
high; c. 1850–1858; $100–135.

Cup and saucer, molded porcelain, both with scalloped rims and
polychrome-glazed floral decoration, maker's mark; Onondaga Pottery Company, Syracuse, New York; cup, 3.75
inches high; c. 1888–1915; $85–115.

Cup and saucer, molded Belleek porcelain, scalloped rims and
ribbed sides, interiors in pink glaze with gilding, maker's
mark; Ott & Brewer, Trenton, New Jersey; cup, 3 inches
high; c. 1885–1892; $230–330.

Cuspidor, molded porcelain with polychrome-glazed embossed
floral decoration; New England Pottery Company, Boston,
Massachusetts; 7.5 inches in diameter; c. 1885–1895;
$125–200.

Darning egg, molded Parian porcelain, Negroid head breaking
through surface of eggshell; United States Pottery Company, Bennington, Vermont; 2.5 inches long; c. 1847–1858;
$175–250.

Dish, molded and hand-worked Belleek porcelain with basketry
sides and base, rim decorated with molded polychrome-

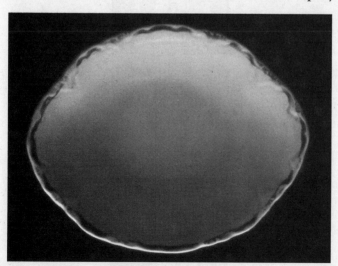

*Dish, oval molded porcelain with gilded rim, New Jersey or Ohio, c. 1870–1900, 6 inches
long; $45–60.*

glazed flowers; Ceramic Art Company, Trenton, New Jersey; 8.5 inches in diameter; c. 1889–1896; $400–600.

Dish, molded artificial or soft paste porcelain with embossed floral patterns hand-decorated in polychrome glazes, printed maker's mark; Lenox, Incorporated, Trenton, New Jersey; 10.2 inches in diameter; c. 1890–1910; $90–130.

Dish, molded heart-shaped Belleek porcelain vessel with scalloped rim; Willets Manufacturing Company, Trenton, New Jersey; 7 inches across; c. 1879–1890; $275–350.

Egg cup, molded Parian porcelain footed vessel with embossed pond lily decoration; United States Pottery Company, Bennington, Vermont; 2 inches high; c. 1847–1858; $125–175.

Ewer, molded vessel with long, tapering neck and scalloped rim, embossed leaf patterns; United States Pottery Company, Bennington, Vermont; 8.5 inches high; c. 1847–1858; $185–265.

Figurine, molded Parian porcelain Greek mythological group based on the tragedy *Oresteia,* impressed maker's marks; by

Figurine, molded classical female figure, New York or New Jersey, c. 1860–1890, 9 inches high; $130–180.

Carl Muller, Union Porcelain Works, Brooklyn, New York; 18.5 inches high; 1877; $14,000–17,000.

Figurine, molded Parian porcelain bust of the Greek goddess Athena; Union Porcelain Works, Brooklyn, New York; 10 inches high; c. 1880–1900; $3,000–4,000.

Figurine, molded robin on branch, porcelain stained in polychrome mat colors, maker's mark; Edward Marshall Boehm, Incorporated, Trenton, New Jersey; 11 inches high; c. 1950–1980; $900–1,300.

Figurine, molded Parian porcelain representation of recumbent spaniel; United States Pottery Company, Bennington, Vermont; 2 inches high; c. 1847–1858; $85–135.

Figurine, molded Parian porcelain recumbent greyhound on plinthlike base; Vermont or New Jersey; 5.5 inches long; c. 1850–1870; $200–300.

Figurine, molded Parian porcelain bust of Washington, impressed maker's mark; New York City Pottery, New York, New York; 20 inches high; 1876; $9,000–14,000.

Figurines, molded Parian porcelain; pair of rustic figures, Vermont or Massachusetts, c. 1850–1880, 10 inches high; $150–225/pair.

Figurine, molded Parian porcelain representation of woman's hand, ruffled base; United States Pottery Company, Bennington, Vermont; 5 inches high; c. 1847–1858; $130–180.

Figurine, molded Parian bust of Lincoln; Ott & Brewer, Trenton, New Jersey; 11 inches high; c. 1871–1892; $5,500–7,000.

Figurine, molded Parian porcelain shepherd dog and pup; Trenton China Company, Trenton, New Jersey; 2.5 inches high; c. 1865–1885; $75–100.

Figurine, molded Parian porcelain recumbent cow on rustic base; United States Pottery Company, Bennington, Vermont; 5 inches long; c. 1847–1858; $200–300.

Figurine, molded Parian porcelain praying child kneeling on pillow; United States Pottery Company, Bennington, Vermont; 6 inches high; c. 1847–1858; $125–175.

Figurine, molded Belleek porcelain representation of the Liberty Bell, blue transfer picture of Independence Hall, patriotic slogan and date 1876, printed maker's mark; Columbian

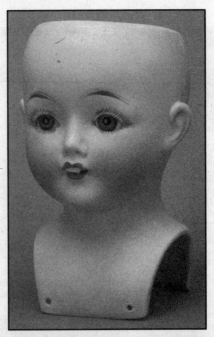

Doll's head, molded, hand-painted bisque porcelain, blown glass eyes; Fulper Pottery Company, Flemington, New Jersey, c. 1915–1925, 4.5 inches high; $125–175.

Paper weight, molded porcelain, Vermont or New Jersey, c. 1850–1880, 4 inches long;
$300–400.

Art Pottery, Trenton, New Jersey; 5 inches high;
c. 1893–1895; $175–275.

Inkwell, molded Parian porcelain in octagonal form with embossed masks decoration and pewter cover; United States
Pottery Company, Bennington, Vermont; 3 inches in diameter; c. 1847–1858; $450–600.

Jar, molded blue-and-white porcelain with embossed acanthus
leaves, turned foot and top embellished with applied fruit;
United States Pottery Company, Bennington, Vermont; 5
inches high; c. 1850–1858; $250–350.
Jar, molded ovoid Parian porcelain with embossed grape and leaf
decoration, matching domed top with applied grapes;
United States Pottery Company, Bennington, Vermont;
4.75 inches high; c. 1847–1858; $200–325.

Loving cup, molded Belleek porcelain with three handles and platinum overlay decoration, stamped maker's mark; Lenox, Incorporated, Trenton, New Jersey; 10 inches high; c. 1896–1905; $300–450.

Miniature pitcher, molded Belleek porcelain with gilded decoration; Ott & Brewer, Trenton, New Jersey; 3 inches high; c. 1885–1895; $150–225.

Miniature vase, molded blue-and-white porcelain with flaring foot and tapering sides, embossed floral pattern; United States Pottery Company, Bennington, Vermont; 2.2 inches high; c. 1850–1858; $80–120.

Miniature creamer, molded Parian porcelain with ovoid body and ear-shaped handle, embossed floral pattern; United States Pottery Company, Bennington, Vermont; 2 inches high; c. 1847–1858; $55–85.

Miniature recumbent sheep, molded Parian porcelain; United States Pottery Company, Bennington, Vermont; 1.2 inches long; c. 1847–1858; $70–95.

Mug, molded tapering cylindrical form, Belleek porcelain with polychrome decoration of fruits and leaves, stamped maker's mark; Willets Manufacturing Company, Trenton, New Jersey; 6 inches high; c. 1890–1909; $275–375.

Mug, molded Parian porcelain vessel with embossed bust of Washington against a blue ground, impressed maker's mark; William Bloor, East Liverpool, Ohio; 5 inches high; c. 1859–1862; $300–400.

Mug, porcelain with embossed representations of drinker and drunk being seized by policeman, handle with eagle head finial; Union Porcelain Works, Brooklyn, New York; 5 inches high; c. 1870–1880; $750–950.

Mug, molded artificial or soft paste porcelain, cylindrical tapering form with embossed polychrome-glazed representation of monk pouring wine into glass, printed maker's mark; Lenox, Incorporated, Trenton, New Jersey; 6 inches high; c. 1900–1910; $350–500.

Mustard pot, molded Parian porcelain with embossed floral decoration and matching bud-shaped top, ear handle; United

Mug, molded porcelain with gilding and blue slip decoration, Vermont or Maryland, c. 1850–1900, 4 inches high; $150–200.

States Pottery Company, Bennington, Vermont; 3 inches high; c. 1847–1858; $200–300.

Perfume vial, artificial or soft paste porcelain with clear glaze, wheel thrown; William Ellis Tucker, Philadelphia, Pennsylvania; 3 inches long; c. 1826–1828; $300–450.

Picture frame, oval molded Belleek porcelain with applied, highly detailed floral pattern; Ott & Brewer, Trenton, New Jersey; 11 inches high; c. 1883–1892; $3,000–3,800.

Pitcher, molded artificial or soft paste porcelain, bulbous body, scalloped rim and large ear-shaped handle, gilded and polychrome-glazed fruit decoration, maker's mark; Tucker & Hulme, Philadelphia, Pennsylvania; 9 inches high; c. 1828–1829; $16,000–22,000.

Pitcher, molded artificial or soft paste porcelain, bulbous body embossed with figure of Bacchus amid grapes and vines, impressed maker's mark; William Boch & Brothers, Brooklyn, New York; 9.5 inches high; c. 1842–1861; $1,500–2,200.

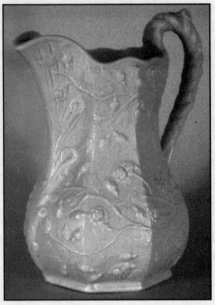

Pitcher, molded porcelain, Baltimore, Maryland, c. 1870–1890, 8.5 inches high; $150–200.

Pitcher, molded porcelain, United States Pottery Company, Bennington, Vermont, c. 1852–1858, 8 inches high; $200–275.

Pitcher, molded Parian porcelain with embossed figures of musicians and revelers, cylindrical form with rustic handle; Bennett Pottery, Baltimore, Maryland; 7.5 inches high; c. 1887–1890; $900–1,400.

Pitcher, molded porcelain with embossed rustic or "Cascade" pattern, handle in form of branch, impressed maker's mark; Christopher Webber Fenton, Bennington, Vermont; 9 inches high; c. 1847–1848; $1,550–1,950.

Pitcher, molded artificial or soft paste porcelain, gilded, embossed representations of cornstalks and ears, handle in form of cornstalk; Charles Cartlidge & Company, Brooklyn, New York; 12 inches high; c. 1844–1856; $2,000–2,750.

Pitcher, molded artificial or soft paste porcelain, embossed polychrome-glazed and gilded leaf decoration with spout in form of flying eagle; Charles Cartlidge & Company, Brooklyn, New York; 13 inches high; c. 1844–1856; $2,500–3,200.

Pitcher, molded Parian porcelain with representations of Cupid

Pitcher, molded porcelain, gilded and slip decorated in magenta, Vermont or New Jersey, c. 1850–1880, 9 inches high; $200–300.

and Psyche; United States Pottery, Bennington, Vermont; 8 inches high; c. 1850–1858; $300–450.

Pitcher, molded porcelain, ovoid form, gilded rim and base, decorated with gold transfer prints of George and Martha Washington; Ott & Brewer, Trenton, New Jersey; 8 inches high; c. 1876; $800–1,200.

Pitcher, molded Parian porcelain, embossed busts of classical figures Homer, Cicero, etc., within garlands, elaborate ear-shaped handle, impressed maker's mark; Union Porcelain Works, Brooklyn, New York; 8 inches high; 1877; $2,200–2,800.

Pitcher, molded porcelain with embossed tulip and sunflower pattern on tan ground, impressed maker's mark; Lyman W. Clark & Company, Boston, Massachusetts; 8 inches high; 1873; $900–1,300.

Pitcher, molded clear glazed porcelain with embossed figures and floral patterns; American Porcelain Manufacturing Com-

Pitchers, molded porcelain glazed in blue: left, *Hanley, England, c. 1840–1860, 9 inches high, $150–250:* right, *United States Pottery Company, Bennington, Vermont, c. 1849–1858, 9.5 inches high, $300–400.*

Pitcher, rare presentation form, molded porcelain, gilded and slip decorated in red and blue, Charles Cartlidge & Company, Greenpoint, New York, c. 1844–1856, 9.5 inches high; $2,500–3,200.

pany, Gloucester, New Jersey; 11 inches high; c. 1854–1860; $1,300–1,800.

Pitcher, molded clear glazed porcelain with transfer busts of George and Martha Washington in gold; Cook Pottery Company, Trenton, New Jersey; 9.5 inches high; c. 1894–1900; $175–250.

Plaque, molded Parian porcelain, embossed bust of woman (Ceres?) holding sickle and sheaf of wheat; Bennett Pottery, Baltimore, Maryland; 8 inches in diameter; c. 1887–1890; $1,200–1,700.

Plate, molded porcelain decorated with polychrome-glazed birds on branches; Union Porcelain Works, Brooklyn, New York; 10 inches in diameter; c. 1890–1910; $75–100.

Plate, molded blue-and-white porcelain with embossed acanthus leaf decoration; United States Pottery Company, Bennington, Vermont; 7.5 inches in diameter; c. 1847–1858; $200–300.

Saucer, molded porcelain, with polychrome transfer decoration, Lenox China Company, Trenton, New Jersey, c. 1910–1930, 5.25 inches in diameter; $30–40.

Platter, molded oval porcelain vessel decorated in blue and gold, scalloped rim, printed maker's mark; Bennett Pottery, Baltimore, Maryland; 10 inches long; c. 1890–1910; $80–100.

Salt shaker, molded egg-shaped and footed Parian porcelain vessel with embossed pond lily decoration; United States Pottery Company, Bennington, Vermont; 3 inches high; c. 1847–1858; $140–190.

Sauce boat, molded artificial or soft paste porcelain, helmet form with flaring base and embossed floral patterns touched in blue; Bonnin and Morris, Philadelphia, Pennsylvania; 7.2 inches long; c. 1769–1772; $18,000–24,000.

Sugar bowl, molded Belleek porcelain with applied lily pads and flowers, cover finial in form of girl's head; Ott & Brewer, Trenton, New Jersey; 5 inches high; c. 1885–1892; $700–900.

Sugar bowl, molded porcelain, bulbous body mounted on four stub feet, decorated in aster pattern, matching top with loop handle; Onondaga Pottery Company, Syracuse, New York; 5.5 inches high; c. 1888–1910; $90–120.

Sugar bowl, molded Belleek porcelain, dragon-form handles, silver overlay on blue ground, maker's stamp; Willets Manufacturing Company, Trenton, New Jersey; 4.5 inches high; c. 1879–1890; $400–550.

Sugar bowl, molded Parian porcelain with vine and flower pattern, rustic handles, matching domed cover; United States Pottery Company, Bennington, Vermont; 4 inches high; c. 1847–1858; $250–350.

Sugar bowl, molded porcelain glazed in blue and gold, matching domed top with Foo Dog handle, stamped maker's mark; Bennett Pottery, Baltimore, Maryland; 6 inches high; c. 1890–1910; $120–170.

Syrup pitcher, molded Parian porcelain with embossed pattern of bird and nest, cast pewter cover; United States Pottery Company, Bennington, Vermont; 6.5 inches high; c. 1853–1858; $350–500.

Teapot, molded Belleek porcelain, gourd form with embossed bamboo shoots, gilded and polychrome-glazed decoration, matching cover; Ott & Brewer, Trenton, New Jersey; 6 inches in diameter; c. 1885–1895; $500–750.

Teapot, molded Parian porcelain Gothic hexagonal-form vessel with matching domed top and gilded banding; United States Pottery Company, Bennington, Vermont; 9.5 inches high; c. 1850–1858; $230–350.

Teapot, molded Belleek porcelain with matching top and embossed platinum-glazed floral decoration, stamped maker's mark; Lenox, Incorporated, Trenton, New Jersey; 5.5 inches high; c. 1900–1920; $125–175.

Toby jug, molded clear-glazed artificial or soft paste porcelain, spouted vessel with embossed man's face and rustic handle, matching cover; Charles Cartlidge & Company, Brooklyn, New York; 6 inches high; c. 1844–1856; $4,000–5,000.

Toddy cup, molded footed vessel with matching domed top and circular handle, gilded banding; United States Pottery

Tea pot, porcelain, Coors Porcelain Company, Coors, Colorado, c. 1910–1914, 8 inches high; $200–275.

Company, Bennington, Vermont; 4 inches high; c. 1850–1858; $275–375.

Tray, molded and hand-shaped Belleek porcelain, oblong with raised scalloped rim, polychrome floral decoration; Willets Manufacturing Company, Trenton, New Jersey; 12 inches long; c. 1879–1890; $230–310.

Trinket box, blue-and-white porcelain molded in the form of a heart with matching top, embossed floral and grape decoration; United States Pottery Company, Bennington, Vermont; 3.5 inches long; c. 1850–1858; $110–160.

Trinket box, molded elongated hexagonal form, blue-and-white porcelain with embossed floral patterns and matching top having applied grapes and leaves; United States Pottery Company, Bennington, Vermont; 5 inches long; c. 1850–1858; $55–85.

Trinket box, molded Parian porcelain, box in form of draped couch, top with representation of reclining woman; United

Trinket or dresser boxes, molded Parian porcelain, United States Pottery Company, Bennington, Vermont, c. 1849–1858: left, *unglazed, 5 inches long, $75–100,* right, *blue slip decorated, 5.5 inches long, $100–135.*

States Pottery Company, Bennington, Vermont; 4.5 inches long; c. 1847–1858; $165–235.

Tureen, molded porcelain with polychrome glaze and gilded floral decoration, oval form with freestanding loop handles and matching domed cover; Onondaga Pottery Company, Syracuse, New York; 9.5 inches long; c. 1888–1910; $125–165.

Umbrella holder, molded porcelain with gilded, embossed floral decoration on a blue ground; Burroughs and Mountford, Trenton, New Jersey; 20 inches high; c. 1880–1890; $250–350.

Vase, turned bulbous porcelain body with long neck and polychrome floral decoration, stamped maker's mark; Greenwood Pottery Company, Trenton, New Jersey; 6.5 inches high; c. 1883–1886; $350–550.

Vase, molded baluster form, porcelain with embossed polychrome-glazed floral sprays, stamped maker's mark; Lenox, Incorporated, Trenton, New Jersey; 9.5 inches high; c. 1930–1950; $150–225.

Vase, molded Parian porcelain in form of hand clutching budding flower; United States Pottery Company, Bennington, Vermont; 6 inches high; c. 1847–1858; $90–130.

Vase, molded Belleek porcelain, bulbous body and long neck with

Vase, molded Parian porcelain decorated in yellow, blue and green slip, Vermont or Massachusetts, c. 1850–1880, 6.5 inches high; $85–135.

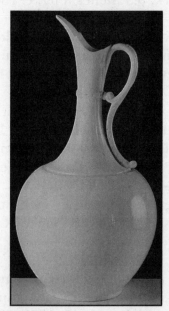

Vase, "Lotus Ware," molded porcelain, Knowles, Taylor & Knowles, East Liverpoool, Ohio, c. 1888–1898, 12 inches high; $1,500–2,100.

polychrome-glazed, applied floral decoration and loop handles, impressed maker's mark; Knowles, Taylor & Knowles, East Liverpool, Ohio; 10 inches high; c. 1880–1889; $450–750.

Vase, Parian porcelain molded in form of ear of corn; United States Pottery Company, Bennington, Vermont; 5 inches high; c. 1847–1858; $75–110.

Vase, molded polychrome-glazed porcelain in the form of a frog grasping base of pitcher plant, impressed maker's mark; Union Porcelain Works, Brooklyn, New York; 6 inches high; c. 1870–1880; $1,700–2,500.

Vase, molded Belleek porcelain in the form of a curving ram's horn, impressed maker's mark; Ott & Brewer, Trenton, New Jersey; 8 inches high; c. 1885–1895; $300–450.

Vase, Belleek porcelain, gilded and polychrome glazed, Ott & Brewer, Trenton, New Jersey, c. 1883–1892, 11 inches high; $2,500–3,200.

Vase, molded Parian porcelain with applied decoration, United States Pottery Company, Bennington, Vermont, c. 1849–1858, 8 inches high; $75–100.

Water cooler, molded porcelain with reeded base and matching top, embossed central floral and geometric patterns, printed maker's mark; Union Porcelain Works, Brooklyn, New York; 18 inches high; 1888; $5,000–7,000.

Whistle, molded Parian porcelain in the form of a carved branch; United States Pottery Company, Bennington, Vermont; 3 inches long; c. 1847–1858; $85–135.

White Earthenware

The term *white earthenware* encompasses a broad area of
ceramics that is distinguished, as the name suggests, by
white or off-white bodies. This ware is made from
naturally occurring clays that are highly plastic, opaque,
and nonvitreous. Closely related is ironstone or
"ironstone china," which, while also a white ware, fires
to an extremely hard, vitrified body. At first glance,
ironstone and some high-fired white earthenware may
resemble porcelain, but, unlike the latter, they are
never translucent.

White earthenware was the first step, both in China
and in Europe, in the development of porcelain, and

327

potters have always striven to produce thinner and whiter bodies that might offer a less expensive substitute for that precious ware. As a consequence, decorative techniques mimic those employed in the field of porcelain. Almost all white wares are cast in molds that often impart an embossed or raised decoration to the body. Some pieces are decorated before being given the typical clear glaze; others, over the glaze after firing. Decoration may be hand-painted, but more often transfer printing is employed. In this technique, a decorative design printed on thin tissue paper is applied to the damp clay body prior to firing. During the firing process the design adheres to the vessel while the paper burns away. Some of the more valuable examples of American white earthenware are those bearing transfer decoration, usually scenes of American history.

White earthenware and ironstone have been used almost exclusively for table and cooking wares. Plates, platters, dishes, bowls, cups and saucers, serving vessels such as casseroles, tea and coffee pots, pitchers, creamers, and sugar bowls will be found in some abundance. Less common are items like figurines, inkwells, foot warmers, and pie plates.

Much of this pottery will bear a manufacturer's mark, usually stamped or printed on the bottom. However, these marks may not always be immediately recognized as American. Due to public preference for similar English wares, many pre-1900 American makers employed cyphers, such as the English lion rampant or a crown along with company initials, rather than fully spelling out a piece's American origin. As a consequence, most collectors employ a ceramics-mark book, such as Kovel's *Dictionary of Marks: Pottery and Porcelain,* to ferret out the domestic products.

American white wares offer a collector's paradise. Even though they were not made in any quantity until the second half of the nineteenth century, they were produced in vast numbers thereafter. As a result, it is not difficult to acquire a substantial and varied collection. Moreover, competition is minimal. With the exception of transfer-printed examples that have historical or political associations, and the very early New Jersey pieces, few people have shown an interest in the area. Even ironstone collectors seem to prefer the English examples. So if you want variety, low prices, and no fakes or restored pieces, this is your field!

WHITE EARTHENWARE PRICES

Bedpan, molded white earthenware; Ohio or Illinois; 13 inches long; c. 1890–1920; $15–20.

Bedpan, molded white earthenware, printed maker's mark; Crown Pottery Company, Evansville, Indiana; 12.5 inches long; c. 1885–1905; $20–30.

Bowl, molded white earthenware with paneled sides, printed maker's mark; Cook Pottery Company, Trenton, New Jersey; 7.5 inches in diameter; c. 1895–1915; $25–35.

Bowl, molded white earthenware with hand-painted floral decoration and scalloped rim, printed maker's mark; Peoria Pottery Company, Peoria, Illinois; 7 inches in diameter; c. 1889–1902; $55–75.

Bowl, molded ironstone with embossed floral pattern, stamped maker's mark; Brockman Pottery Company, Cincinnati, Ohio; 9 inches in diameter; c. 1887–1910; $45–65.

Bread tray, molded ironstone, oval with upturned ends and em-

Bowls, serving, oval molded white ironstone, New Jersey or Ohio, c. 1860–1890, 6 to 8 inches long, $20–30 apiece.

Serving bowls, molded white ironstone, New Jersey or Ohio, c. 1870–1910; Left to right: oval, 9 inches long, $20–30; rectangular, 9.5 inches long, $25–35; round, 9 inches in diameter, $15–25.

Bowls, molded white earthenware with so-called cut-sponge decoration, both by Mayer Pottery Company, Beaver Falls, Pennsylvania, c. 1881–1885; left, oval baker or serving dish, 8 inches long, $200–275; right, saucer, 5 inches in diameter, $100–150.

bossed floral decoration, printed maker's mark; Bloor, Ott & Brewer, Trenton, New Jersey; 10 inches long; c. 1865–1873; $175–235.

Bread tray, molded white earthenware, oblong with handle at each end; Ohio; 11 inches long; c. 1880–1910; $55–75.

Butter dish, molded ironstone, oblong with matching domed top

White ironstone, molded wares, New Jersey or Ohio, c. 1870–1910. Left to right: *oval serving bowl, 8.5 inches long, $20–25; covered butter dish, 5 inches in diameter, $40–55; egg cup, 2.75 inches high, $3–6.*

having acorn finial; Mercer Pottery Company, Trenton, New Jersey; 7 inches long; c. 1880–1900; $45–70.

Butter dish, molded ironstone, oblong with matching domed top having U-shaped lift handle, printed maker's mark; Steubenville Pottery Company, Steubenville, Ohio; 6.75 inches long; c. 1882–1902; $55–75.

Chamber pot, molded ironstone, bulbous body with rustic handle, printed maker's mark; Mayer Pottery Manufacturers Company, Beaver Falls, Pennsylvania; 6 inches high; c. 1890–1910; $35–50.

Chamber pot, molded ironstone, paneled body with embossed Gothic devices, matching cover with flame finial, banding in blue and gold; United States Pottery Company, Bennington, Vermont; 9 inches high; c. 1850–1858; $150–225.

Chamber pot, molded ironstone with matching domed cover; Ohio or Pennsylvania; 8.75 inches high; c. 1880–1910; $55–75.

Chamber stick, molded white earthenware, scalloped tray, candle

White ironstone, molded wares, New Jersey or Ohio, c. 1870–1910. Left to right: *covered child's chamber pot, 7 inches in diameter, $20–30; serving bowl, 11 inches in diameter, $25–35; pitcher, 9 inches high, $30–45.*

Coffeepot, molded white earthenware, Trenton, New Jersey, c. 1870–1900, 9.5 inches high, $60–85.

holder in form of curved pipe, gilded and decorated with gray-and-blue transfer print of "The Maples, Rutland, Vermont," printed maker's mark; Hampshire Pottery, Keene, New Hampshire; 7 inches long; c. 1885–1900; $150–225.
Coffeepot, molded white earthenware with matching domed top and square handle, overall blue glaze decorated freehand

with birds and flowers, printed maker's mark; J.E. Jeffords &
   Company, Philadelphia, Pennsylvania; 10 inches high;
   c. 1870–1890; $125–175.
Coffeepot, molded white earthenware with transfer-printed floral
   pattern and matching top, printed maker's mark; Goodwin
   Brothers, East Liverpool, Ohio; 9 inches high;
   c. 1876–1893; $70–95.
Chocolate cup, molded white earthenware, narrow cylindrical
   body with fluted base and foliated ear handle, impressed
   maker's mark; J.S. Taft & Company, Keene, New Hampshire; 3.5 inches high; c. 1879–1883; $65–90.
Commemorative bread tray, molded ironstone, oval with openwork handles and embossed wording: "GIVE US THIS
   DAY/OUR DAILY BREAD," pink transfer decoration of
   main exhibition building at Philadelphia Centennial,
   printed maker's mark; Trenton Pottery Works, Trenton,
   New Jersey; 12 inches long; 1876; $165–235.

*Commemorative ware, 1876 Centennial, molded white ironstone with black transfer deco-
ration, Onondaga Pottery Company, Syracuse, New York, 1876: cup and saucer, 3.5
inches high, $120–160; pitcher, 14 inches high, $300–450.*

Commemorative cup and saucer, molded ironstone with polychrome-glazed banding and facsimile signature of George Washington with dates 1774–1874, printed maker's mark; Glasgow Pottery, Trenton, New Jersey; cup, 2 inches high; c. 1874; $115–145.

Commemorative mug, molded white earthenware with gilded borders and gray transfer print of President Theodore Roosevelt; New Jersey or Ohio; 6 inches high; c. 1901–1909; $135–185.

Commemorative plate, molded white earthenware, scalloped border and blue transfer print of log cabin and three busts of President William Henry Harrison; New Jersey or Maryland; 10 inches in diameter; c. 1840–1842; $300–450.

Commemorative plate, molded white earthenware with black transfer print of Presidents Garfield and Arthur; New Jersey; 10 inches in diameter; c. 1880; $125–175.

Commemorative plate, molded white earthenware with black transfer print of President Benjamin Harrison; New Jersey; 9.5 inches in diameter; c. 1888; $80–130.

Plate, molded white earthenware with green transfer decoration commemorating launching of yacht, Onondaga Pottery Company, Syracuse, New York, 1902, 10 inches in diameter, $150–200.

Commemorative plate, molded white earthenware with black transfer print of assassinated President William McKinley and printed information on his life and death; New Jersey; 9 inches in diameter; c. 1901; $70–95.

Commemorative plate, molded white earthenware decorated with transfer print of Wanamaker store in Philadelphia, printed maker's mark; Buffalo Pottery, Buffalo, New York; 5 inches in diameter; 1911; $65–85.

Commemorative platter, molded white earthenware with polychrome transfer print of White House surrounded by busts of ten Presidents set in reserves; Ohio; 11 inches long; c. 1909–1910; $450–650.

Commemorative platter, molded white earthenware decorated with blue transfer print of Cumberland Gap, Virginia, and illustrations of famous locomotives, issued at 100th anniversary of Baltimore & Ohio Railroad, printed maker's mark; Lamberton Works, Trenton, New Jersey; 10 inches long; c. 1927–1943; $125–165.

Compote, molded white earthenware with blue transfer-decorated floral patterns, shallow footed bowl, printed maker's mark;

Compote (rare), molded white ironstone, Coxon & Company, Trenton, New Jersey, c. 1865–1880, 11 inches in diameter, $60–80.

Maddock Pottery Company, Trenton, New Jersey; 9.5 inches high; c. 1893–1910; $65–85.

Cow creamer, molded ironstone in form of standing cow with tail curled over back and mounted on oblong base; United States Pottery Company, Bennington, Vermont; 7 inches long; c. 1850–1858; $450–700.

Cow creamer, molded white earthenware with gray marbleized glaze; L.B. Beerbower & Company, Elizabeth, New Jersey; 7 inches long; c. 1880–1885; $300–450.

Cracker jar, molded white earthenware, bulbous jar with fluted base, matching top, and two freestanding handles, hand-painted floral decoration; New England Pottery Company, Boston, Massachusetts; 10 inches high; c. 1886–1895; $180–270.

Creamer, molded white earthenware with mat orange glaze, impressed maker's mark; Greenwood Pottery Company, Trenton, New Jersey; 4 inches high; c. 1868–1886; $40–60.

Creamer, molded white earthenware with commemorative transfer print decoration of Admiral Dewey, Cook Pottery Company, Trenton, New Jersey, c. 1895–1900, 4.5 inches high, $80–110.

Creamer, molded white earthenware glazed in blue and gold, printed maker's mark; Wheeling Pottery Company, Wheeling, West Virginia; 3.7 inches high; c. 1887–1905; $55–75.

Creamer, molded white earthenware with blue transfer-printed Oriental scene, "Blue Willow" type; Pennsylvania or Ohio; 3.6 inches high; c. 1900–1920; $25–35.

Cup and saucer, molded ironstone decorated with ocher transfer print of Independence Hall at the Philadelphia Centennial, printed maker's mark; American Crockery Company, Trenton, New Jersey; saucer, 6 inches in diameter; 1876; $90–130 the pair.

Cup and saucer, molded ironstone, printed maker's mark; Chittenango Pottery Company, Chittenango, New York; cup, 2.5 inches high; c. 1897–1903; $20–30 the pair.

Figurine, molded white earthenware slipper with square toe and low heel; New Jersey; 5.5 inches long; c. 1880–1890; $45–75.

Cup, molded white earthenware with blue transfer decoration in the Chinese manner, Midwestern, c. 1900–1930, 3 inches high, $5–8.

Footbath, molded oval ironstone vessel with flaring rim and free-standing handle at each end, decorated with banding and scrollwork in blue and gold; United States Pottery Company, Bennington, Vermont; 16 inches long; c. 1850–1858; $200–300.

Fruit basket, molded and hand-worked ironstone, open lattice-work pattern with scalloped rim and octagonal base resting on four stub feet; United States Pottery Company, Bennington, Vermont; 8.5 inches in diameter; c. 1850–1858; $300–450.

Gravy boat, molded ironstone, helmet form with large ear handle, printed maker's mark; Cook Pottery Company, Trenton, New Jersey; 9 inches long; c. 1895–1915; $30–40.

Gravy boat, molded ironstone, helmet form, printed maker's mark; Chittenango Pottery Company, Chittenango, New York; 8.5 inches long; c. 1897–1902; $20–30.

Inkwell, molded ironstone in form of phrenological head, inkwell in square base, decorated in blue-and-black glaze; United States Pottery Company, Bennington, Vermont; 5.5 inches high; c. 1850–1858; $1,000–1,500.

Gravy boat, molded white ironstone with blue Masonic transfer decoration, Sterling Pottery Company, East Liverpool, Ohio, c. 1900–1920, 9 inches long, $20–30.

Juicer, molded ironstone, two-part with fluted top and octagonal base, printed maker's mark; Thomas Maddock's Sons, Trenton, New Jersey; 4.5 inches high; c. 1905–1925; $45–65.

Miniature or child's tea set, molded ironstone teapot, creamer, sugar bowl, six cups and saucers, and six cake plates, printed maker's mark; Ott & Brewer, Trenton, New Jersey; teapot, 5.5 inches high; c. 1870–1890; $200–300 the set.

Miniature or toy saucer, molded white earthenware with brown transfer design of children and animals, printed maker's mark; New Jersey Pottery Company, Trenton, New Jersey; 3 inches in diameter; c. 1870–1880; $15–20.

Mortar and pestle, ironstone, pestle with turned wooden handle; United States Pottery Company, Bennington, Vermont; mortar, 7 inches in diameter; c. 1850–1858; $100–140.

Mug, molded cylindrical white earthenware vessel decorated with polychrome transfer print of monk, printed maker's mark;

Mug, molded white ironstone, New Jersey or Ohio, c. 1860–1880, 4 inches high, $20–30.

New Jersey or Ohio; 3.5 inches high; c. 1893–1905; $80–110.

Mug, molded cylindrical ironstone decorated with band of green glaze at rim, printed maker's mark; Shenango Pottery Company, New Castle, Pennsylvania; 3.3 inches high; c. 1900–1930; $5–8.

Paperweight, molded ironstone in form of recumbent poodle on rectangular base; United States Pottery Company, Bennington, Vermont; 4 inches long; c. 1850–1858; $165–245.

Pie plate, molded white earthenware, printed maker's mark; L.B. Beerbower & Company, Elizabeth, New Jersey; 12 inches in diameter; c. 1880–1900; $55–80.

Pie plate, molded ironstone; Midwestern; 10.5 inches in diameter; c. 1890–1920; $30–45.

Pitcher, molded ironstone with bulbous body decorated with embossed figures of King Gambrinus and Uncle Sam, im-

White ironstone, molded wares, New Jersey or Ohio, c. 1870–1910. Left to right: *mortar and pestle, Carr China Company, Grafton, West Virginia, c. 1900–1920, 4 inches high, $15–20; pie plate, Massachusetts, c. 1880–1910, 11 inches in diameter, $20–30; mixing bowl, Anchor Pottery, Trenton, New Jersey, c. 1890–1900, 10 inches in diameter, $25–35.*

Pie plate, molded white ironstone, Crescent Pottery Company, Trenton, New Jersey, c. 1881–1902, 10 inches in diameter, $30–45.

Pitcher, molded white ironstone, Cook Pottery Company, Trenton, New Jersey, c. 1894–1910, 8 inches high, $45–65.

pressed maker's mark; Greenwood Pottery Company, Trenton, New Jersey; 9 inches high; c. 1868–1886; $800–1,200.

Pitcher, molded white earthenware with broad base and narrow upper body, gilded handle and gray transfer-printed decoration of "The Maples, Rutland, Vermont"; Hampshire Pottery, Keene, New Hampshire; 5.5 inches high; c. 1885–1900; $55–75.

Pitcher, molded white earthenware with embossed representation of the death of Colonel E.E. Ellsworth at Alexandria, Virginia, in 1861; Millington, Astbury & Poulson, Trenton, New Jersey; 8.5 inches high; c. 1861–1865; $800–1,200.

Pitcher, molded ironstone decorated with gold transfer prints of Memorial Hall and Horticultural Hall at the Philadelphia Centennial, Ott & Brewer, Trenton, New Jersey; 8 inches high; 1876; $250–400.

Pitcher, molded ironstone with bulbous body and braced ear handle, gilding and polychrome-glazed floral decoration surround owner's name in script within reserve; United States Pottery Company, Bennington, Vermont; 10 inches high; c. 1850–1858; $250–350.

Pitcher, molded white earthenware with beer foam strainer in spout, gilded and glazed in pink and white (so-called

Pitchers, molded white ironstone, New Jersey or Ohio, c. 1860–1920, 4 to 9 inches high; $25–55 each.

White ironstone, molded wares, New Jersey or Ohio, c. 1870–1910. Left to right, *egg cup, 3 inches high, $4–7; pitcher, 9.5 inches high, $35–50; plate, 10 inches in diameter, $3–7.*

Pitcher, molded white earthenware with gilded decoration, New York, c. 1870–1900, 8 inches high, $60–75.

"Sweetheart" pitcher); Peoria Pottery, Peoria, Illinois; 10.5 inches high; c. 1889–1902; $225–325.

Plate, molded white earthenware with scalloped border, blue transfer print of classical scene (Canova pattern), printed maker's mark; American Pottery Company, Jersey City, New Jersey; 9 inches in diameter; c. 1835–1845; $275–350.

Plates (tourist souvenirs), molded white earthenware with polychrome painted decoration, Midwestern, c. 1930–1950, 5 to 7.5 inches in diameter, $5–15 apiece.

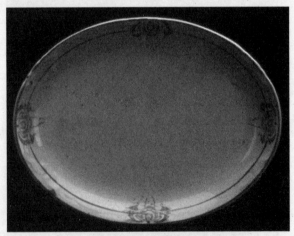

Bone plate, molded white earthenware with blue transfer decoration in the Aesthetic Movement style, East End Pottery, East Liverpool, Ohio, c. 1880–1900, 7.5 inches long, $10–15.

Plate, molded white earthenware with blue transfer-printed
Chinese scene, so-called "Blue Willow" pattern, printed
maker's mark; Buffalo Pottery, Buffalo, New York; 10 inches
in diameter; c. 1901–1914; $45–60.

Plate, molded ironstone, printed maker's mark; Akron China

Plate, molded white ironstone, Ohio or New Jersey, c. 1870–1910, 9.5 inches in diameter,
$5–10.

Plate, molded, polychrome painted white earthenware, the Roycrafters, East Aurora, New
York, c. 1920–1930, 10 inches in diameter, $150–200.

Company, Akron, Ohio; 10 inches in diameter;
c. 1895–1905; $15–25.

Plate, molded ironstone decorated with polychrome-glazed floral
pattern, printed maker's mark; Cook & Hancock, Trenton,
New Jersey; 10 inches in diameter; c. 1881–1902; $20–25.

Plate, molded white earthenware with blue banded rim, impressed
maker's mark; American Pottery Company, Jersey City, New
Jersey; 9.5 inches in diameter; c. 1840–1845; $225–275.

*Plate, molded octagonal white earthenware with polychrome transfer decoration, New York
or New Jersey, c. 1880–1910, 8.5 inches across, $5–10.*

*Plates, molded white ironstone, New Jersey or Ohio, c. 1870–1910, 6 to 8.5 inches in
diameter, $5–10 apiece.*

Plate, molded white earthenware, embossed floral pattern, printed maker's mark; New Milford Pottery Company, New Milford, Connecticut; 9.5 inches in diameter; c. 1896–1900; $20–30.

Platter, molded white earthenware with scalloped rim and hand-painted floral decoration, printed maker's mark; Peoria Pottery, Peoria, Illinois; 12 inches long; c. 1889–1902; $65–85.

Platter, molded ironstone, oval with scalloped rim, hand-painted scene of woman in interior, printed maker's mark; Glasgow Pottery, Trenton, New Jersey; 10 inches long; c. 1895–1910; $200–300.

Platter, molded white earthenware, printed maker's mark; George S. Harker & Company, East Liverpool, Ohio; 12 inches long; c. 1880–1905; $25–35.

Powder box, molded white earthenware, round with inset neck and disklike top, decorated with brown transfer print of the Vermont State Capitol building, Hampshire Pottery, Keene, New Hampshire; 3.3 inches in diameter; c. 1885–1900; $80–110.

Platters, molded white ironstone, New Jersey or Ohio, c. 1870–1910, 9 to 12 inches long: top, $35–45; bottom, $45–60.

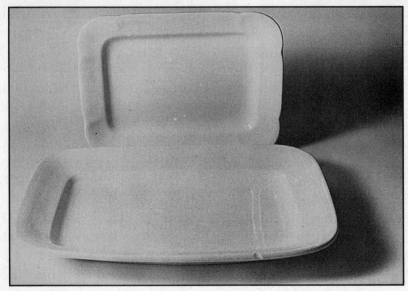

Platters, molded white ironstone, New Jersey or Ohio, c. 1870–1910; 8 to 11 inches long, $15–30 apiece.

Platter, molded white ironstone, New Jersey or Ohio, c. 1870–1910, 11 inches long, $20–35.

Platter, octagonal, blue transfer decorated white earthenware, scene of Pickett's charge at Gettysburg, Bennett Pottery, Baltimore, Maryland, c. 1870–1880, 14 inches long, $500–750.

Rose bowl, molded bulbous form with scalloped rim, white earthenware decorated with brown transfer print of the Vermont State Capitol, stamped maker's mark; Hampshire Pottery, Keene, New Hampshire; 3 inches high; c. 1885–1905; $70–95.

Serving dish, molded ironstone, oval with flaring lip; Tempest, Brockman & Company, Cincinnati, Ohio; 8.5 inches long; c. 1870–1880; $60–80.

Serving dish, molded white earthenware, oval, printed maker's mark; Vodrey Pottery Company, East Liverpool, Ohio; 10 inches long; c. 1896–1910; $35–45.

Serving dish, molded ironstone, oblong with flaring lip, printed maker's mark; Maryland Pottery Company, Baltimore, Maryland; 10 inches long; c. 1888–1905; $40–60.

Shaving mug, molded white earthenware with removable soap tray, gilded and decorated with gray-and-blue transfer print of "Soldiers' Monument, Brattleboro, Vermont," printed maker's mark; Hampshire Pottery, Keene, New Hampshire; 3.8 inches high; c. 1885–1890; $150–200.

Molded white earthenware glazed in a pale yellow, "Luray Pastels," Midwestern, c. 1930–1940. Left to right: desert bowl, 4.5 inches in diameter, $4–7; platter, 12 inches long, $20–25; cup and saucer, 3.5 inches high, $12–18/set.

White ironstone, molded wares, New Jersey or Ohio, c. 1870–1910. Left to right: oval covered serving dish, 10 inches long, $35–45; salad plate, 6 inches in diameter, $4–7; creamer, 5 inches high, $15–20.

Shaving mugs, molded white earthenware with gilding and polychrome transfer decoration, New Jersey or Ohio, c. 1870–1910. Left to right: barber tools, 5 inches high, $200–250; dog with bird, 4 inches high, $125–175; embossed "My Husband", 4 inches high, $60–85.

Shaving mug, molded ironstone with paneled sides, rustic handle, and gilding including owner's name; United States Pottery Company, Bennington, Vermont; 3.75 inches high; c. 1850–1858; $110–160.

Shaving mug, molded ironstone decorated with black transfer print of mounted horsemen, printed maker's mark; Ott & Brewer, Trenton, New Jersey; 3.5 inches high; c. 1871–1893; $75–95.

Slop jar, molded ironstone with paneled sides, bulbous base, and flaring rim, freestanding handles and matching domed top, decorated in blue-and-gold banding and scrollwork; United States Pottery Company, Bennington, Vermont; 17 inches high; c. 1850–1858; $400–600.

Slop jar, molded white earthenware with two freestanding handles and matching domed top, overall transfer decoration in the Moorish manner with busts of women set in reserves, printed maker's mark; Chesapeake Pottery, Baltimore, Maryland; 14 inches high; c. 1880–1910; $225–325.

Slop jar, molded white earthenware with embossed floral pattern and matching domed top, printed maker's mark; Wellsville China Company, Wellsville, Ohio; 15 inches high; c. 1880–1910; $60–85.

Soap dish, molded oblong ironstone open box with scalloped demilune backsplash having two holes for hanging on wall, printed maker's mark; Thomas Maddock's Sons, Trenton, New Jersey; 5.5 inches long; c. 1905–1925; $50–75.

Soap dish, molded oval bowl-shaped ironstone vessel with domed top and removable perforated soap tray, gilded decoration; United States Pottery Company, Bennington, Vermont; 5 inches long; c. 1850–1858; $90–130.

Soap dish, molded oblong ironstone vessel, ridged top with drain holes, printed maker's mark; Edwin M. Knowles China Company, East Liverpool, Ohio; 6 inches long; c. 1901–1910; $55–70.

Soup plate, molded white earthenware with hand-painted floral decoration, printed maker's mark; Peoria Pottery, Peoria, Illinois; 8 inches in diameter; c. 1889–1902; $35–45.

Soup plate, molded white earthenware, printed maker's mark; Homer Laughlin China Company, East Liverpool, Ohio; 9 inches in diameter; c. 1897–1920; $20–30.

Soup bowl, molded white ironstone, Greenwood Pottery Company, Trenton, New Jersey, c. 1886–1910, 8.5 inches in diameter, $5–10.

Soup plate, molded ironstone, printed maker's mark; Bennett Pottery, Baltimore, Maryland; 9 inches in diameter; c. 1885–1915; $30–40.

Sugar bowl, molded white earthenware in bulbous form with two freestanding handles and matching domed top, blue glazed, printed maker's mark; New England Pottery Company, Boston, Massachusetts; 4.3 inches high; c. 1886–1888; $80–110.

Sugar bowl, molded ironstone, bulbous body, freestanding handles and matching domed top, printed maker's mark; Cartwright Brothers, East Liverpool, Ohio; 5 inches high; c. 1890–1910; $45–65.

Sugar bowl, molded ironstone with bulbous body and matching domed top, printed maker's mark; Wheeling Pottery Company, Wheeling, West Virginia; 4.75 inches high; c. 1880–1910; $40–60.

Teapot, molded square white earthenware body with matching top, decorated with dark gray transfer print of "Dead Creek Bridge, Vergennes, Vermont," impressed maker's mark; Hampshire Pottery, Keene, New Hampshire; 5.8 inches high; c. 1885–1900; $125–175.

Teapot, molded white earthenware, bulbous form decorated with embossed classic bust in leafy reserve, matching domed cover; Swan Hill Pottery, South Amboy, New Jersey; 6.5 inches high; c. 1880–1900; $135–200.

Teapot, molded ironstone, bulbous form with matching domed top and printed maker's mark; Warwick China Company, Wheeling, West Virginia; 5 inches high; c. 1887–1915; $35–50.

Tea set, molded white earthenware teapot, creamer, and sugar bowl, all with bulbous bodies and delicate ear handles, impressed maker's mark; Hampshire Pottery, Keene, New Hampshire; tea pot, 5.5 inches high; c. 1880–1890; $250–325 the set.

Toothbrush holder, cylindrical molded white earthenware vessel decorated with red transfer-printed floral decoration,

Tea pot, molded white earthenware with transfer printed decoration in red and green and tin "make do" handle, Ohio, c. 1860–1880, 7 inches high, $70–90.

printed maker's mark; Maddock Pottery Company, Trenton, New Jersey; 5 inches high; c. 1895–1915; $35–50.

Tumbler, molded white earthenware, cylindrical, decorated with brown transfer view of Hot Springs, South Dakota, interior, impressed maker's mark; J.S. Taft & Company, Keene, New Hampshire; 4.25 inches high; c. 1878–1883; $100–130.

Tureen, molded ironstone, round footed vessel with two freestanding handles and matching domed top, printed maker's mark; Mercer Pottery Company, Trenton, New Jersey; 8 inches in diameter; c. 1870–1890; $65–85.

Tureen, molded ironstone, oval footed vessel with two freestanding handles and matching domed top, printed maker's mark; Crown Pottery Company, Evansville, Indiana; 9.5 inches long; c. 1891–1910; $80–120.

Vase, molded bulbous white earthenware vessel with two freestanding handles, hand-painted scene of church in winter,

Milk pan, molded white earthenware, New Jersey or Maryland, c. 1860–1890, 14 inches in diameter, $65–85.

printed maker's mark; City Pottery Company, Trenton, New Jersey; 9 inches high; c. 1860–1880; $200–325.

Vase, molded ironstone china with bulbous base and flaring rim, printed maker's mark; City Pottery, New York, New York; 9.5 inches high; c. 1875–1888; $100–150.

Vase, molded baluster-form white earthenware vessel with hand-painted floral decoration, printed maker's mark; New England Pottery Company, Boston, Massachusetts; 11 inches high; c. 1886–1895; $165–255.

Vase, molded white earthenware, bulbous body with serrated rim, hand-painted, gilded polychrome decoration, printed maker's mark; Steubenville Pottery Company, Steubenville, Ohio; 7 inches high; c. 1890–1900; $200–300.

Washbowl and pitcher set, molded ironstone with gilded rims and bases, owner's name in gold; United States Pottery Company, Bennington, Vermont; pitcher, 11 inches high; c. 1850–1858; $300–450.

Washbowl and pitcher set, molded ironstone china, printed maker's mark; Shenango Pottery Company, New Castle, Pennsylvania; pitcher, 11.5 inches high; c. 1900–1920; $60–85.

Rolling pin, molded white earthenware with blue slip decoration, Midwestern, c. 1900–1930, 11 inches long, $110–140.

Egg cup, molded white earthenware, New Jersey, c. 1910–1940, 3 inches high, $4–7.

Washstand set, molded white earthenware with polychrome-glazed floral decoration, nine-piece set including pitcher and washbowl, hair receiver, toothbrush box, mug, slop jar, etc., printed maker's marks; Burroughs and Mountford, Trenton, New Jersey; pitcher, 11 inches high; c. 1879–1895; $450–600 the set.

Whistle, molded white earthenware in form of bird, impressed maker's mark; William H. Young, Trenton, New Jersey; 2.6 inches long; c. 1853–1857; $700–900.

Egg cup, Fiesta Ware, molded white earthenware with an ivory glaze, Homer Laughlin pottery, Newell, West Virginia, c. 1936–1958, 3.25 inches high, $10–15.

SCRODDLED WARE

Perhaps the least known of all American ceramic
products is scroddled or agate ware, a body produced
by mixing together several clays which would fire to
different hues, resulting in a variegated body. Most
commonly seen are combinations of white, brown, blue,
and gray, though sometimes pink and black are found.
The lighter color, usually white or gray, forms the
background through which run seams of a darker
brown or black, just as in marble, which the ware is
designed to imitate. Wheel-thrown or cast, the final
product was either left unglazed or given a clear glaze
composed of ground flint and feldspar.

Scroddled ware was developed in England, and the earliest as well as the most prolific nineteenth-century American manufacturer was the United States Pottery Company in Bennington, Vermont. Indeed, nearly all marked or otherwise identifiable examples from this era can be traced to this factory.

In the early twentieth century, several other firms produced similar wares, most notably the Niloak Pottery Company of Benton, Arkansas (c. 1909–1946). Whereas United States Pottery had turned out pitchers, cuspidors, and toilet sets, Niloak produced a wide variety of ware including vases, mugs, flower pots, candlesticks, match holders, and umbrella stands.

Scroddled ware should be distinguished from similar-looking pottery that is merely given a coat of marbleized varicolored slip. In the former, the colors pass completely through the piece. In the latter, they are simply a finish for a uniformly colored ceramic body. Marbleized wares have been made throughout Europe and in England and frequently are seen at antiques shows. American nineteenth-century scroddled ware, on the other hand, is quite rare and may often be overlooked by dealers and collectors familiar with the common and readily available Niloak products.

Other than confusion with marbleized bodies, scroddled ware presents few problems for collectors. There are no known fakes or period reproductions. While early scroddled examples, particularly if marked, can command high prices, Niloak products are quite inexpensive.

SCRODDLED WARE PRICES

Bottle, wheel-thrown, elongated ovoid, blue, brown, and white, impressed maker's mark; Niloak Pottery Company, Benton, Arkansas; 10.5 inches high; c. 1909–1946; $70–95.

Bowl, wheel-thrown, blue, brown, red, and white; Niloak Pottery Company, Benton, Arkansas; 10 inches in diameter; c. 1909–1946; $80–120.

Cuspidor, molded diamond pattern in brown and white; United States Pottery Company, Bennington, Vermont; 8.5 inches in diameter; c. 1853–1858; $650–900.

Cuspidor, molded shallow vessel bordered with seashell forms, brown and white; United States Pottery Company, Bennington, Vermont; 8 inches in diameter; c. 1853–1858; $500–700.

Figurine, molded sitting poodle, gray and white; Dalton, Ohio; 8 inches high; c. 1860–1890; $700–800.

Figurine, molded bottle in the form of a woman's high-button shoe, gray, black, and white; Ohio; 7 inches high; c. 1860–1880; $250–350.

Figurine, molded creamer in form of standing cow, brown and white; United States Pottery Company, Bennington, Vermont; 6.5 inches long; c. 1853–1858; $2,000–2,800.

Flask, molded in form of book, impressed maker's mark, gray and pink; United States Pottery Company, Bennington, Vermont; 10.5 inches high; c. 1853–1858; $2,500–3,200.

Jardiniere, molded in the form of a large cup with pedestal base and scalloped rim, black, brown, and white; Ohio; 12 inches high; c. 1870–1890; $300–450.

Mug, wheel-thrown, slightly ovoid vessel with ear handle, brown, blue, and cream; Niloak Pottery Company, Benton, Arkansas; 6 inches high; c. 1909–1946; $65–80.

Pitcher, molded with embossed diamond pattern on semi-ovoid body, ear handle, brown and white; United States Pottery Company, Bennington, Vermont; 5 inches high; c. 1853–1858; $300–400.

Pitcher, molded squat rustic shape with foliate handle, impressed maker's mark, brown and white; United States Pottery Company, Bennington, Vermont; 8.5 inches high; c. 1853–1858; $700–950.

Pitcher and bowl set, molded scroddleware, United States Pottery Company, Bennington, Vermont, c. 1849–1858, 12 inches high; $2,000–3,000.

Pitcher, wheel-thrown ovoid vessel with ear handle, red, blue, brown, and white, impressed maker's mark; Niloak Pottery Company, Benton, Arkansas; 9.5 inches high; c. 1909–1946; $90–120.

Pitcher and bowl set, molded, twelve-sided bowl, pitcher in diamond pattern with ringed neck and foliate handle, reddish brown and gray; United States Pottery Company, Bennington, Vermont; pitcher, 11 inches high; bowl, 13.5 inches in diameter, c. 1853–1858; $2,000–3,000 the set.

Planter, rounded wheel-thrown body, pink, blue, gray, and white, impressed maker's mark; Niloak Pottery Company, Benton, Arkansas; 8 inches in diameter; c. 1909–1946; $45–60.

Slop jar, molded ovoid body in diamond pattern with large scroll handles, matching domed cover, embossed maker's mark, brown and white; United States Pottery Company, Bennington, Vermont; 12.5 inches high; c. 1853–1858; $1,200–1,800.

Teapot, molded cylindrical reeded body with Gothic handle and dome-shaped cover with large U-shaped lift, gray and white; Ohio; 9.5 inches high; c. 1870–1890; $550–750.

Toby pitcher, molded in form of sitting man holding bottle and pitcher, brown and white; United States Pottery Company, Bennington, Vermont; 6.5 inches high; c. 1853–1858; $2,800–3,500.

Umbrella stand, wheel-thrown tubular vessel with flaring foot, brown, blue, and cream, impressed maker's mark; Niloak Pottery Company, Benton, Arkansas; 18 inches high; c. 1909–1946; $150–200.

Vase, molded octagonal tulip form with pedestal base and scalloped rim, brown, gray, and white; United States Pottery

Vase, scroddleware, Niloak Pottery Company, Benton, Arkansas, c. 1910–1940, 8 inches high; $35–50.

Company, Bennington, Vermont; 10 inches high; c. 1853–1858; $1,600–2,200.

Vase, wheel-thrown semi-ovoid vessel with flaring rim, brown, white, and blue, paper label with maker's name; Niloak Pottery Company, Benton, Arkansas; 5.5 inches high; c. 1909–1946; $30–45.

Vase, wheel-thrown tubular vessel with flaring foot, red, blue, and cream, impressed maker's mark; Niloak Pottery Company, Benton, Arkansas; 9 inches high; c. 1909–1946; $60–85.

SEWER TILE WARE

The term *sewer tile ware* has been coined by collectors to describe a variety of interesting pieces made from the same ceramic body used in the manufacture of common drain or sewer tiling. Both redware and stoneware clays have been employed in tile manufacture, and a piece of sewer tile ware may be composed of either. The finish is usually a plain salt glaze or a shiny brown iron-bearing glaze.

Unlike other American ceramics, sewer tile ware does not have a long history. In the late nineteenth century, as the great stoneware manufactories of the Northeast and Midwest gradually went out of business,

365

many potters found work at shops making sewer pipes for the expanding cities and drain tile for farmers' fields.

This was tedious work. Everything was cast in molds, and there was little opportunity for self-expression. Some of the former potters, however, found an outlet for their creativity in the making of figurines and useful objects such as pitchers, vases, humidors, and umbrella stands from the clay and glazing materials they had at hand, much as glassblowers produced their "end-of-the-day" wares.

Many of these pieces were cast in molds based on Staffordshire animal figures or even pieces of pressed glass, and frequently reflected the use of popular Victorian decorative devices, such as scratching or "combing" the surface to make it resemble a tree trunk.

Considering the relatively brief period of this work (c. 1880–1950), it is remarkably varied. Some examples are entirely hand-modeled. Others, as mentioned, are cast in molds or reflect a combination of molding and modeling. Relatively few, however, show signs of being thrown on a wheel. Befitting their personal nature, many pieces of sewer tile bear the names or initials of their makers as well as dates. There are also a few stamped with the marks of the tile factories where they were produced, though it seems unlikely that even these were made for sale. Unlike all other American ceramics, sewer tile ware was not a commercial product. It was made for pleasure or as a gift.

The great bulk of this ware was produced in a few states, with Ohio, New York, and Pennsylvania being the primary sources; and outside this area, it is rarely encountered or recognized. In part, this is due to the fact that, as yet, only a few collectors and dealers have begun to focus on the field. Some do not find the colors or the sometimes crude appearance appealing. More simply do not recognize the ware for what it is—true ceramic folk art and the last expression of the utilitarian American potters' craft.

Yet sewer tile ware offers several advantages to the collector. Examples are often one of a kind, something that can seldom be said of other American ceramics. Moreover, even these unique examples are reasonably priced, with few pieces in this field bringing more than $500, and most substantially less. Also, since demand is limited, there is at present no danger of reproductions or fakes. Even restored pieces are uncommon.

Ashtray, molded in form of fireplace with chimney and base, all incised to resemble bricks, signed and dated salt-glazed redware; Midwestern; 8 inches long; 1946; $85–135.

Ashtray, modeled circular form to accommodate two pipes, signed and dated salt-glazed redware; Midwestern; 4 inches in diameter; 1944; $50–75.

Ashtray, circular molded form with three cigarette rests and embossed manufacturer's mark, stoneware with a tan glaze; by Cannelton (Indiana) Sewer Pipe Company; 6 inches in diameter; c. 1930–1950; $65–85.

Ash tray, hand-formed sewer tile ware in form of owl, Ohio or Pennsylvania, c. 1900–1930, 6 inches high; $125–175.

Bank, round dome-topped vessel with coin slot and embossed owner's name, molded salt-glazed brown stoneware; Ohio; 4 inches in diameter; c. 1890–1910; $150–200.

Bank, modeled in form of cowbell, incised name and date, salt-glazed redware; Ohio; 7.8 inches high; 1920; $175–250.

Bank, molded in the form of an apple, incised owner's name, salt-glazed redware; Ohio; 4.5 inches high; c. 1900–1910; $165–235.

Bank, modeled in the form of an apple with pinprick name and date, reddish-brown glazed stoneware; Ohio; 4 inches in diameter; 1907; $180–230.

Bank, modeled in the form of a sitting pig, salt-glazed redware; Midwestern; 10 inches high; c. 1910–1940; $85–135.

Baseball, miniature replica in salt-glazed yellow clay; Midwestern; 2.5 inches in diameter; c. 1900–1920; $110–150.

Birdhouse, square slab constructed with peaked roof and two circular entrances, salt-glazed redware; Midwestern; 11 inches high; c. 1920–1940; $75–100.

Birdhouse, circular modeled form with domed top and combed surface, single circular entrance with perch; Ohio; 7 inches high; c. 1910–1930; $90–130.

Birdhouse, unusual gourd shape, modeled with single circular entrance and combed surface; Midwestern; 5 inches high; c. 1900–1920; $80–110.

Bookends, molded in the form of roosting owls, salt-glazed redware with name and date; Ohio; 5.5 inches high; 1929; $250–325.

Brick, miniature, cast with figure of buffalo and embossed reference to church donation, unglazed redware; Buffalo, Kansas; 3 × 1.75 inches; c. 1890–1910; $175–250.

Brick, miniature, cast with embossed figure of beaver and advertising logo; Beaver Clay Manufacturing Company, New Galilee, Pennsylvania; 3.2 × 1.6 inches; c. 1890–1920; $145–185.

Bucket, made from a section of cast sewer pipe, cylindrical with iron wire handle, greenish salt-glazed stoneware; Bexar County, Texas; 10 inches high; c. 1900–1920; $75–125.

Candlestick, modeled tubular shape with flared base and combed surface, salt-glazed redware; Midwestern; 8 inches high; c. 1900–1920; $75–100.

Cup, modeled teacup with applied ear handle, salt-glazed redware; Midwestern; 2 inches high; c. 1920–1940; $30–45.

Doorstop in the form of a recumbent lion, molded stoneware with a metallic brown glaze, impressed maker's mark; by the Grand Ledge (Michigan) Sewer Pipe Company; 9 inches long; c. 1890–1920; $400–550.

Doorstop in the form of a recumbent frog, molded stoneware with a brown glaze; Ohio; 6.5 inches long; c. 1890–1920; $200–275.

Doorstop in the form of a recumbent horse, modeled salt-glazed redware; Ohio; 7 inches long; c. 1920–1950; $75–100.

Doorstop in the form of a crouching cat, molded salt-glazed redware; Ohio; 11 inches long; c. 1900–1920; $175–250.

Doorstop in the form of a sitting spaniel, salt-glazed stoneware

Goblet, molded sewer tile ware, based on pressed glass forms, New York or Pennsylvania, c. 1890–1915, 6.5 inches high; $110–150.

molded to resemble a Staffordshire mantel figure; Ohio; 13 inches high; c. 1890–1910; $150–200.

Doorstop in the form of a pointer, molded salt-glazed redware; Ohio; 12 inches long; c. 1910–1930; $180–240.

Doorstop in the form of a fish with tail in air; molded salt-glazed redware; Midwestern; 10.5 inches long; c. 1920–1940; $130–170.

Doorstop in form of owl on stump, molded tan salt-glazed stoneware; Ohio; 14 inches high; c. 1900–1920; $225–300.

Doorstop, modeled in the shape of a snapping turtle, incised claws and shell, salt-glazed redware; Midwestern; 10.5 inches long; c. 1900–1920; $155–195.

Figurine, molded in the form of an Indian child holding tomahawk, incised initials, salt-glazed redware; Ohio; 10 inches high; c. 1920–1940; $275–350.

Figurine, molded in the form of a recumbent alligator, salt-glazed redware; Ohio; 16 inches long; c. 1900–1930; $250–325.

Figurine, molded in the form of head of man wearing World War I German helmet, Bristol and brown glazed earthenware; Midwestern; 4.5 inches high; c. 1915–1925; $235–285.

Figurine, molded in the form of a low boot, salt-glazed brown

Figurines, hand-formed sewer tile ware heads, Ohio or Pennsylvania, c. 1890–1920: left, 4.5 inches high, $150–200; right, 4 inches high, $175–225.

earthenware; Midwestern; 4 inches high; c. 1890–1920; $55–85.

Figurine, molded in the form of a pair of slippers, dark brown glazed stoneware, incised date; Midwestern; 5.5 inches long; 1938; $70–110.

Figurine, molded in the form of a man's head emerging from shoe, brown slip-glazed stoneware; Midwestern; 3 inches high; c. 1920–1940; $65–95.

Figurine, molded in shape of cat with tail erect, salt-glazed brown stoneware; Midwestern; 3 inches high; c. 1900–1920; $70–95.

Figurine, molded in form of sleeping cat, salt-glazed redware; Ohio; 8 inches long; c. 1890–1910; $210–260.

Figurine, molded in form of sitting cat, salt-glazed redware; Midwestern; 6 inches high; c. 1900–1930; $160–190.

Figurine, molded in form of sitting cat with head cocked to side, salt-gazed redware; Ohio; 15 inches high; c. 1920–1940; $300–375.

Figurine, molded in the form of a Scottie dog, salt-glazed redware; Midwestern; 4 inches long; c. 1930–1950; $45–75.

Figurine, molded in the form of a recumbent shepherd dog, salt-glazed redware; Midwestern; 5 inches long; c. 1930–1950; $55–85.

Figurine, modeled and molded in the form of a sitting bulldog, incised name and date, salt-glazed tan stoneware; Ohio; 4 inches high; 1927; $100–130.

Figurine, molded in the form of a crouching dog, incised name and date, brown metallic glazed stoneware; Midwestern; 5.5 inches high; 1945; $65–90.

Figurine, modeled in the form of standing poodle dog, tan salt-glazed stoneware; Midwestern; 3.75 inches high; c. 1930–1950; $45–65.

Figurine, finely molded in the form of a basset hound, salt-glazed redware; Ohio; 14 inches long; c. 1920–1940; $270–340.

Figurine, molded in the form of a spaniel, salt-glazed redware; Ohio; 3.75 inches high; c. 1880–1910; $225–275.

Figurine, molded in the form of a collie dog, tan salt-glazed stoneware; Ohio; 9 inches high; c. 1900–1920; $200–250.

Figurine, molded in the form of a duck, incised feathers, salt-glazed redware; Ohio; 13 inches long; c. 1910–1930; $265–335.

Figurine, molded in the form of a recumbent fawn, salt-glazed brown stoneware; Midwestern; 4 inches long; c. 1920–1940; $70–95.

Figurine, molded in the form of a crouching squirrel, stoneware with tan metallic glaze; Midwestern; 5.5 inches long; c. 1910–1930; $55–75.

Figurine, molded in the form of a sitting pig, brown glazed stoneware; Midwestern; 2 inches long; c. 1900–1940; $40–65.

Figurine, molded in the form of a squatting ape, salt-glazed redware; Ohio; 8.5 inches high; c. 1900–1930; $240–290.

Figurine, modeled in the form of an elephant, salt-glazed redware; Midwestern; 9.5 inches long; c. 1920–1940; $110–160.

Figurine, molded in the form of an eagle, incised feathers, salt-glazed redware; Ohio; 7 inches high; c. 1900–1930; $175–245.

Figurine, molded in the form of a turkey, Bristol and brown glazed stoneware; Midwestern; 7.5 inches high; c. 1920–1940; $135–185.

Figurine, molded in the form of an owl, salt-glazed redware; Midwestern; 5 inches high; c. 1920–1940; $120–160.

Figurine, molded and modeled in the form of a crow sitting on a stump, salt-glazed redware; Midwestern; 9.5 inches high; c. 1900–1920; $130–180.

Figurine, modeled in the form of a sitting groundhog, incised initials, salt-glazed redware; Midwestern; 8.5 inches high; c. 1910–1930; $110–140.

Figurine, molded in the form of a walking raccoon, salt-glazed redware; Midwestern; 3 inches long; c. 1920–1950; $55–85.

Figurine, molded in the form of a crouching rabbit, salt-glazed stoneware; Ohio; 2 inches long; c. 1920–1940; $35–50.

Folk art, hollow cast brick incised with bird flying among branches, incised name and date, salt-glazed redware; E. Lamcille, Louisville, Ohio; 3 × 6 inches; 1893; $250–325.

Football, molded replica of full-size football, reddish-tan stoneware with a salt glaze; Ohio; 6 × 12 inches; c. 1930–1950; $190–240.

Head of Indian, modeled with headdress, tan glazed stoneware; Midwestern; 5.5 inches high; c. 1900–1930; $100–140.

Head of man, modeled salt-glazed redware; Midwestern; 7.5 inches high; c. 1900–1920; $120–160.

Head of man wearing sombrerolike hat, crudely modeled, salt-glazed yellow clay; Midwestern; 7 inches high; c. 1920–1940; $50–75.

Head of man, modeled from a brick, jack-o'-lantern type features, salt-glazed yellow clay; Canton, Ohio; 4 × 7 inches; c. 1900–1920; $110–150.

Head of Indian, finely molded with headband and bear claw necklace, tan glazed stoneware; Barberton, Ohio; 10 inches high; c. 1920–1930; $400–500.

Head of Liberty, modeled bust with inscribed date, salt-glazed redware; Midwestern; 9.5 inches high; 1918; $300–400.

Head of Lincoln, molded two-dimensional bust, salt-glazed red-and-yellow clay; Ohio; 5 inches high; c. 1910–1930; $210–270.

Humidor, modeled straight-sided vessel with combed surface, flat top with incised "Tobacco" and crossed pipes, brown

Humidor, wheel-turned and hand-formed sewer tile ware, New York or Ohio, c. 1900–1920, 6.5 inches high; $100–140.

glazed stoneware; Ohio; 7.5 inches high; c. 1920–1940; $115–155.

Key, modeled skeleton-type key with impressed location, salt-glazed redware; Uhrichsville, Ohio; 8 inches long; 1918; $130–180.

Lamp, electrical, modeled tree-form shaft with combed surface, salt-glazed redware; Midwestern; 16 inches high; c. 1920–1940; $225–300.

Lamp, electrical, modeled tree-form shaft combined with two match holders, all with combed surface, incised date, salt-glazed redware; Midwestern; 9 inches high; 1928; $200–250.

Lamp, electrical, modeled tree-form shaft with applied figures of two dogs and treed raccoon, combed surface, tan glazed stoneware; Ohio; 11.5 inches high; c. 1920–1935; $325–400.

Match holder, modeled in form of three stumps in front of which appears a fox or dog watching a snake, salt-glazed redware; Midwestern; 8 inches long; c. 1890–1920; $160–230.

Match holder, modeled in form of two hollow stumps with combed surfaces, incised name and date; Gnadenhutten, Ohio; 5.5 inches long; 1941; $130–180.

Match holder, well-modeled four-part set including holders and ashtrays on tray, all combed, signed, and dated, green glazed stoneware; Ohio; 6 × 12 inches; 1931; $250–350.

Match and pipe holder, hand-modeled, heart-shaped, incised name, salt-glazed redware; Midwestern; 5 × 6 inches; c. 1920–1940; $60–85.

Match holder and ashtray, two well-modeled holders and heart-shaped ashtray resting on heart-shaped base, stoneware with dark brown glaze; Ohio; 7.5 × 7.5 inches; c. 1910–1930; $170–230.

Match holder, molded in form of crouching beaver with holder in back, unglazed yellow clay, embossed with maker's mark; Beaver Clay Manufacturing Company, Beaver, Pennsylvania; 5 inches long; c. 1900–1920; $140–190.

Match holder, molded in form of hollow tree trunk, stamped maker's mark, salt-glazed redware; Evans Pipe Company, Uhrichsville, Ohio; 3.5 inches square; c. 1920–1940; $75–100.

Match holder, molded in the form of a hollow disk with applied figure of crouching dog, tan salt-glazed stoneware; Midwestern; 3 inches high; c. 1900–1930; $70–95.

Mug, molded with ear-shaped handle, salt-glazed redware; Midwestern; 5 inches high; c. 1910–1930; $60–85.

Mug, modeled with flaring lip, incised name and date, salt-glazed redware; Ohio; 5.5 inches high; 1925; $95–145.

Paperweight, molded in the form of a spaniel's head, salt-glazed redware; Ohio; 4 inches in diameter; c. 1880–1910; $200–300.

Paperweight, molded in the form of a flattened piece of sewer pipe, embossed advertising logo, salt-glazed tan stoneware; Monmouth Mining & Manufacturing Company, Monmouth, Illinois; 4 inches long; c. 1900–1920; $80–120.

Paperweight, modeled in the form of a man's head, salt-glazed redware; Midwestern; 3 inches in diameter; c. 1890–1910; $125–175.

Paperweight, molded in the form of an Egyptian head, impressed maker's mark, salt-glazed redware; Nelsonville (Ohio) Sewer Pipe Company; 4.5 inches high; c. 1920–1930; $225–300.

Paperweight, molded in the form of a scarab, salt-glazed redware, impressed maker's mark; Robinson Clay Products Company, Akron, Ohio; 3 × 4.5 inches; c. 1915–1925; $120–160.

Pin tray, molded and modeled oval tray backed by recumbent lion, salt-glazed redware; Ohio; 6 inches long; c. 1910–1930; $160–210.

Pitcher with applied frog and human figures, molded and modeled dark brown glazed stoneware with incised date and dedication; by William Hirzel, Rochester (New York) Sewer Pipe Factory; 7 inches high; 1889; $200–300.

Pitcher, ovoid, hand-thrown unglazed stoneware with combing to resemble bark; made by J.W. Moore at the Stark Brick Com-

Pitcher, molded and hand-formed sewer tile ware with Bristol-glazed interior, New York or New Jersey, c. 1900–1920, 8 inches high; $70–95.

Pitcher, molded sewer tile ware with applied decoration, New York, c. 1910–1930, 9 inches high; $165–235.

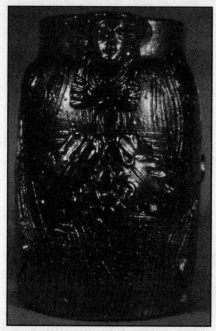

Pitcher, molded sewer tile ware with applied decoration, Rochester, New York, c. 1900–1920, 9.5 inches high; $135–175.

pany, Canton, Ohio; 13.5 inches high; c. 1940–1945; $135–185.

Pitcher, hand-thrown with combed surface and applied horseshoe, brown glazed stoneware; New York; 10 inches high; c. 1900–1910; $90–120.

Planter in the form of a tree stump with branches, body combed to resemble bark, incised name of owner, molded salt-glazed tan stoneware; by an employee of the Summit Sewer Pipe Company, Akron, Ohio; 22 inches high; c. 1920–1930; $200–275.

Planter or flower pot in the form of a modeled tree stump with combed body and heart-shaped reserve inscribed with name and date, salt-glazed redware; Midwestern; 7 inches high; 1945; $140–180.

Planter in the form of a molded tree trunk covered with applied cast figures of crouching monkeys, combed surface, reddish-brown salt-glazed stoneware; Ohio; 10 inches high; c. 1920–1940; $400–500.

Plaque, eagle on national shield, molded salt-glazed redware; Ohio; 12 inches high; c. 1890–1910; $300–400.

Plaque, eagle with outspread wings, molded salt-glazed stoneware; Midwestern; 10 inches high; c. 1910–1930; $150–225.

Plaque, round modeled disk with applied molded flowers, salt-glazed redware; Ohio; 6.5 inches in diameter; c. 1890–1920; $80–110.

Plaque, molded head of woman with 1920s hairdo, salt-glazed redware; Midwestern; 7 inches in diameter; c. 1920–1930; $100–160.

Salt and pepper shakers, tubular form tapering toward center, incised flowers and initials, salt-glazed stoneware; Ohio; 3 inches high; c. 1930–1950; $125–175 the pair.

Sample piece of sewer pipe, molded with impressed maker's mark, salt-glazed stoneware; John H. Rich Sewer Pipe Works, Red Wing, Minnesota; 4 inches high; c. 1893–1896; $100–140.

Skull, modeled hollow form, incised initials, salt-glazed redware; Ohio; 4.5 × 5.5 inches; c. 1910–1930; $145–195.

Soap dish, slab-formed hanging dish, salt-glazed redware; Midwestern; 5 inches long; c. 1900–1920; $80–110.

Umbrella stand, molded tubular form combed to resemble tree bark, brown glazed stoneware; Midwestern; 23 inches high; c. 1890–1920; $135–185.

Vase, molded cylindrical form with slight taper from base, salt-glazed redware; Midwestern; 5.5 inches high; c. 1900–1930; $60–90.

Vase, molded in the form of a duck, salt-glazed redware with inscribed name; Midwestern; 5 inches high; c. 1920–1940; $85–125.

Vase, molded in the form of a tree trunk with applied roses and leaves on a combed surface, inscribed name and date, salt-glazed redware; Ohio; 9 inches high; 1936; $185–245.

GLOSSARY

Pottery and porcelain collectors have a common
language of terms that they use to refer to various
ceramic bodies and how they are made and fired. It is
important for every collector to become familiar with
these terms, both to understand the hobby and to
receive the respect from others in the field that such
knowledge brings.

ALBANY SLIP   A glaze made from water and a unique form of clay found near Albany, New York. It was used primarily as an interior glaze for stoneware but was also often employed to glaze entire objects. Clay with similar properties is found in Texas, Michigan, and California.

APPLIED DECORATION   Ceramic decoration consisting of small hand-shaped or -cast elements such as flowers and leaves that are applied to a ceramic body before firing; most often used to decorate porcelain.

ARTIFICIAL PORCELAIN   A combination of kaolin or similar clays and ground glass designed to resemble true porcelain; also known as soft paste.

ASH GLAZE   A Southern stoneware glaze made by mixing wood ashes and water to produce lye, which is then combined with sand, ground glass, or clay to produce a streaky yellow to dark brown finish.

BELLEEK   A form of extremely thin-walled, delicate, off-white porcelain developed in Ireland and brought to a high state at some American potteries.

BISQUE   A ceramic body fired without being previously glazed; the term is most often applied to bisque or biscuit porcelain. See also Parian.

BRISTOL SLIP   An opaque white slip containing zinc oxide used to glaze stoneware; most ware so finished dates after 1880.

CASTING   See Molding.

CERAMIC   A mineral-based substance or combination thereof which can be fired at high temperature to a hard body.

CLAY   An earth or combination of earths, malleable when wet and solid after firing or baking.

COBALT OXIDE   A naturally occurring compound used to produce the blue glaze employed in stoneware decoration; hence, the term *Cobalt blue.*

COGGLE WHEEL   A freely turning wood- or metal-toothed wheel with a short handle; used to decorate soft clay prior to firing.

COLESLAW DECORATION   A form of applied decoration consisting of many extruded strands of clay or porcelain; most often used to mimic hair or fur on ceramic animals like Rockingham lions.

CRAZING   Myriad tiny cracks in a glazed ceramic body produced by the differing rates at which the body and the glaze contract over time; often a sign of age in pottery and porcelain.

DRAPE MOLDING   A method of shaping a ceramic body by placing a sheet of clay over a wooden or clay mold and then pressing it into shape and trimming off the excess; often used to make redware pie plates.

EARTHENWARE   A slightly porous ceramic body fired at a relatively low temperature; redware is an earthenware.

EMBOSSED DECORATION   Slightly raised decoration formed as the soft clay conforms to the mold; not separately applied.

EXTRUDER   A simple mechanical device through which clay is forced to make such things as coleslaw decoration and ridged handles.

FAIENCE   See Majolica.

FINIAL   A cast or hand-shaped protuberance that serves as the handle for a sugar bowl or teapot cover; often acorn-shaped.

FIRING   The process of baking a ceramic body in a kiln or oven until hard.

FLINT ENAMEL   A streaky polychrome glaze produced by covering a white or yellowware body with clear glaze and then dusting it with colored metallic oxides that run as the piece is fired.

GLAZE   A mixture of water, clay, and various metallic oxides that is applied to a ceramic body prior to firing; heat causes this to vitrify, sealing the body and giving it a glasslike finish.

GREENWARE   The potter's term for unfired or unbaked pottery.

IMPRESSED DECORATION   Decoration created by pressing a shaped wood or metal stamp into the soft clay body prior to firing.

INCISED DECORATION   Freehand decoration created by using a stylus or stick to scratch designs or pictures into the soft clay body prior to firing.

IRONSTONE   A hard, vitrified, nonporous white earthenware body; also referred to as hotel china or semi-porcelain.

KAOLIN   A fine white clay often used in porcelain manufacture.

KILN   The potter's term for the oven in which a ceramic body is fired; made of brick or stone and may take various forms.

LEAD GLAZE   A clear glasslike glaze made from lead oxide, water, and clay; usually employed to glaze redware.

LEON SLIP   See Albany slip.

MAJOLICA   A relatively soft earthenware body covered with an opaque white tin glaze and then polychrome-decorated with contrasting glazes. Most American majolica is molded.

MAKER'S MARK   The name of a pottery manufacturer which may be imprinted into a ceramic body, incised or printed on it, or written on in slip.

MANGANESE OXIDE A metallic oxide which when mixed with slip and fired produces a black to brownish-purple glaze; used on both redware and early stoneware.

MOCHA Refers to pottery, usually yellowware, having various slip decorations resembling those of the moss agate or "mocha stone."

MODELING Forming a clay body by hand, usually with small tools.

MOLDING The process of forming a clay body by pressing soft clay or pouring liquid clay into a mold and allowing it to harden; also referred to as casting.

OVERGLAZE DECORATION Decoration, usually painted or printed, which is applied after a first bisque firing. Usually a second, cooler firing is employed to fix the decoration.

PARIAN Unglazed porcelain with a slightly grainy surface; somewhat resembles marble and often used for statuary.

PIERCED DECORATION Decoration achieved by cutting patterned areas out of the clay body to produce openwork; most common on porcelain and early Pennsylvania redware.

PORCELAIN A hard, white, vitrified, translucent ceramic body composed primarily of kaolin and feldspar (hard paste); addition of other materials such as bone ash (bone china) or ground flint produces a different body. See Artificial Porcelain.

POTTER'S WHEEL A wooden and metal device on which ceramic objects are shaped as they turn. In the most simple form, it consists of two disks joined by a shaft. As the lower is turned by the foot, the upper, upon which rests the clay to be shaped, also revolves.

POTTERY The general term for ceramics produced from clay or a combination of clays; may also refer to the potter's shop.

Redware   A porous, relatively coarse, and brittle ceramic body made from clay that fires to a reddish hue.

Rockingham   A mottled brown glaze usually applied to a yellowware body; also, the ware itself. Use of the term *Bennington* for such ware is incorrect.

Salt Glaze   A shiny, glasslike pebbled glaze on stoneware produced by throwing salt into the hot kiln, where it combines with silica in the stoneware body to form a bonded finish.

Scroddled ware   A ceramic body produced by mixing several clays that fire to different colors.

Sewer Tile Ware   Pieces of pottery made from coarse redware or stoneware clay and given a dark brown glaze; usually made by men working in factories producing sewer or drain tile.

Sgrafitto   A form of pottery decoration in which the ceramic body is covered with a layer of opaque slip and designs are then scratched through this to expose the contrasting red clay body.

Slip   Clay mixed with water in a suspension.

Soft Paste Porcelain   See Artificial Porcelain.

Sponged Decoration   Slip decoration applied with a sponge or other applicator to a ceramic body prior to firing; may be patterned or random.

Spongeware   Pottery, typically a yellowware or stoneware body, decorated by sponging. Sponged white earthenware is less common.

Stenciled Decoration   Slip decoration applied to a ceramic body by brushing it on through a cutout paper or metal pattern.

STONEWARE   A high-fired, vitrified ceramic body of great hardness and density and varying in hue from brown to an off-white; may be glazed and decorated in various ways.

TIN GLAZE   An opaque white glaze containing tin oxide; often used on majolica.

TRANSFER DECORATION   A decorative technique employing printed designs on paper which are applied to a ceramic body before firing. During firing, the design is transferred to the piece as the paper burns away. A common white earthenware decoration.

UNDERGLAZE DECORATION   Slip or transfer decoration applied to a ceramic body before it is glazed and fired.

VITREOUS   Glasslike in appearance; a term often applied to glazes and highly fired ceramic bodies.

WHEEL-THROWN   A potter's term for ware thrown by hand on the potter's wheel rather than molded.

WHITE EARTHENWARE   An opaque, nonvitreous white ceramic body that is given a clear glaze and fired at a high temperature.

WHITE WARES   A generic term for the body of wares encompassed within the categories of white earthenware and ironstone.

YELLOWWARE   A hard, impervious ceramic body which fires at a high temperature to a strong yellow to off-white hue.

BIBLIOGRAPHY

As the old saying goes, knowledge is power, and any price guide will be of most use to those who thoroughly understand the field they are pricing. Accordingly, I have provided a brief bibliography of books that will provide readers with information that will help them to understand and evaluate American ceramics. This list is by no means inclusive. Many good books have not been included, either because they are out of print and unavailable or because they have been superseded by more recent texts.

Adamson, Jack E., *Illustrated Handbook of Ohio Sewer Pipe Folk Art*. Zoar, Ohio, privately printed, 1973.

Altman, V., and S. Altman, *The Book of Buffalo Pottery*. New York, Crown Publishers, Inc., 1969.

Barber, Edwin A., *Marks of American Potters*. Philadelphia, Patterson & White Company, 1904; reprinted, Southampton, New York, The Cracker Barrel Press, 1972.

Barret, Richard C., *Bennington Pottery and Porcelain*. New York, Bonanza Books, 1958.

Bivins, John, Jr. *The Moravian Potters in North Carolina*. Chapel Hill, University of North Carolina Press, 1972.

Branin, M. Lelyn, *The Early Makers of Handcrafted Earthenware and Stoneware in Central and Southern New Jersey*. Rutherford, New Jersey, Fairleigh Dickinson University Press, 1988.

————. *The Early Potters and Potteries of Maine*. Middletown, Connecticut, Wesleyan University Press, 1978.

Burrison, John A., *Georgia Jug Makers: A History of Southern Folk Pottery*. Ann Arbor, Michigan, University Films International, 1973.

Dearolf, Kenneth, *Wisconsin Folk Pottery*. Kenosha, Wisconsin, Kenosha Public Museum, 1986.

DePasquale, Dan, and Gail and Larry Peterson, *Red Wing Stoneware*. Paducah, Kentucky, Collector Books, 1985.

Gallo, John, *Nineteenth and Twentieth Century Yellowware*. Richfield Springs, New York, Heritage Press, 1985.

Greer, Georgeanna H., *American Stonewares: The Art and Craft of Utilitarian Potters*. Exton, Pennsylvania, Schiffer Publishing Ltd., 1981.

Guilland, Harold F., *Early American Folk Pottery*. Philadelphia, Chilton Press, 1971.

Horne, Catherine Wilson, ed., *Crossroads of Clay: The Southern Alkaline Glazed Stoneware Tradition*. Columbia, South Carolina, The University of South Carolina, 1990.

Ketchum, William C., Jr., *Pottery & Porcelain: The Knopf Collectors' Guides to American Antiques*. New York, Alfred A. Knopf, 1983.

————. *American Country Pottery: Yellowware & Spongeware*. New York, Alfred A. Knopf, 1987.

————. *American Redware*. New York, Henry Holt and Company, 1991.

————. *American Stoneware*. New York, Henry Holt and Company, 1991.

Klamkin, Marian, *American Patriotic and Political China*. New York, Charles Scribner's Sons, 1973.

Leibowitz, Joan, *Yellowware—The Transitional Ceramic*. Exton, Pennsylvania, Schiffer Publishing, Ltd., 1985.

Martin, Jim, and Betty Cooper, *Monmouth-Western Stoneware*. Des Moines, Iowa, Wallace-Homestead Book Company, 1983.

Ramsway, John, *American Potters and Pottery*. Boston, Hale, Cushman & Flint, 1939; reprinted, New York, Tudor Publishing Company, 1947.

Robacker, Earl F. and Ada F., *Spatterware and Sponge: Hardy Perennials of Ceramics*. South Brunswick and New York, A.S. Barnes, 1978.

Schwartz, Marvin D., and R. Wolfe, *A History of American Art Porcelain*. New York, Renaissance Editions, 1967.

Smith, Howard, *Index of Southern Potters*. Mayodan, North Carolina, The Old America Company, 1982.

Spargo, John, *Early American Pottery and China*. New York, The Century Company, 1926; reprinted, Rutland, Vermont, Charles E. Tuttle Company, 1974.

Watkins, Lura, *Early New England Potters and Their Wares*. Cambridge, Massachusetts, Harvard University Press, 1950; reprinted, Hamden, Connecticut, Archon Books, 1968.

Webster, Donald Blake, *Decorated Stoneware Pottery of North America*. Rutland, Vermont, Charles E. Tuttle Company, 1971.

Wiltshire, William E., III, *Folk Pottery of the Shenandoah Valley*, New York, E.P. Dutton, 1975.

INDEX

A

Advertisements, stoneware, 8

Albany slip, meaning of, 380

Ale jugs, Rockingham ware, 224

Ant traps
    redware, 158
    stoneware, 8

Apple butter jars, redware, 94

Applied decoration, meaning of, 380

Artificial porcelain, meaning of, 380

Ash glaze, meaning of, 380

Ashtrays
    redware, 94
    sewer tile ware, 367
    stoneware, 8

B

Baking dishes
    spongeware, 265–267
    stoneware, 8
    yellowware, 177

Banks
    flint-enamel ware, 224
    redware, 95–96
    Rockingham ware, 224
    sewer tile ware, 368
    spongeware, 267
    stoneware, 8–9
    yellowware, 178

Barber's bowl, redware, 97

Baskets
    majolica, 163
    porcelain, 303–304
    redware, 97
    stoneware, 9